BEVERLY HILLS PUBLIC LIBRARY

3 5048 00756 3115

WITHDRAWN

ΙΙ022311

ALSO BY LEO DAMROSCH

Jean-Jacques Rousseau: Restless Genius

*The Sorrows of the Quaker Jesus: James Nayler and the
Puritan Crackdown on the Free Spirit*

Fictions of Reality in the Age of Hume and Johnson

The Imaginative World of Alexander Pope

*God's Plot and Man's Stories: Studies in the
Fictional Imagination from Milton to Fielding*

Symbol and Truth in Blake's Myth

The Uses of Johnson's Criticism

Samuel Johnson and the Tragic Sense

TOCQUEVILLE'S DISCOVERY OF AMERICA

ADULT
973.5
Damrosch

TOCQUEVILLE'S

DISCOVERY OF

AMERICA

Leo Damrosch

FARRAR, STRAUS AND GIROUX

New York

Beverly Hills Public Library
444 N. Rexford Drive
WITHDRAWN
Beverly Hills, California 90210

Farrar, Straus and Giroux
18 West 18th Street, New York 10011

Copyright © 2010 by Leo Damrosch
Map copyright © 2010 by Jeffrey L. Ward
All rights reserved
Distributed in Canada by D&M Publishers, Inc.
Printed in the United States of America
First edition, 2010

A portion of chapter 1 originally appeared in
The Wall Street Journal Weekend Edition.

Library of Congress Cataloging-in-Publication Data
Damrosch, Leopold.
    Tocqueville's discovery of America / Leo Damrosch.— 1st ed.
       p.   cm.
    Includes bibliographical references and index.
    ISBN: 978-0-374-27817-5 (hardcover)
    1. Tocqueville, Alexis de, 1805–1859—Travel—United States.   2. United
States—Description and travel.   3. National characteristics, American.   I. Title.

E165.D16 2010
973.5'6—dc22

2009031894

Designed by Abby Kagan

www.fsgbooks.com

1   3   5   7   9   10   8   6   4   2

CONTENTS

ILLUSTRATIONS

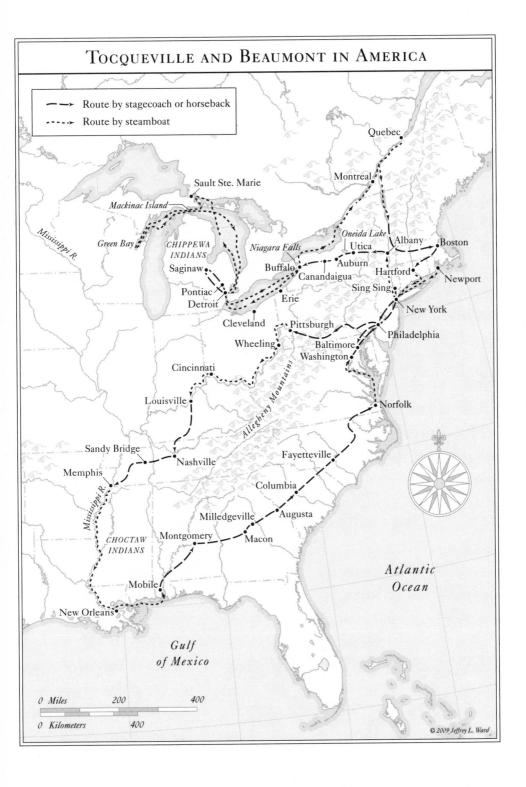

TOCQUEVILLE AND BEAUMONT IN AMERICA

- – – → Route by stagecoach or horseback
- · · · → Route by steamboat

Mississippi R.

Quebec

Montreal

Sault Ste. Marie

Mackinac Island

Green Bay

CHIPPEWA INDIANS

Oneida Lake
Utica   Albany   Boston

Niagara Falls

Saginaw

Buffalo   Auburn
Canandaigua   Hartford

Newport

Pontiac

Erie

Sing Sing

Detroit

Cleveland   Pittsburgh

New York

Philadelphia

Wheeling   Baltimore
Washington

Cincinnati

Allegheny Mountains

Norfolk

Louisville

Sandy Bridge   Nashville   Fayetteville

Memphis

Mississippi R.

Columbia

Milledgeville   Augusta

CHOCTAW INDIANS   Montgomery   Macon

Mobile

Atlantic Ocean

New Orleans

Gulf of Mexico

0 Miles   200   400

0 Kilometers   400

© 2009 Jeffrey L. Ward

TIME LINE OF THE AMERICAN JOURNEY

1831

APRIL	2	depart from Le Havre
MAY	9	arrive in Newport
	11	New York City
	30	Sing Sing (to June 8)
JUNE	9–29	New York City
	30	steamboat to Albany
JULY	1–4	Albany
	5–7	Mohawk Valley
	8	Oneida Lake (Frenchman's Island)
	9–13	Auburn (Elam Lynds)
	14–15	travel westward
	16–18	Canandaigua (John C. Spencer)
	19	Buffalo
	20–22	steamboat on Lake Erie
	22–23	Detroit
	24–30	to Saginaw and back
	31	Detroit

AUG.	1–13	steamboat on Lake Huron (Sault Sainte Marie, Green Bay)
	14	Detroit
	15–16	steamboat on Lake Erie
	17	Buffalo
	18–19	Niagara Falls
	20–23	steamboat to Montreal
	24–25	Montreal
	26–31	Quebec City
SEPT.	1–2	Montreal
	3	travel south
	4–6	Albany
	7	travel east
	9	Boston
OCT.	3–8	Hartford
	9–11	New York City
	12–28	Philadelphia
	29	Baltimore and Carrollton (to Nov. 6)
NOV.	7–20	Philadelphia
	21–25	westward to Pittsburgh
	26	steamboat on the Ohio
	27	steamboat wreck, near Wheeling
	28–30	steamboat on the Ohio
DEC.	1–4	Cincinnati
	5–8	steamboat on the Ohio
	9	Louisville
	10–11	overland to Nashville
	12–16	overland to Memphis (illness at Sandy Bridge)
	17–24	Memphis
	25–31	steamboat on the Mississippi

1832

JAN.	1–3	New Orleans
	4	travel through the South
	18	Washington (to Feb. 2)
FEB.	3	Philadelphia
	4–19	New York City
	20	set sail for France (arrive late March)

PREFACE

In the spring of 1831, Alexis de Tocqueville began a nine-month journey through the United States with his friend Gustave de Beaumont. Tocqueville was twenty-five years old, an apprentice magistrate at Versailles, and fascinated by the American experiment with democracy. Four years later he would publish *Democracy in America*, which was immediately recognized as a classic and continues to be quoted throughout the political spectrum for its insights into American culture. It has been called "certainly the greatest book ever written by anyone about America," and modern writers have constantly resorted to it—for example, David Riesman in *The Lonely Crowd*, Robert Nisbet in *The Quest for Community*, and Robert Bellah in *Habits of the Heart* (a title taken from a phrase of Tocqueville's, "les habitudes du coeur").

Tocqueville met and questioned hundreds of Americans on his journey, some famous—Daniel Webster, John Quincy Adams, Sam Houston—and some obscure; many important ideas in *Democracy in America* were originally suggested by people he talked with. He wrote to his brother after his first few weeks in New York, "Ideas come in, as it were, through our pores, and we learn as much in drawing rooms or taking walks as when we're shut up in our study." He soon discovered that whereas in Europe it was impolite to ask probing questions, the typical American was "a pitiless questioner" and perfectly willing to answer such questions as well as to ask them. As for Tocqueville, Beaumont said about him, "He had the very rare talent of knowing how to listen well just as much as how to speak well." Tocqueville also believed that coming from abroad gave him an advantage: "A foreigner often learns important truths at the hearth of his host, who might conceal them from his friends."

Tocqueville was not just a great listener; he was a man in motion, and it is no accident that he found his way to his masterpiece by traveling. Beaumont especially admired the energy with which his friend pursued his quest. "Repose was contrary to his nature, and even when his body wasn't moving, his intelligence was always at work . . . The slightest loss of time was unpleasant to him. This way of thinking kept him in continual anxiety; he pressed this passion so far during his journeys that he never arrived at a place without first making sure of his means of getting away, which made one of his friends comment that he was always leaving before he arrived." He was interested in everything, and tireless in acquiring knowledge. He once told Beaumont, "You are always on fire, but you catch fire for only one thing at a time, with no curiosity or interest for everything else . . . I have an ardent and insatiable curiosity that constantly pulls me off my path to the right or the left." Sheldon Wolin, in the most impressive modern study of Tocqueville, calls the notebooks he kept during his travels "a registry of unending surprise."

Tocqueville was a sensitive, ambitious, and at times troubled young man taking in a nonstop barrage of impressions in a strange land. The America he encountered was no abstract embodiment of democracy, but a turbulent, competitive, rapidly changing society. During the 1830s the nation was still young. It had recently elected its first populist president in Andrew Jackson, it was expanding aggressively westward, and it was deeply conscious of class, regional, and racial tensions, forebodingly aware that civil war might one day tear it apart. This book seeks to bring that traveler and that world to life, through Tocqueville's own highly perceptive observations at the time and through the wealth of comments on Jacksonian America made by a host of contemporaries, especially other foreign visitors who published book-length accounts. Their perceptions help to build up a panoramic view of America in the 1830s, and they illuminate—often by contrast—the powers of observation and sympathy that made Tocqueville such a superb interpreter of American culture. By accompanying him on his journey, we can share in his personal discovery of America during an era of immense significance in the history of our nation, yet one that has received little attention amid the outpouring of books on the Revolution and the Civil War.

Democracy in America is not a rigidly systematic book, and modern interpreters sometimes complain that its key concepts can be inconsistent or fuzzy. They were bound to be, at a time when the whole basis of society was being reimagined throughout the Western world; it has been well said that Tocqueville's book is "not so much a book of answers as a book of questions." And while he was certainly interested in theory, it was in no abstract or academic way. For him theorizing was a necessary tool for making sense of the enormous social and political changes his generation was living through; as a modern commentator says, "Everything he wrote was intensely practical. His major books were political acts, the acts of a citizen."

What Tocqueville eventually created was not an account of "Americans" as a unique national type, but a structural explanation of some profound reasons why democracy, by its very nature, tends to produce certain characteristics in its citizens. In important ways, as he understood very clearly, the young nation enjoyed unique advantages of history and geography that the Old World could never share. The eighteenth-century founders had inherited a centuries-old tradition of liberty in colonies that had no hereditary aristocracy, and their break with England required no violent revolution such as France had to endure. Millions of acres of land were available for settlement in America, and the absence of powerful neighboring states made it unnecessary to maintain a large army or to impose centralized control. By contrast, in postrevolutionary France the very word "democracy" had a bad name, suggestive of mob rule; there was still a king, a powerful central government, and a huge army; and the number of eligible voters for the legislature was minuscule. When Tocqueville wrote a chapter titled "Of the Government of Democracy in America," he started by acknowledging how provocative those words would seem to French readers: "I know I am treading on burning coals. Every word in this chapter is bound to offend in some way the various parties that divide my country."

Indeed, it would be hard to exaggerate the differences between the America and the France of that time. A number of Tocqueville's aristocratic relatives had been guillotined in a violent class-based revolution, and his own parents had barely escaped execution. Over the space of forty years France had been a hereditary monarchy, a radical democracy, a dictatorship with imperial ambitions, a monarchy again, and (in the last few months) an uneasy sort of semi-democracy whose future seemed much in doubt. By contrast, America was astonishingly stable, and Tocqueville was determined to learn why.

The goal of *Democracy in America*, then, was to dig down to bedrock in order to locate principles that other nations might incorporate. In his introduction Tocqueville declared, "In America I saw more than America; I sought there an image of democracy itself . . . I have attempted to see, not differently, but further than the political parties do. While they are concerned with the next day, I have wanted to ponder the future." A number of his predictions turned out to be uncannily prophetic—his insights have been called "almost frighteningly prescient"—but that is only incidental to his achievement. The years to come would bring enormous changes that he could not have foreseen, and in any case it was never his intention to be a prophet. "In the picture of the future," he wrote, "chance always creates an area of obscurity that the eye of intelligence has no way of penetrating." (The America of the twenty-first century differs in profound ways from the America of the early nineteenth, and if Tocqueville's analysis still resonates, it is because of its uncanny intellectual power.)

Throughout their nine-month journey, Tocqueville and Beaumont were true collaborators, constantly comparing notes and working out ideas. They complemented each other socially as well, since the reticent and sometimes melancholic Tocqueville relied on his gregarious friend to break the ice. Beaumont was the more active and athletic of the two, but Tocqueville too showed extraordinary stamina. Early on it was he who insisted on giving Beaumont swimming lessons in the Hudson, as Beaumont reported to his mother, "with all the determination of a friend who knows how unfortunate my position would be if I should happen to fall into the middle of a great American river." At one point it looked as if that skill would be required, when a steamboat they were on split against a rock and foundered among ice floes. Altogether they visited seventeen of the then twenty-four states, as well as three regions that would later become states (Michigan, Wisconsin, and West Virginia). In those days Ohio was at the brink of the frontier, and Wisconsin was a trackless forest beyond the pale of civilization.

Theirs was hardly the most exotic journey of the era—in December of the same year, the twenty-two-year-old Charles Darwin set sail in the *Beagle*, at a moment when Tocqueville and Beaumont were relaxing on a Mississippi steamboat—but in the context of French culture and politics it was exotic enough. At a deep level, in fact, there was a real similarity between Tocqueville and Darwin. Unlike superficial travelers, they both wrote compellingly because they were so keenly observant— Darwin of the natural world, with glances at society, and Tocqueville of society, with glances at nature. And if he was discovering America, Tocqueville had the exceptional insight to grasp that the nation itself was engaged in ongoing self-discovery. At one point during the trip he jotted in his notebook, "There is not a country in the world where man takes possession of the future more confidently, or feels with more pride that his intelligence makes him master of the universe, which he can reshape to his liking. It's a movement of mind that can only be compared to the one that brought about the discovery of the New World three centuries ago. In fact one could say that America is being discovered a second time." And in *Democracy in America* he declared, "This new society I have sought to depict and want to judge is only just being born. The passage of time hasn't yet determined its shape; the great revolution that created it is still going on."

In historical hindsight the 1830s did indeed represent a major turning point. In Sean Wilentz's words, "A momentous rupture occurred between Thomas Jefferson's time and Abraham Lincoln's that created the lineaments of modern democratic politics." Beyond the world of politics, unprecedented economic changes were under way; one major history of the period is centered on the "market revolution" and another on the "communications revolution." Tocqueville and Beaumont had firsthand experience of both. Gordon Wood observes that by contrast with the expectations of the founders, "by the 1820s America had become the most egalitarian, individualistic, and money-making society in western history." That was exactly what fascinated Tocqueville and inspired his most penetrating insights. And those insights were made possible by his intense engagement, during an event-filled nine months, with America and Americans.

There are brief accounts of Tocqueville's journey in biographies by André Jardin and Hugh Brogan, which necessarily devote most of their space to his later political career in France. As for a full treatment of his American experience, it has been seventy years since that was last attempted. In his 1938 book, *Tocqueville and Beaumont in America*, George Wilson Pierson provided an invaluable accounting of the more than two hundred people Tocqueville is known to have met, but of course he lacked what a writer today can gratefully draw upon, the work of scores of distinguished historians and political scientists on Jacksonian America and on Tocqueville's thought.

Like everyone who writes about Tocqueville, I have made use of the great Tocqueville collection in the Beinecke Library at Yale, which contains much that is not yet in print, and I have been helped especially by Eduardo Nolla's magnificent annotated edition of *De la démocratie en Amérique*, which came out nearly twenty years ago but has been little used by American writers, though that will certainly change when a promised English translation appears. Nolla's notes are filled with fascinating material from the thousands of pages of drafts that Tocqueville accumulated as he labored on his book, including ones that Tocqueville filed under the English heading of "Rubish," and at many points these have helped me to tell his story. Nearly all of these, together with the majority of passages I quote from Tocqueville's and Beaumont's letters, have never appeared in English before.

It should be mentioned also that studies of Tocqueville's thought disagree about the relation of the first part of *Democracy in America* to the second. Some have argued that the two parts—published in 1835 and 1840—are so different that, as the title of one book has it, there are really "two democracies." Tocqueville himself said that there was certainly a difference in emphasis, since the first part analyzes American institutions and the second ranges more widely in social behavior and mores. And he acknowledged as well that because he hoped to influence political thought and action in France, the second has more to say about democracy in general than about America specifically. Nevertheless, he declared firmly, "The two parts complement each other and form but a single work," and for our present purpose that seems right. I quote often from *Democracy in America* when it draws directly on insights acquired during the journey, and on occasions when it seems important to distinguish between the 1835 and the 1840 texts, I do so.

A word about translations. There are several good English versions of *Democracy in America*, not so many of Tocqueville's other writings, and none at all of some important ones, including most of his letters. I have made my own translations of everything that I quote from French, for two reasons: first, to try to capture the rhythm and clarity of prose that is lucid in the original but often sounds convoluted and ponderous in English; and second, to present a Tocqueville who speaks with a single voice rather than with the inconsistent voices of different translators. It's worth noting also what writers on Tocqueville usually ignore, that the many dialogues with Americans in his notebooks are rendered in French. Without altering the meaning, I have tried to make his Americans sound less stilted and formal than they tend to be when Tocqueville's French is retranslated into English.

It should be noted also that the illustrations in this book are as nearly contemporary with Tocqueville's journey as possible, and that none shows anything he would not have seen.

ACKNOWLEDGMENTS

My thanks to my agent, Tina Bennett, for believing in this project from its inception; to Eric Chinski, for trenchant editorial advice that improved the manuscript greatly; to Joyce Van Dyke, for making improvements in clarity and narrative pace on every page; and to Daniel Williams, for invaluable help in locating out-of-the-way sources and images.

TOCQUEVILLE'S DISCOVERY OF AMERICA

1

WHERE TOCQUEVILLE WAS COMING FROM

Alexis de Tocqueville came from an aristocratic family whose two branches represented both kinds of nobility in prerevolutionary France, the chivalric and the bureaucratic. The Tocquevilles inherited a title gained long ago by military prowess; an ancestor had taken part in William the Conqueror's invasion of England. On the maternal side were judges and civil servants, ennobled more recently for professional service to the Crown. Alexis's mother Louise's grandfather was the truly distinguished Chrétien-Guillaume de Lamoignon de Malesherbes, who as official censor in the mid-eighteenth century had worked to protect great writers such as Voltaire and Rousseau, and who said he spent his whole life "in what would be called in other countries the opposition party." Malesherbes died at the guillotine, punished for loyally serving as defense counsel when his king was on trial for his life. Alexis honored his memory and thought of him as an inspiring role model, not least in resisting the seductions of power.

Malesherbes was not the only relative who was executed, and Alexis, who was born in 1805, grew up hearing frightening stories of how the revolutionary idealism of 1789 degenerated four years later into the cruel Reign of Terror, when Robespierre's dreaded Committee of Public Safety ordered the execution of thousands of "counterrevolutionaries" (historians believe the total may have been as high as forty thousand). Many members of Tocqueville's mother's family were beheaded, and she and his father, Hervé, survived only because three days before they were scheduled to die, the implacable Robespierre and his allies were overthrown by a coup. When Hervé, who was twenty at the time, emerged from prison, his hair had gone completely white, and Louise was afflicted with mental illness for the rest of her life. From her Alexis inherited fluctuations of mood and emotional sensitivity— he has been called a repressed romantic—and from Hervé he got an energetic and impulsive temperament. As he once told his brother Édouard, "It's that restlessness of mind, that consuming impatience, that need for repeated lively sensations that our father has, sometimes to a rather childish degree. This disposition gives great élan at certain times, but most of the time it torments without cause, agitates fruitlessly, and makes those who possess it very unhappy."

Alexis was far more promising than his two older brothers, with whom he always maintained affectionate relations. Hippolyte, the eldest, had a not very successful military career and then an unremarkable one in the civil service; the middle brother, Édouard, left the army to marry an heiress and devoted himself thereafter to running his estate. Young Alexis, meanwhile, was educated at home by a kindly but not very demanding old priest named the abbé Christian Lesueur, who had been his father's tutor before him. By the time Alexis was ten years old, he had been exposed to a good deal of history at first hand. His father took him to Paris to witness the celebration after Napoleon's defeat at Waterloo, and he wrote to his tutor, "Why didn't you come with us? How you would have shouted 'Vive le roi!'" Soon afterward they were granted a formal audience with the newly restored monarch, Louis XVIII.

Under that king and his successor, the inept Charles X, Hervé de Tocqueville held a series of positions in which he served as an active and imaginative administrator, developing modernizing programs in agriculture, transportation, and education. But he was very much an aristocrat of the old school, sympathetic to extreme royalists who wanted the ancien régime restored to its old privileges. His two eldest sons shared his convictions; Alexis did not.

Alexis spent his childhood in Normandy, where his family had its roots, and in Paris, until 1817, when he was twelve years old and his way of life changed dramatically. His father was appointed prefect, or governor, of the Moselle region in eastern France, with headquarters at Metz. He sent for Alexis and placed him in the first school he had ever attended, where he immediately excelled. Most important, liberated from the tutelage of the lovable but deeply conservative Lesueur, Alexis learned to think for himself. He began devouring books by eighteenth-century skeptics in his father's library, and at sixteen he experienced a shattering loss of religious faith that still haunted him when he described it to a confidante thirty-five years later: "Then doubt entered my soul, or rather it rushed in with incredible violence, not just doubt about this or that, but universal doubt. Suddenly I experienced the sensation that people who have been through an earthquake describe, the ground shaking beneath their feet, the walls around them, the ceiling above them, the furniture they're touching, the whole of nature before their eyes. I was seized by the blackest melancholy, and by extreme disgust for life without even knowing life yet, and I was overwhelmed with distress and terror at the sight of the road that lay ahead of me in the world."

What rescued him were his earliest sexual adventures. "Violent passions pulled me out of this state of despair, and turned my gaze away from these mental ruins and toward sensory objects." (After his death his widow considered this confession so shocking that she got Beaumont, who had been collecting his friend's correspondence, to return it to her, and she destroyed it. It survives only because Beaumont's wife was so struck by it that she surreptitiously made a copy.) Tocqueville was handsome, charming, and appealing to women, but virtually nothing is known about his early relationships. One of his biographers, however, discovered the birth certificate of a child born of a transient union with a servant, and at about the same time Tocqueville had a passionate affair with a middle-class girl whom his patrician family would never have accepted for his spouse. A remarkable letter survives from his cousin and lifelong friend Louis de Kergorlay, written in 1823, when Alexis was seventeen, which contrasts their erotic temperaments. "I see that you catch fire suddenly, like gunpowder," Kergorlay said, "and that the important thing is not to put a match to you. With me it's completely different. It's a subdued, confused, and habitual feeling that never leaves me, and tickles me quite apart from any objects that arouse it, which is to say, this or that woman. I feel less unbridled lust than you do, and more love . . . But since, unlike yours, my soul has more to do with this than my body does, I'm far more demanding. I'm waiting for the woman who will be right for me, the way the Jews await the Messiah." What prompted Kergorlay's rather preachy letter (he was only eighteen himself) was not just a high-minded resolve to remain pure until marriage, but a hint Alexis had dropped that he was planning to fight a duel over an affair of honor. It is not known whether the duel ever took place, but if it did, perhaps his father, the prefect, hushed it up.

As for the religious doubts, they troubled Tocqueville for the rest of his life. In a rather abstract way he continued to be, or wanted to be, a believer, but more accurately he was an agnostic lamenting the loss of the faith of his earliest years. One of his favorite authors was Pascal, whose *Pensées* spoke eloquently to his dread of emptiness and to his compulsion to be always active. "Nothing is so intolerable to man," Pascal wrote, "as to be completely at rest, without passions, without business, without diversion, without work. He then feels his nothingness, his desertion, his insufficiency, his dependence, his weakness, his emptiness. Immediately from the depth of his heart will emerge ennui, gloom, sadness, distress, vexation, despair." For someone with Tocqueville's volatile temperament, intellectual labor would become a lifelong escape from anxiety and doubt; as Beaumont said, "Mental activity was like a sanctum for him, in which he took refuge to escape the unrest and sorrows of the soul." A few years after Tocqueville's death the American Charles Eliot Norton wrote that he "was born a thinker . . . his mind was large and calm." The wisdom and calm were hard-won.

When his school studies were finished, Tocqueville moved in with his mother in Paris—she had refused to go to Metz—and began to study law. He found the subject arid and tedious, but he stuck with it for two years and got his degree. For relief he made a two-week tour of Sicily with his brother Édouard, and on the trip he kept a huge notebook (now mostly lost) that would turn out to be a trial run for his note taking in America five years later.

Hervé de Tocqueville was transferred twice after his stint in Metz, the second time to Versailles, and in 1827 he got his twenty-two-year-old son appointed as an unsalaried *juge-auditeur*, or apprentice magistrate, there. Alexis found the work unexpectedly stimulating, though he was rather startled by his own competitiveness, and frustrated by his awkwardness as a speaker. He wrote to his cousin Kergorlay, who was an army officer by then, "I recognize daily that I have a need to come out on top that is going to torment me cruelly all my life. And I have another defect at present: I'm having a hard time getting used to speaking in public. I grope for words and cut my ideas short. I see people all around me who reason badly and speak well, and that puts me in a continual rage."

It might seem that Alexis had chosen the wrong profession altogether, since he told Kergorlay that he had no intention of becoming "a legal machine" like his pedantic colleagues. But he had discovered that

ALEXIS DE TOCQUEVILLE
In this portrait, made when Tocqueville was in his thirties, the artist has caught his characteristic expression of reserve, bordering almost on diffidence.

immersion in complex details could be intellectually absorbing. "I'm no longer bored; you can't imagine what it's like to turn your attention seriously on a single point. Inevitably, you end up getting interested in the work. Thus the law, which disgusted me in theory, doesn't affect me that way in practice. All my faculties unite to find a solution or a means to it, I feel my mind active and expanding, and the result is the same *bien-être* I've experienced in my heart when I was in love and it made me feel alive." Gaining close familiarity with different legal codes turned out to be invaluable training for Tocqueville's inquiries in America.

It was at Versailles that Tocqueville met Gustave de Beaumont, a fellow magistrate three years older than himself, and formed a lifelong friendship. Beaumont came from the Loire Valley west of Paris, and just as the Tocqueville family had a château at Tocqueville, the Beaumonts had one at Beaumont-la-Chartre (known today as Beaumont-sur-Dême). He, too, was the youngest of three brothers, and the others had become army officers just as Tocqueville's had. Right from the start there was an exceptionally close bond, as Tocqueville confirmed a year later, "a friendship between us that, I don't know how, was born already long-standing." He was well aware that Beaumont's gregarious good cheer was an invaluable stimulant. A wit said years afterward that the two complemented each other "like the decanter of vinegar and the decanter of oil."

Early in their friendship Tocqueville wrote, "You've taught me, my dear Beaumont, to bend my stiff back, and I hope that with time you'll make it even more supple. If firmness is a good thing, stiffness never is, and I believe I have both the good quality and the defect. I'll turn myself over to you on this point—prune and trim as you see fit." A few months later he added, "You have more chance of being recognized and valued than I, with my externally cold and not very sociable character . . . Whatever may happen to us, the thing is done, we're united, and it very much seems that it's for life." Nevertheless, they always addressed each other—and their parents—with the formal *vous*, reserving *tu* for relatives in their own generation and for a few childhood friends.

The two young men pursued flirtations at Versailles, which had to be conducted with extreme discretion with the sternly chaperoned

GUSTAVE DE BEAUMONT
Beaumont evidently seeks an
authoritative pose, with no
hint of his usual gaiety.

French girls. Tocqueville told Beaumont that whenever he called at the house of a girl he was interested in, he was told that no one was at home. But eventually he managed to intercept her with her mother at a fair. "Fortunately, the mother never passed a bookstall without pausing. When she was inspecting a book and I could see she wasn't looking, I went and stood by the daughter and picked up a book myself; as soon as the mother was reading hers, I shot the girl *un regard assassin,* a killing look. When the mother took off her lorgnette, I quickly resumed reading, with that saintly expression you're familiar with. This was repeated five or six times." Eventually, the mother noticed him, chatted cheerfully, and issued an invitation to visit; but sure enough, when he showed up, he was informed that she and her daughter had unfortunately gone out.

Two years before that episode, in 1828, he met the woman who would much later become his wife. Her name was Mary Mottley; she was an Englishwoman six (or possibly nine) years older than himself, living in France with her mother. Mary, or Marie, as he always called her, was highly intelligent and spoke excellent French, and the attraction was soon so intense that Tocqueville resolved on marriage, but he knew that her foreignness and lack of social standing would provoke vehement resistance from his aristocratic parents. For the time being, therefore, he kept the relationship totally secret from everyone but his closest friends.

In 1830 came a dramatic event that proved to be a turning point in the careers of both Tocquevilles, father and son. Reacting against an unexpected electoral victory by the liberal opposition, Charles X issued a series of decrees that dissolved the legislature, tightened voting qualifications to ensure conservative majorities, and abolished freedom of the press. The streets of Paris immediately filled with barricades—the insurrection is celebrated in Delacroix's famous painting *Liberty Leading the People*—and Charles withdrew his decrees, but it was too late. The Duke of Orléans, who had liberal sympathies in spite of his aristocratic lineage, was acclaimed king as Louis-Philippe I. Nearly all members of the Tocqueville and Beaumont families believed that this new king was completely illegitimate, and Hervé immediately resigned his post, ending his career in government.

Much to the outrage of their families, however, the young Tocqueville and Beaumont did not resign. With painfully divided feelings, but determined not to throw away the chance of public service, they took an oath of loyalty to Louis-Philippe. Tocqueville wrote to Marie, whom he would not feel free to marry for another five years, "My conscience doesn't reproach me at all, but all the same I'm deeply wounded, and I'll number this day among the unhappiest of my life . . . I'm at war with myself. It's a new state, horrible for me . . . How my voice altered when I pronounced those words! I felt my heart beating as if my chest would burst."

Looking back after Tocqueville's death, Beaumont commented that his friend might have had a very conventional career but for the shock of 1830. "His name, his family, his social position, and his career marked out for him the path to follow . . . Young, agreeable, connected with all the great families, with looks that would allow him to aspire to the finest matches, which were already being proposed to him, he would have married some rich heiress. His life would have flowed easily and decently in the regular performance of his duties within a circle circumscribed in advance, with the well-being that a great fortune provides, in the midst of the serious concerns of the law and the peaceful satisfactions of private life." But Tocqueville was temperamentally restless and aspiring. He wanted to accomplish something great, and now history was offering him an opportunity, if only he could decide how to use it. As he had told Beaumont even before the 1830 crisis, "The passions of politics agitate my feelings so much that I feel I'm literally another man when I experience them." Beaumont recalled nostalgically a quarter of a century later, "Those who never saw that period, and who know only the indolence and indifference of today, will find it hard to comprehend the ardors of that time."

Loyalty oath or not, the new government was suspicious of aristocratic employees who might be covertly disaffected, and Tocqueville and Beaumont were well aware that their position was precarious. More largely, there was widespread anxiety in the face of an unpredictable future, the notorious *mal du siècle*, or "sickness of the age." As the poet and playwright Alfred de Musset later recalled in memorably purple prose, "Behind them was a past forever destroyed, still quivering on its ruins with all the fossils of the centuries of absolutism; before them the dawn of a vast horizon, the first glimmerings of the future; and between these two worlds, like the ocean that separates the Old World from young America, something vague and floating, a stormy sea full of wreckage, traversed from time to time by some far-off white sail or some ship puffing heavy smoke—in short, the present century."

Before long Tocqueville and Beaumont thought of a shrewd solution. In order to keep clear of political booby traps, it would be a good idea for them to get out of France, and if they could travel on official government business, their loyalty might seem less in doubt. Prison reform was then being widely debated throughout Europe, where jails were still simply holding tanks in which prisoners of both sexes mixed freely, educated each other in criminal skills, and bribed the jailers to bring them luxuries. Still worse, the crime rate had been rising steadily for years, and reformers were therefore urging that imprisonment be made an unpalatable deterrent and that inmates be reeducated for useful lives when they returned to society.

The new regime was uneasy about most of the ideas for reform that

were in the air, and it seized on prisons as a safely noncontroversial issue. As Michel Foucault says in his great book *Discipline and Punish*,
"The prison has always formed part of an active field in which projects,
improvements, experiments, theoretical statements, personal evidence
and investigations have proliferated." In America a brand-new system
was being established in which huge penitentiaries—the name implied
encouragement to repent—isolated inmates from each other and gave
them useful work to do. So Tocqueville and Beaumont proposed to
their superiors that they be dispatched to America to study the penitentiaries, pointing out that "books of theory abound, but practical
works are nowhere." As Tocqueville told a friend at the time, it was a
subject "which has nothing political about it, and which relates only to
the good of society in general." Still better, "We'll be journeying all
over the Union in the name of France, and that will give us an indisput-
able advantage over all other travelers." The government accordingly
commissioned them to undertake an eighteen-month expedition (it
was later cut short to nine months) on condition that the young investigators travel on their own money.

Privately, they had a much larger aim in view, as Tocqueville told
another friend shortly before sailing. "We're going with the intention of
examining, in detail and as scientifically as possible, all the workings
of that vast American society that everyone talks about and no one
knows." Four years later, when the first part of *Democracy in America* was
about to come out, he admitted frankly to Kergorlay that "the penitentiary system was a pretext; I used it as a passport that could give me
access everywhere in the United States." In fact the great book was the
result of a series of accidents: Tocqueville happened to be the right
person in the right place at the right time. But it was also the result of
ambition and hard work; he knew how to turn accidents to advantage.

So Tocqueville and Beaumont bustled around, getting equipped for
the journey. They purchased leather trunks, fine hats, and fowling
pieces for shooting birds. Beaumont, who had artistic inclinations, also
brought sketchbooks and a flute. On April 2, 1831, they embarked at
Le Havre with 180 fellow passengers on a sailing ship, itself named the
Havre. It was a *paquebot*, a term borrowed from the English "packet

boat" to denote a vessel that had a government contract to carry pack-
ets of mail and that sailed on fixed dates instead of waiting for a full
cargo. Steamships didn't yet have the power or endurance to cross the
Atlantic.

The duration of the voyage necessarily depended on winds and
weather; one acquaintance said that a previous crossing had taken an
appalling sixty-six days. Tocqueville enjoyed the grandeur of the ocean,
though. One stormy night he propped himself against the bowsprit
and watched the waves glow with brilliant iridescence as the ship cut
through them. Another time, when passengers were taking potshots at
a barrel floating by, "it was I who had the honor of putting a hole in it."
Less satisfactory were the social encounters. Most of the passengers
were Americans whom he found tiresome, and there was no avoiding
them—"it's what one might call distilling boredom drop by drop." The
casual social style also took some getting used to. "Having to live on
top of each other and see each other constantly establishes an inconsid-
erateness and freedom of which one has no idea on terra firma." Beaumont's flute was welcome, and when his fellow passengers called for
dancing, he proposed a *contredanse* in which men and women faced
each other in lines, going through five dance styles in succession. "I
was the orchestra, and getting up on a chair, I directed the ball marvel-
ously—*pantalon, pastourelle, poule, galop,* and *valse* came one after another with extreme rapidity."

On board ship, both friends quickly discovered that their English
needed work. In a letter to his family that Beaumont kept adding to
during the voyage, he admitted ruefully, "Although I already knew how
to order bread in that language, I feel now the difference between
knowing a foreign language superficially and studying it more deeply.
It's of the utmost importance for us to know English right down to our
fingertips and to understand it idiomatically, so as to sense all the fine
points and to grasp all the nuances of expression. Without that, we'll
never be sure of our observations, because we won't know for certain
that we understand what they're saying to us. So we're putting our
minds through torture to achieve that goal." An attractive young American, a Miss Edwards, was willing to help with the torture, correcting

their mistakes during long conversations. Beaumont hastened to add (he was writing to his family), "Notwithstanding her eighteen years, her freshness, her kindness, and all the charms of her person, our relations are entirely fraternal. I'm using the expression accurately, since she's actually like a sister to me—which is not without merit, since she's really pretty and very witty."

For much of each day Tocqueville and Beaumont stayed in their shared stateroom and put themselves through a heroic program of study, with particular attention to books on the law and on American prisons. Spending so much time together, they found that the relationship was wearing well. "Tocqueville is a truly distinguished man," Beaumont noted, "with lofty ideas and nobility of soul. The more I know him, the more I love him. Our lives have been placed side by side, and it's evident that our destinies are and will be in common."

At last North America came into view. They were scheduled to land in New York, but just as they were approaching the entrance to the harbor, the wind shifted and began to blow directly against them. Since supplies were running low, the captain decided not to wait for a favorable wind but to head eastward and set his passengers ashore at Newport, Rhode Island. There the *Havre* docked at long last, on May 9, after thirty-eight days at sea.

2

FIRST IMPRESSIONS: NEW YORK CITY

Newport in those days was a modest and charming town; the vast palaces of the Gilded Age were still half a century in the future. "It's a collection of little houses the size of chicken coops," Tocqueville wrote to his mother, "but with a neatness that's a pleasure to see, which we have no notion of in France." What especially struck him and Beaumont was the casualness of the customs office, their first indication that America was far less bureaucratic than France. "They inspected our baggage with very little attention," Beaumont reported, "and it's evident that the customs officers in Newport bear no resemblance to French ones."

Excitement awaited in a huge steamboat, the *President*, that would carry them to New York. The steamboat was an American invention that was barely beginning to catch on in Europe, and Tocqueville was astonished at this behemoth. "It's impossible to give an idea of the interior of this immense machine," he wrote to his mother. "Suffice it to say that it contains three great saloons, two for men and one for women, where four, five, and often eight hundred people eat and sleep comfortably."

"We've arrived," Beaumont wrote after they landed, "at a sort of hotel known as a boardinghouse. It's nothing else than a pension." Once they got to their room and realized how exhausted they were, they retired at four in the afternoon and slept for sixteen hours straight. Their boardinghouse was located in a desirable neighborhood. "In New York," Beaumont explained, "there's a place called Broadway, which more or less means *grande rue*, where from noon to three o'clock you're sure to find all the elegant women of New York."

Some establishments that would remain famous were already in existence, such as Brooks Brothers and Lord & Taylor, and Wall Street was the financial center, but New York was a disappointment compared with European cities. "The appearance of the town is bizarre for a Frenchman," Tocqueville reported, "and not very pleasing. You see neither domes nor church towers nor grand edifices, so you feel as if you're still in a suburb." The skyline totally lacked today's grandeur, and after Beaumont got to Boston, he contrasted the two cities to New York's disadvantage: "It's on flat terrain, and no matter from what side you look at it, it presents nothing to the eye but a single line of houses. Boston, on the contrary, is built on uneven and hilly terrain, so when you see the city from a distance, it presents charming points of view."

Still, New York was the largest American city by far, with more than 200,000 inhabitants (Philadelphia and Boston, the next largest, had 60,000 each). The settled area extended only from the southern tip of

BROADWAY FROM THE BOWLING GREEN, 1828

Manhattan up to Canal Street in what is now Chinatown. The rectangular grid of streets didn't yet exist, and what would eventually become Third Avenue was a muddy lane leading to the remote village of Harlem. On one occasion Tocqueville and Beaumont were entertained at the country estate of an acquaintance from the *Havre*, which was set among farms on the bank of the East River. Today that location is East Sixty-fourth Street. The farms might even seem to have invaded the city. An English visitor deplored the "miserable wooden cottages" scattered throughout, even along Broadway, and was disgusted to find that "swine innumerable roam at large." The beasts were indeed a menace, bowling over small children, but poor families depended on them for food and let them scavenge for garbage until it was time to slaughter them; riots defeated every official attempt to clear them out.

What most startled foreign travelers was the incessant bustle and noise. A Scottish visitor complained pompously, "The streets of New York are not to be perambulated with impunity by either the lame, the blind, or the exquisitely sensitive in their olfactory nerves; to use an American expression, a person must be 'wide-awake' not to dislocate his ankles by the inequalities and gaps in the side-pavements, or break his legs by running foul of the numberless and immoveable encumbrances with which they are occupied." More approvingly, Walt Whitman noted the continual activity and noise: "What can New York—noisy, roaring, rumbling, tumbling, bustling, stormy, turbulent New York—have to do with *silence*?" Europeans were shocked, too, by the summer heat, and were solemnly told that healthy people sometimes dropped dead on account of drinking cold water. (One visitor commented sagely, "Water should not be drunk immediately from the well, but should be allowed previously to stand for a few minutes in the air. It should be taken in small mouthfuls, and these heated in the mouth for two or three seconds before swallowing.")

New Yorkers turned out to be flattered to be the subject of an official French delegation, and a relentless social whirl was immediately under way for Tocqueville and his friend. "We're showered with courtesies and overwhelmed with visits," Beaumont wrote to his brother Jules. "In the midst of all this we have to find time to work and above all to think, and really that's not easy to do." They accomplished it by rising at seven, "you well know thanks to what beneficent instrument," an alarm clock that Jules had thoughtfully provided, which had already proved its efficiency on shipboard with "an infernal racket that overpowers the noise of the sea and the whistling of the wind."

The research was serious enough. They spent their mornings studying books at the Athenaeum at the corner of Pine and Broadway. A big box in the Tocqueville collection at Yale is filled with hundreds of pages of notes, interspersed with masses of statistics that he laboriously extracted from disorganized prison records. He wrote to a friend, "We're accomplishing an enormous labor on the prisons. Will it be useful? I don't know, but I flatter myself that it will be complete." And he added, "I can tell you, it's by the sweat of our brow." Still more valuable were insights about America gained in conversation, and it was an advantage to have a big project in view, since it gave focus to social encounters and made people eager to talk. "We continue to acquire material for our great work," Beaumont wrote. "We go about constantly questioning the people we encounter, we squeeze whoever falls into our hands, and at night we write up what we've heard during the day."

The companions were beginning to think that something grander than a prison report might result from their experiences, and they both began to keep copious notes on topics of all kinds. Tocqueville's impressions were recorded in little notebooks that he folded and stitched by hand. They were not a true diary and are not especially lively reading from cover to cover, but they were never meant to be. They were raw material, a record of everything that might somehow be useful later. Beaumont wrote admiringly after Tocqueville's death, "One can scarcely imagine the activity of body and mind that consumed him like a burning fever and never slackened. Everything was a subject for observation. He would ask in advance, in his head, all the questions he hoped to resolve . . . Whenever an idea occurred to him, he noted it down without delay, no matter where he was, because he had observed that the force of first impressions can never be recovered if one lets them slip away." Inspired by his friend's example, Beaumont later wrote to his sister, "I've become such an intrepid and indefatigable observer that my notes are taking on enormous size, and my journal is inordinately long." That journal is now lost, but much of its material went into Beaumont's letters and into his novel *Marie*.

In effect, they were becoming investigative reporters. "Since our arrival here," Tocqueville reported cheerfully after a month, "we've become the most pitiless questioners in the world." A measure of their intellectual energy is Beaumont's dismissive opinion of the French consul and his family: "They are agreeable people, and they immediately invited us to dinner, but there's nothing to be gained from their conversation. They know nothing of the country they're in, and they're absolutely devoid of powers of observation." Whatever his limitations, the consul was at least a cultivated and intelligent man, unlike a couple of young French noblemen who announced that they planned to tour the country but also expressed a horror of American society. Beaumont was disgusted by their shallowness. "I'd like to know what use their trip will be . . . I conclude from this that they'll get to know the roads and inns wonderfully well. We tried to get them to talk; I don't know that there are any emptier fools on earth."

It wasn't all work. There were endless dinner parties and balls, and the companions soon found that they hadn't brought enough formal clothes. Since American gloves were expensive and flimsy, Tocqueville wrote home for two dozen pairs of *gants glacés*—leather cured in olive oil, eggs, and distilled alcohol—and half a dozen pairs in chamois. It embarrassed him to have to depend on family support, since the French government had declined to subsidize the trip. "Tell Papa," Tocqueville wrote to his old tutor the abbé Lesueur, "that up to now we haven't incurred a single expense that wasn't absolutely *necessary* in the full meaning of the word . . . I assure you I earnestly desire to weigh as lightly as possible on his budget, and I'll make every effort to do so."

The travelers found themselves constantly among the rich and locally famous, many of whom were people of real distinction. The banker Nathaniel Prime, who showed them genial hospitality at his country retreat, was reputed to be the wealthiest man in New York. The Swiss-born Albert Gallatin, who spoke perfect French, had been secretary of state and the treasury under Jefferson and Madison, as well as ambassador to France and England, president of the Bank of New York, and founder of the American Ethnological Society. James Kent, a former chief justice of New York, was an unrivaled authority on the law.

Especially valuable was Edward Livingston, once a military aide-de-camp to Andrew Jackson and now his secretary of state. Livingston's energies were waning by now, and in any case his talents had always been more intellectual than political ("He is a polished scholar," said his old friend Jackson, "an able writer, and a most excellent man, but he knows nothing of mankind"). However, he had once been a senator from Louisiana, and as an expert on the legal history of that state he was of great help interpreting differences between the French legal system and the American. Livingston was personally charming, too, as were many of the dignitaries Tocqueville got to know, and he had a stunning Creole wife, who elicited Beaumont's appreciative comment: "Madame John Livingston is a charming woman who couldn't be nicer—or more flirtatious, though I'll never know if the flirtatiousness goes any further than that."

The young Frenchmen were a perfect team. Beaumont was a cheerful extrovert, able to charm any group of strangers, while Tocqueville was easily excited by ideas that interested him and a compelling conversationalist with intelligent companions of any social class. It was among less intelligent people—and they encountered many in high society—that he was at a disadvantage. Long after the journey he acknowledged ruefully, "Whenever someone fails to strike me with something unusual in mind or feelings, I, so to speak, do not see him. I've always thought that mediocre men, just as much as people of merit, have noses, mouths, and eyes, but I've never been able to fix in my memory their particular version of these features . . . I respect them, for they lead the world, but they bore me profoundly."

Actually, Tocqueville was making a real effort to be agreeable, and the flattering attentions were bringing him out of his shell. After the first month an amused Beaumont drew up a formal deposition:

I the undersigned, being an expert in politeness and courtesy and a candid friend of Master Alexis de Tocqueville, that is to say readier to tell him his faults than to speak of his good qualities, do certify the following facts: the said Master Alexis, who could previously have been reproached for a social style that was rather too cold and reserved, and too indifferent toward people he doesn't care for, . . . has accomplished a complete reform in his manners. Now he is affable and gracious toward all, as agreeable with old women as with young ones, and he puts himself out in society even for those whose looks displease him.

By way of evidence Beaumont described Tocqueville sitting by the piano while an untalented lady performed, smiling happily and applauding energetically at the end of each piece. On another occasion, Tocqueville let his mind wander until a song was finished, and he admitted afterward in a letter home, "Remembering that one was supposed to laugh, I did so quite loudly. At this outburst of merriment everyone stared at me, and I was covered with confusion when I realized that the comic song I'd been listening to ended five minutes ago, and that the one that made me so jolly was the most plaintive and sentimental in the entire American repertoire." Beaumont, who prided himself on his flute playing, complained that Americans performed music horribly. "An American told me, 'We like music the way children like noise.' If any harmony does attempt to emerge in this insensitive milieu, it's smothered at birth by the chilly, muffled atmosphere around it, the way a sound dies out in flat country where there are no echoes."

There were official duties, too. Energized by the discovery that they wanted to inspect American prisons, the authorities eagerly dragged them to institutions of confinement of every kind. In a carriage provided by their hosts, they visited during the course of a single day a reformatory for juveniles, an insane asylum, an establishment for deaf-mutes, a poorhouse, and the prison on Blackwells Island (now known as Roosevelt Island) in the East River. By way of compensation, at the poorhouse they were treated, perhaps not very tactfully, to a lavish banquet for twenty-five guests. The Frenchmen were shocked by the gulf between American manners and the ones they were accustomed to. There seemed to be no wine, oysters appeared at the end instead of the beginning, and fish was served before meat—"in a word," Tocqueville wrote home, "complete barbarism." Worst of all, when wine did arrive at last, each guest rose in turn to offer a toast to the visitors, who were supposed to drink in response. Realizing that to repeat this performance two dozen times would leave him helplessly drunk, Tocqueville contrived to take tiny sips and managed to survive. But just when he thought it might be time to leave, there was an even more off-putting sequel. Cigars on plates were served, and in a massive cloud of smoke the toasts began all over again. "Each person's features relaxed a tiny bit, and they gave themselves over to the heaviest gaiety in the world."

American stolidity, indeed, was a constant theme in visitors' accounts. In the eastern part of the country especially, faces were inexpressive. Even courting couples, one observer commented, appeared to be "wearing all unconsciously the masks which custom had prescribed, and onlookers who did not know the secret would think them cold and indifferent." A German immigrant whom Tocqueville got to know well, Francis Lieber, claimed that "there is little of what is called *fun* in America," though his testimony may be suspect, since his own writings are ponderously facetious. As for the ebullient Charles Dickens, who visited America a decade after Tocqueville, conversations there roused him to rage—"such deadly leaden people, such systematic plodding weary insupportable heaviness."

Some comments by Beaumont show that what he missed most of all was the playful, witty repartee he was accustomed to at home. "They don't chat in the United States the way they do in France. The American always argues. He has no knowledge of the art of lightly skimming the surface of topics in a large group, where each one puts in a remark, brilliant or dull, heavy or light, where one person finishes a phrase begun by someone else, and where everything is touched on but never in depth." Tocqueville, on the other hand, with his innate seriousness and passion for ideas, found that the American social style made meaningful conversation easier. Years afterward he told an English friend, "The sole object of the people I was raised by was amusement and diversion. They never talked about politics, and I believe they scarcely thought about them . . . One studied how to please as today one would study how to gain wealth or power." For Tocqueville there was no contradiction between serious topics and enjoyable conversation. He had remarked to a friend a year before the American trip, "To keep the mind in motion, to make one want to reflect, to raise questions in passing for reflection to explore—that, in my opinion, is the purpose of conversation."

What Tocqueville found less appealing was the bombastic style that Americans of that era affected. In *Democracy in America* he recalled, "An American doesn't know how to converse; he debates. He doesn't discourse; he holds forth. He always speaks to you as if he were addressing a meeting, and if he happens to get worked up, he will say 'Gentlemen!' when he's talking to a single person." Like other travelers, too, Tocqueville was exasperated by the Americans' tendency to boast about their country and to extort compliments from visitors. "The people here seem to me to be stinking with national conceit," he wrote to his mother three days after arriving in New York. But as time went on, he would recognize that what looked like vanity was actually insecurity. "The slightest praise delights them, and the greatest seldom satisfies them. They harass you continually to force you to praise them, and if you resist all their attempts, they praise themselves." The English, on the other hand, weren't insecure enough. "Toward the entire world the Englishman displays a reserve filled with disdain and ignorance. His pride has no need to be fed; it lives off itself." John Stuart Mill, who would become a close friend of Tocqueville's in later years, pointedly contrasted "the frank sociability and amiability of French personal intercourse, and the English mode of existence in which everybody acts as if everybody else (with few, or no, exceptions) was either an enemy or a bore."

The companions' command of English was improving fairly rapidly—"we've had to give up our own language completely, no one speaks it," Tocqueville wrote shortly after arrival—but it was still a work in progress. "It's often pitiful to listen to us, but eventually we do make ourselves understood, and we understand everything. People assure us that in the end we'll be speaking remarkably well." A letter in English some weeks later shows a confident, though not exactly idiomatic, command of the language: "Mr. de Tocqueville thanks Mister Francis for the good advises which are contained in his letter and which it is his intention to follow. Mr. de Tocqueville will never forget the cares and the kind attendance which have been given him by Doct. Francis." The letter containing the "good advises," unfortunately, is lost. Beaumont admitted more candidly, "We're making progress, but it happens every day that we make strange mistakes, and we're never quite sure what people are telling us." They even misheard a day of the week and failed to show up for an elaborate banquet in their honor. "You'll conclude from this," Beaumont wrote ruefully to his mother, "that we're still not very good at English, and I'll readily agree. Yet in France we would have the reputation of speaking like Londoners, because we say with such aplomb things that are expressed as badly as they could possibly be."

By the time he wrote *Democracy in America*, after marriage to an Englishwoman and extended visits with English friends, Tocqueville's mastery of the language was perfect, and he had come to understand that there was no such thing as a single "American" speech. Instead, there was an immense range, from windy rhetoric to salty colloquialism. "I've often noticed that Americans, who in general conduct their business in language that is clear, crisp, and unadorned, and often vulgar in its extreme simplicity, readily turn bombastic when they reach for a poetical style. Then they show themselves relentlessly pompous from one end of a speech to the other." Far from being a snob, Tocqueville enjoyed the pithiness of ordinary American speech, as did the English writer Captain Frederick Marryat, who thought it amusing that Americans called shops "stores" and divided cities into "blocks," but who appreciated an eating house sign in Illinois that read, "Stranger, here's your chicken fixings." Marryat commented perceptively that many Americanisms had originated as regional usages in various parts of England, and he reported with friendly interest expressions that would seem completely unexceptionable today: "*Bad* is used in an odd sense: it is employed for awkward, uncomfortable, sorry—'I have felt quite bad about it ever since.'" "*Right away*, for immediately or at once, is very general." "*To make tracks*—to walk away." Moreover, Marryat, who was fond of a good joke, was surprised that so many visitors called Americans humorless, and suspected that they were often having their legs pulled without realizing it.

Beyond the technicalities of law and government, it was American society that interested Tocqueville and Beaumont, and as their acquaintances on shipboard had predicted, they found it overwhelmingly commercial. This was a regular leitmotif at the time. According to the German immigrant Francis Grund, "Business is the very soul of an American. It is as if all America were but one gigantic workshop, over the entrance of which there is the blazing inscription '*No admission here, except on business.*'" Many Americans agreed. Sarah Hale deplored the "materialism, competitiveness, and acquisitiveness" of "this bank-note world," and Washington Irving, the most popular author of his generation, coined the expression "the almighty dollar," which he called "that great object of universal devotion throughout our land."

Beaumont commented disparagingly after his first week in New York, "The Americans are a nation of merchants, devoured by a hunger for wealth that brings many far from honorable passions along with it, such as greed, fraud, and bad faith. They seem to have but one single thought here and one single goal, which is to make their fortune." But after further acquaintance he began to understand that although Americans sought wealth, they at least had no class of idle parasites. He wrote to his brother, "There are no rich people in the sense we ordinarily give the word. By that we generally mean those who have no other occupation than to spend their fortune, and who live off their rents, whether they live in rural seclusion or spend their income in the city."

Tocqueville's thinking followed the same trajectory, but more profoundly. On arriving in New York, he declared, "The more deeply one goes into the American national character, the more one sees that they value everything on earth in response to this sole question: How much money will it bring in?" But he admitted that his opinions were still at the "more or less" stage, and already he was struck by a moral dimension to the pursuit of gain. "The whole world here seems like a malleable material that man turns and shapes to his liking. An immense field, only a small part of which has yet been traversed, lies open here to industriousness. There is no one who may not reasonably hope to attain the pleasures of life, and no one who isn't aware that if he loves hard work, his future is certain." Beaumont was struck by how often he heard "So-and-so is worth ten thousand dollars; someone else isn't worth half as much."

Back home, the wealthy were less crass about their finances, but on the other hand they tended to be complacently parasitical. At its best the French upper class promoted an ethic of public-spirited "virtue," but it was not always at its best, and Tocqueville came to believe that Americans had found an effective equivalent for aristocratic virtue. "A people that seems to live only to get rich can't know how to be virtuous in the strict sense of the word, but they are well behaved. They have none of the vices of the idle rich, and their habits are regular." And however much Tocqueville admired the old ways, he was certain that their day was past, so there was every incentive to understand what made this new kind of society work. In a note labeled "First Impressions," four days after arriving in New York, he wrote a sentence that could serve as the foundation of *Democracy in America*: "The entire society seems to have merged into the middle class."

Insofar as anyone might potentially rise from the bottom of American society to the top, whereas a French peasant was always a peasant and a nobleman always a nobleman, such a formulation made sense. But it seems clear today that Tocqueville underestimated the gulf between bottom and top in America. He was not alone in this. When he claimed that few Americans had large fortunes and that wealth was lost as often as gained, resulting in exceptional social mobility, he was just repeating what everybody told him. Modern research, however, has shown that the myth of rags to riches was indeed a myth. Four percent of the inhabitants of New York City controlled 50 percent of its wealth, and hundreds of families were extremely rich even by European standards. There were two millionaires in New York at a time when a laborer's daily wage was one dollar (a skilled carpenter could make a dollar and a quarter), and there were three hundred people with fortunes of $100,000. In those days someone who had $10,000 in the bank could enjoy a life of elegant leisure, and $3,000 was more than enough for a commodious town house, a country place, servants, a carriage, and so on. Moreover, there was no income tax, and the property tax, typically 1 percent of value, was based on notoriously underestimated assessments. Of course, the wealthy didn't necessarily consider themselves so. John Jacob Astor was heard to say that a man could be as happy with half a million "as if he was rich." As for the "rags" part of the myth, only a tiny percentage of the wealthy were self-made. Most were born into rich families and simply went on getting richer.

At the other end of the scale, ordinary workers were increasingly losing status and security. As Sean Wilentz shows in compelling detail in *Chants Democratic*, employers were increasingly breaking down complex tasks so that unskilled laborers could do them cheaply. In addition, they were less and less likely to participate as master craftsmen alongside their employees. They were simply bosses, whose only connection with employees was the payment of low wages, and the first strikes— short-lived and ineffectual, to be sure—were starting to be organized.

Another sign of change was the reluctance of most Americans to work as household servants, which startled Europeans. Basil Hall, a Scottish naval officer whose *Travels in North America* gave much offense, complained about "the total want of good servants" and concluded that "the whole system of domestic service is deplorable." Another visitor said disapprovingly, "Servants, whether white or black, native or foreign, entertain such notions of equality and independence as fit them but poorly for this station of life, and tend greatly to abridge the comforts of their employers." And a third noted, "'Master' is not a word in the vocabulary of hired people. 'Boss,' a Dutch one of similar import, is substituted. The former is used by Negroes, and is by free people considered as synonymous with slave keeper."

In his notebook Tocqueville commented that servants "say that they're giving *the help* [quoted in English], and they want to be treated like neighbors who have come in temporarily to lend a hand. They have to eat with their masters." When he mentioned to Livingston the "extreme equality" that seemed to prevail, Livingston replied that customs such as the universal shaking of hands were merely routine politeness, like signing "your humble servant" in a letter. "Just like everywhere else," he added, "we have an aristocracy of money, if one can call something an aristocracy that constantly changes and has pretensions but not power." But that was precisely Tocqueville's point. In the aristocratic culture in which he grew up, even the highest servants took for granted that an unbreachable barrier separated them from their masters, while down at the bottom "the French have a word expressly invented for the lowest servants of aristocracy—they call them lackeys." In America there were no masters, only employers, and there were no lackeys; servants simply contracted to perform a particular job. "By nature neither one is inferior to the other; they only become so temporarily as a consequence of the contract . . . Public opinion, which bases itself on the ordinary course of things, puts them on much the same level and creates a sort of imaginary equality between them, regardless of the actual inequality of their conditions." To a Frenchman this was a profound novelty, and in the very first sentence of *Democracy in America* Tocqueville chose to say, "Among the new objects that attracted my attention during my stay in the United States, none struck me more forcibly than the equality of social conditions."

Racial equality, or rather the lack of it, was a different matter. Tocqueville noticed little prejudice at first, but he came to realize that even in the North, black people seldom got to enjoy the few rights they had. A New York law of 1821 had abolished property requirements for white males to vote, but raised them for blacks to a level that disqualified nearly all of them. The French economist Michel Chevalier visited America at about the same time and reported, "An American of the North or South, whether rich or poor, ignorant or learned, avoids contact with blacks as if they carried the plague. Free or slave, well dressed or badly, the black, or man of color, is always a pariah. He is refused lodging in hotels. At the theater and in steamboats he has an allotted space far away from the whites. He is excluded from commerce, because he may not set foot in the stock exchange or banking offices. Everywhere and always, he is eminently unclean." The Scot Thomas Hamilton, a stern conservative in other respects, was revolted by the treatment of black people in the North. "They are subjected to the most grinding and humiliating of all slaveries, that of universal and unconquerable prejudice." Things had actually been getting worse. During his 1825 farewell tour Lafayette was astonished at the increase in prejudice, recalling that during the Revolution black and white soldiers had eaten meals together as a matter of course. After Tocqueville was back in France and working on an important chapter on race relations, he was able to generalize: "In proportion as slavery departs, the

whites grow more afraid of mixing the races and grow more contemptuous. The law is less harsh, but hatred is more so."

For Tocqueville and Beaumont, an especially disconcerting discovery
was the resolute chastity of American women, at least those they would
have liked to pursue. Prostitution was a massive trade in the city, with a
couple of hundred brothels and swarms of streetwalkers; one estimate is
that in New York as many as 10 percent of all women between the ages of
fifteen and thirty were prostitutes at some point in their lives. But the
young Frenchmen prided themselves on respectable liaisons, and these
turned out to be completely taboo. After six weeks Tocqueville wrote to
his brother Édouard, "Would you believe, my dear friend, that since our
arrival in America we have been practicing the most austere virtue? Not
the slightest lapse. Monks—good monks, I ought to say—could do no
more. That's already good, and better yet, it's our intention to do everything we possibly can to persevere right up to the end of the trip." Beaumont's letters often lamented the frustration of flirtation that led nowhere.
His experience at one elegant party inspired a labored witticism:

> It was the first time we had seen a lot of women gathered together. It
> struck me that several were extremely pretty. I can't be certain about
> that, because just one of them occupied me the whole evening—Miss
> Fulton is rightly considered the most beautiful woman in New York,
> and I continually paid her my tribute of admiration. We took charming
> strolls together *au claire de lune.* Alas! It's a hundred to one that I'll
> never see her again. She's the daughter of the famous Fulton, inventor
> of the steamboat. It appears that the great man didn't apply his process
> to the creation of children, because she doesn't seem in the least a
> woman with the vapors ["steamboat" in French is *bateau à vapeur*].

Among Tocqueville's unsorted notes an entertaining anecdote survives.
He was just as taken with Julia Fulton as Beaumont was, "struck as
much by her extreme flirtatiousness as by her dazzling beauty. I ventured to tell her laughingly that she was worthy of being a French-
woman. At once her expression turned severe and her habitually
engaging smile vanished. With great indignation she shot at me the

most ridiculous and unpleasantly prudish glare I've ever seen, cloaking herself in impassive dignity. But don't imagine that what injured her was being taken as a flirt, a criticism she would have accepted willingly. It was being seen as not completely American."

THE TOILETTE

Frances Trollope's friend Auguste Hervieu provided this illustration for her *Domestic Manners of the Americans*, in which Trollope commented, "The ladies have strange ways of adding to their charms. They powder themselves immoderately, face, neck, and arms, with pulverised starch; the effect is indescribably disagreeable by daylight, and not very favourable at any time. They are also most unhappily partial to false hair, which they wear in surprising quantities." Trollope added that although the American women did have pretty feet, "they do not walk well, nor, in fact, do they ever appear to advantage when in movement." Tocqueville and Beaumont, who were regularly smitten with American women, did not share Trollope's disdain.

As for the rigid virtue of married women, it is possible that the visiting Frenchmen took in what they heard more solemnly than it was intended. When a woman got married, Tocqueville reported to his sister-in-law Émilie, she might as well be in a convent. "It's the life of a nun: no more balls, hardly any socializing, a worthy but cold husband for her only company, and it's like this all the way to the life eternal. The other day I ventured to ask one of these recluses how, when all is said and done, a woman manages to pass her time in America. She replied with great sangfroid, 'In admiring her husband.'" Pretty clearly the irony escaped him.

Still, in America people did get married for love, or at least by personal choice, whereas in France marriage was normally a transaction between families. Tocqueville himself had already been forced by parental disapproval to give up a woman from Metz whom he had loved for five years, and he knew he would have an uphill struggle getting his family to accept the middle-class Englishwoman Marie. While he was in America, he indignantly rejected a suggestion by relatives that he consider engagement to someone he had never even met. So it was with strong sympathy that he noted that Americans got married "because they're attracted to each other," and he declared with feeling, "When you want to judge the equality between different classes of people, you always come to the question of how they make their marriages. That's the root of the matter. A sort of equality, resulting from necessity or courtesy or policy, may appear to exist and may deceive the eye. But when one wishes to put this equality into practice through intermarriage between families, that's when one puts one's finger on the sore spot." Tocqueville was doubtless aware that his own parents, who were never very compatible and lived apart for long periods, barely knew each other when their marriage was arranged. Years later he told a nephew that in France "the most important affair in life is decided for the most part more casually than buying a pair of gloves."

Another surprise was the social freedom of unmarried American girls, who were permitted to flirt with men, and even to spend time alone with them. "I have often been startled, and almost frightened, by the remarkable skill and agreeable audacity with which these American girls know how to guide their thoughts and words through the reefs of cheerful conversation . . . Even in the independence of early youth, an American girl never ceases to be her own master. She enjoys all of the permissible pleasures without abandoning herself to any of them, and her reason never lets go of the reins, however slackly she may often seem to hold them." After marriage the fun was decisively over. "A woman's independence is lost forever when she takes on the marriage bond . . . She lives in her husband's home as if in a cloister."

Other travelers noticed this rigid code, but they usually dismissed it as a mere survival of puritanical morals. Tocqueville, as always, wanted to understand how it reflected social structure, and he argued that a commercial democracy would inevitably place very different demands on marriage than the aristocratic milieu he came from. Despite the efforts of the feminist movement that was just then coming into being, his kind of explanation would remain popular for a century to come: a wife was expected to inculcate her children with ethical values and to restrain her potentially wayward husband through affectionate oversight and reproof. "The Americans," Tocqueville would write in *Democracy in America*, "are at once a puritanical nation and a commercial people. So both their religious beliefs and their habits of industriousness lead them to demand self-abnegation from women, and a continual sacrifice of pleasure to business that is rarely expected of them in Europe. Thus in the United States an inexorable public opinion holds sway, carefully confining women within the little circle of domestic interests and duties and forbidding them to venture outside."

Much later during the journey, in a private letter to his sister-in-law Émilie, Tocqueville allowed himself to be more skeptical about marital relations in America:

> I admit that from a certain point of view this country is an El Dorado
> for husbands, and they can almost certainly find perfect happiness as
> long as they have no romantic imagination whatever and expect noth-
> ing more from a wife than to prepare tea and raise children, which as
> everyone knows are the basic duties of marriage. In those two respects,
> American women excel . . . But what still remains to be understood is

how these accomplished women are so different before they enter the exclusiveness of marriage; they are coquettes up to a certain day and never afterward. How to explain such a sudden, total change? I would admit a miracle if it happened just once by chance, but when it keeps on happening, I can no longer understand it. Might one not believe— couldn't one possibly imagine—wouldn't we have some reason to think—you see I'm being circumspect and sufficiently doubtful—that the cure is only apparent, and that the coquetry goes on existing even though they mustn't show it? It's a fact, which all travelers have noticed, that married women in America are nearly always weak and languishing. For my own part, I'm not far from believing that they are sick from suppressed coquetry . . . So that's reason enough to show that, taken all in all, it's better by far to live in France than in America.

"Elles sont malades d'une coquetterie rentrée"—this is very nearly a Freudian theory of sexual repression!

In New York, meanwhile, Tocqueville was writing regularly to Marie Mottley, whom he had secretly promised to marry. Unfortunately, she destroyed all of his letters after his death, and apart from a few excerpts that she chose to preserve, the only surviving trace of their existence is Tocqueville's covert mention of *la voisine*, "the neighbor," to the friend who passed his letters on to Marie. This duty was discharged so loyally that Tocqueville wrote with gratitude, "I thank you for the care you've taken with your *voisine*, whom I still love from the bottom of my heart."

However sincerely he loved Marie, strict fidelity was no part of Tocqueville's plan for himself. By his own admission he had been a tireless pursuer of women, and would continue to be for the rest of his life. After he had been married for eight years he wrote a gloomy letter to Louis de Kergorlay, his cousin and oldest friend, to report that Marie was in despair over his infidelities and that although he still loved her passionately, he doubted that he could ever overcome a desire "which, as too much experience has shown me, gets carried away from time to time to the point of blindness and . . . makes my blood boil just as it did twenty years ago." Tocqueville begged Kergorlay to write to Marie and persuade her to see reason. Actually, Kergorlay had already tried, with arguments that reflect the attitudes of his class. He urged Marie to understand that her husband was guilty of "infidelity of bad habits but not infidelity of the heart," and that masculine morals must not be judged by feminine feelings. Women, he explained, with their purity of mind, might naively expect love and sex to be synonymous, but for men they were fundamentally different. It seems probable, then, that Tocqueville in America was continuously frustrated, not wishing to degrade himself with prostitutes, and disconcerted to find that good girls were permanently off-limits. Throughout the journey he would constantly ask questions about courtship and marriage patterns, and eventually they would play an important role in his analysis of American society.

Perhaps surprisingly, one topic that didn't interest Tocqueville much was New York politics. The system of government fascinated him, but not the ignoble details of influence peddling and vote getting. (A few years later, after taking his seat in the French legislature, he would see much more clearly that in a democracy, politics and government are inseparable.) The grandees he was meeting in New York, who harbored the elitist sentiments that used to be called Federalist and would soon be known as Whig, assured him that Andrew Jackson was a crude and ignorant backwoodsman, a bias that Tocqueville never shook off. Nor did he grasp that with Martin Van Buren from upstate New York as their leader, populist Democrats were developing the first modern political party, on the principle that the will of the majority should always prevail. He seems also to have been unaware of the Tammany Hall machine that already controlled New York City. Under the notorious bosses of the second half of the century, it would draw its power from the rapidly swelling immigrant community, but in the early 1830s it represented the very lawyers, merchants, and financiers whom Tocqueville was meeting.

What Tocqueville did recognize was that American electioneering was extraordinarily confrontational, fueled by a free press such as did not exist in France. With some amazement he copied into his notebook a furiously abusive newspaper attack on Jackson, which he eventually included, in a somewhat toned-down translation, in *Democracy in America*: "Intrigue is his vocation, and will yet overthrow and confound him. Corruption is his element and will yet react upon him to his utter dismay and confusion . . . He must disgorge his winnings, throw away his false dice, and seek the hermitage, there to blaspheme and execrate his folly, for to repent is not a virtue within the capacity of his heart to obtain." Tocqueville didn't realize that Jackson's Nashville estate was called the Hermitage, and translated "seek the Hermitage" as "finir dans quelque retraite," "end up in some place of retirement." And he may not have understood that, as a modern historian says, "such slander endeared Jackson to his followers because they identified with his suffering. To be a Democrat was to be an outsider."

In a deeper sense, though, Tocqueville paid little attention to American politics because they seemed so much less ideological than politics at home. He wrote to his father that in the newspapers "the price of cotton takes up more space than general questions about government." On this his most recent biographer remarks sternly, "He could not have chosen a worse example," since cotton was the chief southern export, the focus of a bitter tariff dispute and of regional tensions that would eventually lead to the Civil War. But Tocqueville's real point was that this compartmentalizing of politics was a great advantage for Americans, "one of the most fortunate people on earth," because they were immune to the ideological earthquakes that were shaking France at that very moment. Immediately before the comment about cotton, he said approvingly, "Politics take up only a small corner of the picture here. I don't doubt that the most apparently peaceful state in Europe is more profoundly agitated by politics than the entire American confederation."

At home, indeed, events were moving fast. Anxiety about developments there, and about how the Tocqueville and Beaumont families might be imperiled, would continue to grow for the rest of their time in America. "While the king of France is sustaining the Chamber of Deputies," Beaumont wrote, "the king of England is dissolving Parliament. And elsewhere, is it true that we're going to wage war against Don Miguel [of Portugal]? Are the great Polish victories over the Russians officially confirmed? And is it known if France, England, and Austria are forming an alliance, as is now being said, on the side of Poland against Russia?" For a modern American reader, these events, with the possible exception of the reform movement in England, are lost in the abyss of time. They serve as a reminder of our inevitable need to simplify history and focus it on ourselves, which is why the perspective of these sympathetic outsiders is especially illuminating.

But now it was time to get on with the work Tocqueville and Beaumont had been commissioned to carry out, and they made arrangements to visit the celebrated Sing Sing penitentiary on the Hudson River. They found the name peculiar, as well they might, and were told it was the name of an Indian chief who once lived there. Just three years old, the new institution had replaced the notorious Newgate Prison in downtown New York, where prisoners of both sexes used to mingle freely, so that according to one observer, "their beastly salacity, in their visual amours, is agonizing to every fibre of delicacy and virtue."

In an age of experiment and reform, schools, prisons, and asylums were must-see destinations for foreign visitors. Americans were proud of their achievements in this area, and the arrival of the French investigators seemed to confirm that the Old World had much to learn from the New. Tocqueville commented less flatteringly that the blandness of American life made any novelty seem extraordinary. "In the United States," he wrote to a cousin, "they have neither wars, nor plagues, nor literature, nor eloquence, nor revolutions, nor fine arts, nor many great crimes—nothing of what excites attention in Europe. In the United States, therefore, they regard the construction of a fine prison like the pyramid of Cheops." He added that his hosts would be amazed if they knew that there weren't a hundred people in the whole of France who understood what a penitentiary was, and that the government itself was probably unaware that it had sent him and Beaumont to find out.

Penitentiaries were a relatively recent invention. Inspired by Enlightenment ideas about the malleability of human behavior, European reformers had been arguing for half a century for a system of punishment that would embody a program of rehabilitation. By the beginning of the nineteenth century various experiments were being made, and the United States was particularly well suited to conduct them, since its prisons were controlled by state and local governments rather than by a central authority as in France, which would have had to institute any changes on a massive nationwide scale.

In the words of the report Tocqueville and Beaumont submitted after returning to France, the defects of the old system included "crowding of prisoners; confusion of different crimes, ages, and sometimes sexes; mingling of indicted and condemned prisoners, criminals, debtors, guilty people, and witnesses; frequent escapes; absence of all discipline; never any silence that might lead criminals to reflect; never any work that might accustom them to earn an honest living; insalubriousness of living quarters that ruins their health; cynical conversations that corrupt them; idleness that depraves; and, in a word, collecting together every vice and every immorality—that is the spectacle presented by the prisons that have not yet started on the road of reform." In 1831 the old system was still the normal one all over Europe, as well as in fifteen of the twenty-four American states.

Tocqueville and Beaumont were familiar in theory with the two main innovations that were being tried. In Philadelphia a system of absolute isolation had been briefly instituted, with the intention of separating prisoners who would otherwise corrupt one another. Far from producing the expected reformation, this method provoked despair. In Tocqueville and Beaumont's words, "Absolute solitude, with nothing to distract or interrupt it, was beyond the strength of man; it consumes the criminal relentlessly and pitilessly, and it doesn't reform, it kills." Following this alarming experience, two modified solutions were proposed. The decision in Philadelphia was to retain isolation cells but give the prisoners productive work to do in them, both to occupy their minds and to prepare them for employment after release. Sing Sing, however, was modeled on the Auburn system, named after a pioneering institution in upstate New York, in which the convicts emerged each day from their cells to work in groups but were still required to maintain absolute silence. The official regulations stated, "They are not to exchange a word with each other under any pretense whatever, nor to communicate any intelligence to each other in writing;

they are not to exchange looks, wink, laugh, or motion to each other." Disobedience was punished by brutal flogging. The favored implement was the "cat," a whip with half a dozen strands of rawhide knotted at the end, but Elam Lynds, the inventor of the Auburn system, preferred to carry a big bullwhip. The chaplain at Sing Sing recalled that when a convict was mistakenly accused of breaking a blacksmith's punch, no statement in self-defense was permitted, and he received a hundred lashes on his bare back with a promise of a hundred more unless he confessed.

Visitors from abroad generally agreed that stern treatment and isolation were entirely appropriate. Dickens, who had had to leave school at twelve and go to work when his father was sentenced to debtors' prison, was an exception, and after his visits to American prisons he was haunted by visions of anguish. The future creator of the unforgettable Abel Magwitch in *Great Expectations* was well aware of the psychic suffering of prisoners, and also of the real possibility of wrongful conviction. More typical was a Scot who visited Sing Sing shortly after it opened and was impressed that even when the prisoners returned to their cells after an eleven-hour workday, "assistant keepers are constantly moving around the galleries, having socks on their feet, that they may walk without noise, so that no convict can feel secure, but that one of the keepers may be at the very door of his cell, ready to discover and report next morning for punishment the slightest breach of silence or order."

What lay behind the system was the famous "panopticon" championed by Jeremy Bentham—he also called it an "inspection-house"—in which the warden would resemble a hidden God. In Bentham's vivid description, he was to lurk "concealed from the observation of the prisoners, unless where he thinks fit to show himself; hence, on their part, the sentiment of an invisible omnipresence." And if he fell short of omniscience as well as omnipresence, it wouldn't be for want of trying.

At Sing Sing, Tocqueville and Beaumont looked on in wonder while nine hundred prisoners, free from chains or fetters, worked in the open air quarrying marble for the Greek Revival mansions that were going up in New York. A mere thirty guards were enough to keep them in order, and the secret, Tocqueville saw, was that the guards operated as a team while the convicts were unable to communicate, and also that they ruled through fear of the lash. "Apart from sleeping in a cell and being flogged," he wrote to a friend, "we lead pretty much the same life as the convicts . . . During the ten days we've been studying them without a break, we haven't managed to catch them exchanging a single meaningful glance or hear a single word, and in short they have apparently surrendered their willpower completely and irrevocably. I remember seeing something similar among the Trappists, but I would never have believed, without witnessing it myself, that force alone could bring about a similar result." After dark the silence was even more eerie. "We have often walked at night through these echoing but mute galleries, where a lamp is forever shining, and it felt like walking through the catacombs. There were a thousand living beings there and yet it was a solitude."

If the silence was disconcerting, the floggings apparently were not. In their report Tocqueville and Beaumont quoted approvingly from an American study of prisons: "The rights of the guard over the detainees' persons are that of a father over his children, a teacher over his pupils, a master over his apprentice, and a sea captain over his crew." To this they added, "Punishment by whipping is in use in the American navy, with no idea of infamy attached to it." What did impress them, though, was the contrast between American ideals and the code of the penitentiary. A leading theme of *Democracy in America* would be that despotic regimes can give people equality but deny them freedom, and Sing Sing was a perfect illustration. In their report Tocqueville and Beaumont wrote trenchantly, "All the inmates are treated alike; there is much more equality in prison than in society . . . Even while society in the United States gives the example of the most extensive liberty, the prisons of that country present a spectacle of the most complete despotism."

In historical hindsight, this system was not really an exception to the way society normally worked, but rather an extension of new techniques of organization and control. For as the 1829 report of the Prison Discipline Society suggested, "unceasing vigilance" could be "a principle of very extensive application to families, schools, academies, colleges, factories, and mechanics' shops." Michel Foucault puts it more challengingly in *Discipline and Punish*, a work that gives close attention to the report on penitentiaries that Tocqueville and Beaumont eventually prepared. "Is it surprising," Foucault asks, "that prisons resemble factories, schools, barracks, hospitals, which all resemble prisons?"

As for the goal of reformation, on closer view that seemed highly dubious. After visiting many such institutions, Tocqueville wrote to his father, "I'm as unsure on this point as you are by your fireside. What I do know for certain is that I wouldn't entrust my purse to one of those fellows." After he left Sing Sing, a district attorney told him, "I don't think an adult criminal will reform, no matter what one does. In my opinion he comes out of our penitentiaries hardened." (In later years the name Sing Sing came to be proverbial for rigorous incarceration, and in 1901 the town thought it best to rename itself Ossining.)

HUDSON HIGHLANDS
This 1840 view, with its contemplative observer in the style of the Hudson
River school that was getting under way at the time, captures the romantic
grandeur that Tocqueville and Beaumont admired.

There were respites from prison life, and Tocqueville began one letter home with an exercise in the picturesque, while he was visiting Livingston's country house in Greenburgh to the south of Sing Sing. "You would never guess, my dear father, from what place I'm writing to you. I'll begin my letter by describing it. I'm at the top of a rather high hill that borders the Hudson. A hundred paces away a country house where we're staying forms the foreground of the landscape. At the foot of the hill flows the river, several miles wide and covered with sails. It grows dim toward the north and disappears amid high blue mountains . . . The whole is illuminated by a magnificent sun which, striking its rays through the humid atmosphere of this country, throws a soft and transparent coloring over everything." What the elder Tocqueville would not have guessed was his son's particular point of vantage. "On top of the highest hill is an enormous plane tree [it must have been a sycamore]. I'm perched in its branches to escape the heat, and that's where I'm writing to you. Beaumont, at its foot, is sketching what I'm describing." A few days later Beaumont reported, "In the evenings at seven we go to swim in the Hudson. I'm beginning to swim passably." He added that after Tocqueville finished his arboreal letter, he wandered off to hunt. "Tocqueville has been waging a war to the death against the American birds. These birds are in general charming. Many are blue, others have black bodies with a yellow ruff that's very pretty. The ones I'm speaking of are very common here; we haven't had many opportunities to shoot them yet." Later there would be plenty of opportunities.

The labor of prison investigation had been tiring, but it was much appreciated by Americans. Before Tocqueville and Beaumont left New York, a notice from the *Westchester Herald*, in the ponderous style of the day, was widely reprinted:

M. de Beaumont and M. de Tocqueville, the distinguished gentlemen composing the Commission, have spent the last two weeks in this place, and after a most laborious and careful inspection of the prison here, its construction, its order, cleanliness, discipline, and regularity,

together with a strict investigation into all the minutiae of its government and its operation, we are gratified with the opportunity of stating
that they are highly pleased with the institution, and they do not hesitate to pronounce it superior, in many of its branches, to any which they
have ever visited in Europe.

But by now they had had their fill of society as well as of prison, and were
ready for adventure. "I'm weary of men," Beaumont wrote, "and above
all of Americans." It was time to explore the interior, or, as Tocqueville
romantically put it, "We will plunge headfirst into the wilderness."

3

"EVERYTHING ATTESTS TO A NEW WORLD"

Tocqueville and Beaumont would spend more than half of their time in America in three cities—fifty-seven days all told during two stays in New York, thirty-two days in Philadelphia, and twenty-six days in Boston. There would also be a week each in Baltimore and Washington. But in between their urban sojourns they proved themselves indefatigable travelers, fully capable of living rough, surmounting emergencies, and appreciating American society in all of its varieties.

When at last, after six weeks in the big city, they journeyed into the western part of New York State, they found new experiences crowding in upon them. Travel in itself was both arduous and exhilarating. A memorable Fourth of July celebration gave insight into the ethos of the young nation. The pace of pioneer settlement was startling. They got their first glimpses of evangelical religion. They encountered their first Native Americans. And they began to form a deeper understanding of the forces that gave America its energy, its promise, and its potential problems.

The trip began with a steamboat ride up the Hudson, made unnecessarily exciting by the captain's decision to race a rival vessel all the way to Albany. His craft was the *North America*, which, when put into service four years earlier, had reduced the New York–Albany run from fifteen hours to ten (the ancestor of all steamboats, Robert Fulton's *Clermont* a quarter of a century before, needed thirty-two hours to make the trip). Steamboats were still fueled by prodigious quantities of wood, and it was considered a great breakthrough some years later when the *North America* was successfully converted to coal. Tocqueville probably didn't know that this particular captain was notorious for winning races by burning double the usual amount of wood while disabling safety valves in order to triple boiler pressure. Over the years, so many over-taxed boilers exploded that racing was eventually made illegal.

HUDSON STEAMBOAT
Long and narrow, steamboats on the Hudson were built for speed.

At five in the morning on July 2 the *North America* docked in Albany; neither Tocqueville nor Beaumont bothered to report who won the race. They were especially exasperated because they had been eagerly expecting to visit West Point—between them they had four brothers in military service—but the captain refused to lose time by making the regularly scheduled stop. "We were in the position," Tocqueville wrote to his mother, "of someone who took the wrong coach and went to Rouen instead of Compiègne, except that one can get out of a coach and not a steamboat." He was impressed, though, by the national talent for technological improvement, which he later summarized in a chapter titled "Why the Americans Are More Attached to the Practical Than to Theory in the Sciences." As an intellectual raised in a culture that prized theorizing highly, he couldn't help feeling that much was missing, but he acknowledged that "these same Americans, who have never discovered a single general law of mechanics, have given to navigation a new machine that is changing the face of the earth." On another occasion he was introduced to the concept of planned obsolescence: a sailor explained that American ships weren't designed to last long because ongoing improvements would make it necessary to replace them. He must have been struck, if he happened to encounter it, by the policy of the *Journal of the Academy of Natural Sciences of Philadelphia*, which directed its contributors "to exclude entirely all papers of mere theory—to confine their communications as much as possible to facts."

In Albany the friends got to observe the celebration of the Fourth of July, and despite a total absence of splendor—Beaumont said the humblest French ceremony would have been more brilliant—the proceedings were moving in their sincerity. Several days later he described them at length:

> One mustn't expect fine uniforms and embroidered costumes; one must reflect upon the great event that the fete commemorates, and see the emblems that engrave it on the people's memory. Here, with great pomp, an American flag that survived the War of Independence, riddled by gunshot, is borne along. There, riding in a carriage at the head of the procession, are three or four old soldiers who fought with Washington, preserved as precious relics by the town and honored by all. Farther off is a richly decorated float bearing the first press that was used to print the Declaration of Independence. All of the industrial and commercial professions, represented by their delegates, have banners on which their trades are inscribed. Nothing would be easier than to ridicule these banners that say "Association of Butchers," "Association of Apprentices," and so on. But when you think about it, these

emblems are very natural among a people who owe their prosperity to commerce and industry . . . In our fetes there is more brilliance, and in those of the United States, more truth.

What Beaumont probably didn't realize was that the tradesmen represented a dying breed, artisans whose emblems and traditions went all the way back to Elizabethan England. Describing a similar parade in Albany a few years earlier, Sean Wilentz says that "artisan independence conjured up, not a vision of ceaseless, self-interested industry, but a moral order in which all craftsmen would eventually become self-governing, independent, competent masters." But as Tocqueville would realize by the time he wrote *Democracy in America*, division of labor and the factory system were beginning to create an entirely new kind of workforce.

Tocqueville, seated next to the lieutenant governor as an honored guest, was deeply moved, and his notebook entry is eloquent in its simplicity:

> Mixture of amusing and serious impressions. Militia on foot and horseback, speeches full of rhetorical excess, pitcher of water on the platform, hymn to liberty in a church. A little of the French spirit. Perfect order prevails. Silence. No police, no authority anywhere. The people's fete. "Marshal of the day" has no restrictive power, yet obeyed. Orderly presentation of trades. Public prayer. The flag present, and old soldiers. Real emotion.

Coming from a country where order was ostentatiously enforced by soldiers and police, Tocqueville found their absence remarkable. As a modern commentator observes, authority had been internalized as a set of shared obligations and habits, and there was no need for a show of force.

The celebration culminated in a young lawyer's reading of the Declaration of Independence, and Tocqueville responded warmly to Jefferson's text. "When it invoked the justice of its cause, and expressed the noble resolve to die or else set America free, it was as if an electric current made every heart vibrate. This was not in the least, I assure you, a theatrical performance. In this reading of promises of independence so well kept, in this return by an entire people to the memory of its birth, in this union of the present generation with the one that is no more, sharing for the moment its noble passions—in all of this there was something profoundly felt and truly great." The fundamental theme of *Democracy in America* would be that habits and beliefs are more important than laws are in sustaining liberty. Tocqueville would write there, "Love of country is a sort of religious cult to which people grow attached through its observances." On this very day, as it happens, a new song was receiving its first performance in a church in Boston: "My country, 'tis of thee, sweet land of liberty, of thee I sing."

What may seem surprising is that Tocqueville showed little interest in the state government in Albany. The reason was that it hardly seemed to exist. "We expected to stay several days in Albany," he wrote, "because that town is the capital of New York State. The administration is established there, and the legislature meets there. We hoped to obtain valuable information on whatever central government there is in this country. The offices and registers were all open to us, but as far as *government* goes, we're still looking for it. Really it doesn't exist at all."

ALBANY

The artist has done his best to make the provincial capital impressive, a sort of Istanbul of the Empire State (which was already using that epithet).

To be sure, the impressive capitol building of today didn't yet exist—it was completed in 1899, when Theodore Roosevelt was governor—but Tocqueville was seeing (or not seeing) what he wanted to. Administration in France was centralized to an extraordinary degree that paralyzed local initiative. It was impossible to repair a church or town hall anywhere in France without submitting an elaborate proposal to the Ministry of the Interior, which would pass it along to a *conseil de bâtiments civiles*, which would issue a directive to the prefect of the province in question, who would give it to his subprefect, who would eventually get back to the mayor of the town in question. All along the way, armies of clerks would copy and recopy an ever-swelling mass of paperwork.

Tocqueville himself believed that decentralization not only cut through red tape but also encouraged citizen involvement in a crucial way, so he was always on the lookout for evidence for it, even at the very top. A note jotted in a stagecoach reads, "The greatest merit of the United States government is that it's *powerless* and *passive*." With his indifference to practical politics, he seems not to have recognized Van Buren's control of the machine known as the Albany Regency and his skill at consolidating support for Jackson. Still less did he appreciate Jackson's ability to lead the federal government in political battle, and he was apparently unaware of the tension between New York City and the rural hinterland. But as an expert on the period comments, "New York politics baffled contemporary observers, as well as later students, by their extraordinary complexity." Throughout the nation, indeed, this was an era of extremely confusing political transition. The Republican Party as we know it did not yet exist; it would be born in Lincoln's time, in the 1850s. The earlier Republican Party of Jefferson had fractured and was in the process of regrouping as the populist Democratic Republicans of Jackson and Van Buren (later known simply as Democrats), with their opponents likewise regrouping as the National Republicans of Adams and Clay (later known as Whigs).

In any case, what Tocqueville meant by a political party was very different from the routine scramble for office and patronage. He agreed with a lawyer who told him, "In truth, there are now no parties in the

United States; everything is reduced to a question of men—those who have power and those who want it, the ins and the outs." To someone who had just lived through the French upheaval of 1830, and whose parents had narrowly escaped death in the cataclysm of 1789, American controversies did seem trivial. When a dinner companion described some mildly turbulent electioneering, Tocqueville said feelingly, "You argue like a man who has never seen a people agitated by real, profound political passions. Everything here has been on the surface so far. There are no great material interests at stake."

America was thus insulated from the intense ideological oppositions that shook Europe, and Tocqueville admitted to some regret at the low rhetorical temperature. In a stagecoach he wrote, "What I call great political parties are ones that attach themselves to principles and not just their consequences, to generalities and not just particular cases; on the whole they have nobler features, more generous passions, stronger convictions, and a franker and bolder style than the others." When Beaumont read a revised version of this sentiment in the manuscript of *Democracy in America*, he queried in the margin, "Is this theory safe from criticism? You call *great parties*, then, only those that rest on a political theory, and you refuse the name to those that are based on *immense interests*. This is arbitrary." Arbitrary or not, it was a quite accurate assessment of American practice at the time. The author of a classic study of Jacksonian politics says, "American parties are above all electoral machines, engaged in nominating and electing candidates, rather than, as Edmund Burke put it, being 'a body of men united for promoting by their joint endeavours the national interest upon some particular principle in which they are all agreed.'"

A few miles outside Albany the travelers stopped at a favorite tourist destination, a meetinghouse of the Shaker sect. Inspired by a visionary from England named Ann Lee, the Shakers had begun as a splinter movement known originally as the Shaking Quakers because of their ecstatic dancing; they asserted equality of the sexes and total celibacy while awaiting the imminent end of the world. A group of them immigrated with their leader, now known as Mother Ann, to western New

York in the 1770s, calling themselves the United Society of Believers. By 1830 there were some two dozen Shaker villages in rural areas all the way from Illinois to Maine.

Tocqueville and Beaumont watched the proceedings with bemused fascination (back in France, Tocqueville referred to them, a bit oddly, as "shakery quakers"). They were more sympathetic than most visitors, including Harriet Martineau, who thought that the worshippers were pathetic victims of brainwashing: "Their soulless stare at us, before their worship began, was almost as afflicting as that of the lowest order of slaves; and when they danced they were like so many galvanized corpses." Beaumont also described how the congregation sat motionless for several minutes and then agitated their bodies violently for a full hour, but he went on to say that their sincerity was obvious, and he wrote down an old man's concluding remarks: "Worldly interest and vain curiosity have attracted you here; may you take beneficial impressions away! Who among you can say he is as happy as we? Happiness lies neither in wealth nor in the pleasures of the senses; it consists above all in reason. Everyone seeks in vain for the truth, and we alone have found it on earth." Tocqueville, however, still regarded the rituals of Catholicism as the norm, in spite of how uncertain his personal beliefs had become. "Can you imagine, my dear mother," he wrote, "what aberrations the human spirit can fall into when it's abandoned to itself? There was a young American Protestant with us who said as we left, 'Two more spectacles like this one and I'm turning Catholic.'" To be sure, he knew that his pious mother would appreciate hearing that.

To some extent Tocqueville did eventually recognize that evangelical fervor had deep roots in class resentment. Even if everyone might potentially hope to get rich, most never would, and they knew it. It was among these people—backwoods farmers, the urban poor, slaves—that preachers were gaining throngs of converts, denouncing (in the words of a Baptist statement) "an inordinate desire of earthly things, or what belongs to our neighbors, and a dissatisfaction with what we have, a rapacity in obtaining wealth, and a tenaciousness in keeping it." In *Democracy in America*, Tocqueville would write that when a society is preoccupied with material goods, some people are bound to "throw

SHAKERS DANCING

themselves frantically into the world of the spirit." But he saw this behavior as aberrant, if not crazy—"from time to time bizarre sects arise that try to open extraordinary paths to eternal happiness, and religious madness is very common"—and he dismissed itinerant Methodist preachers as little better than salesmen "qui colportent de place en place la parole divine," "who go from place to place peddling the Lord's word." He seems not to have appreciated that for thirty years America had been experiencing a sustained revival known as the Second Great Awakening, or that western New York had caught fire so often that it became known as the Burnt-Over District. The charismatic preacher Charles Grandison Finney, who coined the phrase, later recalled that in 1831, precisely when Tocqueville was in the area, there was launched "the greatest revival of religion throughout the land that this country had then ever witnessed."

Nathan Hatch's classic study, *The Democratization of American Christianity*, suggests that evangelicals were in open rebellion against the learned clergy of the older denominations, with their authoritarian style and theology. In contrast to formal language and solemn hymns, they offered colloquial eloquence and ecstatic singing. Especially striking were the Methodist camp meetings. In a thinly settled area that might well have no church buildings yet, a preacher's platform would be put up in the forest, surrounded by benches and tents to be used by hundreds of participants for a week or more. Many a traveler left horrified accounts of the emotionalism on display there, and Tocqueville was no exception, though his account recalled an indoor scene in a Methodist chapel:

> I saw on a raised platform a young man whose thunderous voice made the ceiling ring. His hair stood on end, his eyes seemed to dart fire, his lips were pale and trembling, and his body was shaking all over . . . He spoke of the depravity of man and the inexhaustible resources of divine vengeance . . . He depicted the Creator as ceaselessly occupied with heaping up human generations in the gulf of hell, tirelessly creating sinners and then inventing tortures for them . . . I fled, disgusted and stricken with terror. "Author and preserver of all things," I said to myself, "is it possible you can recognize yourself in the hideous portrait these creatures are painting here?"

In this area of experience, in short, Tocqueville's objectivity failed him. Not only did he exaggerate the irrationality of evangelical religion, but he missed its social role in addressing anxieties of the American people that would be central to his own analysis.

Traveling onward through western New York State, the companions reached the Mohawk Valley, where Beaumont recalled that *The Last of the Mohicans* was set. But as Tocqueville reported in his notebook, the wilderness was rapidly undergoing domestication:

> In general the whole countryside has the appearance of a forest with some clearings in it. Strong resemblance to lower Normandy. Every sign of a new country, man making attempts that are as yet ineffectual to conquer the forest. Cultivated fields covered with saplings, tree trunks in the midst of the crops. In a single field a mélange of bushes and trees of a thousand species, plants sown by man, various grasses growing on their own. Streams on all the slopes, left to themselves.

New country inhabited by an old people. Nothing wild except the ground. Dwellings clean and well cared for, shops in the midst of the forest, newspapers in isolated cabins.

In Normandy there would have been no stumps in the fields, wild plants would have been carefully excluded, trees limited to a few favored species, and streams diverted into channels. What surprised Tocqueville most was the civilized demeanor of the inhabitants— "nouveau pays peuplé par un vieux peuple," "a new country inhabited by an old people."

NEWLY CLEARED LAND

The British traveler Basil Hall commented that "the newly-cleared lands in America have, almost invariably, a bleak, hopeless aspect." Like other foreigners, he was especially offended by split rail fences, "at best a poor substitute for hedges and hedgerows." Leaving stumps in the field actually made economic sense for farmers who wanted to cultivate as large an acreage as possible, and to sell out before long and move on.

Those newspapers in the cabins were significant, too. English visitors, accustomed to a relatively small number of papers that all had conservative editorial policies, thought that America was being ruined by gutter journalism, with its shameless character defamation. Marryat had personal experience of extortion when the notorious *Herald* sent him a copy of the paper with an abusive account of him and a note attached: "Send twenty dollars, and it shall be stopped." Tocqueville, coming from a land of censorship, saw things very differently: "So long as someone can speak freely in even one public place, it's as if he were speaking publicly in every village." And in the margin of the *Democracy in America* manuscript he wrote, "After the people themselves, the press represents the most irresistible power that exists in America." The ubiquity of newspapers was in fact the fruit of a deliberate policy going back to the nation's founding. To encourage far-flung regions to bond together, Congress promoted an excellent postal system and subsidized the cheap circulation of papers (which were, as a rule, weeklies outside the big cities). They now made up 90 percent of the mail but paid only 10 percent of postal fees. In 1790 there had been seventy-five post offices in the entire country, in 1815 there were three thousand, and by 1830 there were eight thousand. Since there was no home delivery, post offices also became village gathering places.

As the travelers pressed on, they were appalled at the dreadful condition of the roads. Here it seemed undeniable that the centralized French system was better. Roads in America were the responsibility of a confusing patchwork of state, county, and local authorities, and when Tocqueville questioned one distinguished informant, he was told that "a great constitutional question" was involved. Establishing interstate highways had been a major element of the "American System" that John Quincy Adams and his allies had tried to promote, with political as well as economic implications. "We are under the most imperious obligations," John C. Calhoun declared fifteen years earlier, "to counteract every tendency to disunion. Let us, then, bind the republic together with a perfect system of roads and canals. Let us conquer space." But that kind of federal intervention was precisely what backwoods settlers feared, evidence, in their opinion, that big government was usurping states' rights and invading people's lives.

Tocqueville was also surprised to discover that during his whole time in America "I never saw a single person in his own carriage or with his own horses. The richest people travel in public conveyances, with no servants." So it was by stagecoach that he and Beaumont proceeded. The vehicles had a primitive suspension system of leather straps that didn't do much to absorb violent jolts, and as many as nine passengers sat crowded together on crude benches, with a tenth next to the driver on top (Dickens complained that the drivers were surly, refused to converse, and constantly spat). Windows were covered with leather, not glass. Accidents were common; one Cincinnati resident was overturned thirteen times in three years.

A STAGECOACH ON THE MOUNTAINS
This illustration appeared in an edifying book published by the American Sunday School Union with the comment, "The company is generally various and pleasant, and often improving. We can seldom fail to do or get good wherever we are."

Tocqueville was astonished at the casualness with which long journeys were contemplated. "In this country they have an incredible disregard for distances," he wrote to his family. "They don't say it's 250 miles to someplace, but twenty-five hours." Traveling would soon become much easier, and its duration would shrink; this was the very end of what Harriet Beecher Stowe, thirty years later, called "the ante-railroad times." But in 1831 it would have taken quite a prophet to foresee the triumph of the railways.

The route west took Tocqueville and Beaumont along the whole length of the Erie Canal, but they paid little attention to it; what they wanted was to escape civilization, not to witness its advance into the forest. At last they could behold the virgin land they had encountered in the fiction of François-René de Chateaubriand—a cousin of Tocqueville's mother—and of James Fenimore Cooper. Tocqueville reported, "I believe that in one of my letters I complained that there is scarcely any wood in America. I must now make amends. Not only is there wood, and woods, but the entire country is still one vast forest with some clearings in its midst. When you climb a steeple, there's nothing as far as the eye can see but trees, agitated by the wind like waves in the sea. Everything attests to a new world."

Best of all, they were approaching a place Tocqueville had longed to see ever since boyhood, when he read about it in a book called *Geographical and Pedagogical Stories for Young People*. The story was that an aristocratic émigré fleeing from the French Revolution—a character with whom he naturally identified—settled with his beloved wife on a little island in Oneida Lake, north of the village that would become Syracuse. They stayed there for some years, raising crops and children, and then disappeared, no one could tell where. Tocqueville and Beaumont successfully located the island, known as Frenchman's Island after its romantic inhabitants (it has that name to this day). Better yet, they encountered an old woman who remembered the couple, and who said that after they left, she visited the island and found an apple tree and vine they had planted. She had a boat they could borrow, and in great excitement they rowed out to the island. Tocqueville recorded in his notebook:

> We discover an old apple tree in the middle of the island. Nearby, a vine, gone wild, was entangled right into the top of the surrounding trees, like a liana. The house used to be there. No trace remains. We write our names on a plane tree. We set out again. Profound silence on

the island, broken only by the birds that live in freedom there. We walk over the entire island without finding any trace of the two beings who had made it their universe. This expedition has interested and moved me more deeply than any I've made, not just in America, but since I first began to travel.

Afterward Tocqueville wrote up a longer account of the experience, in which he acknowledged that the story had long held a place in his imagination as a fantasy escape. Thinking of the Frenchman and his bride, he wrote, "How often have I envied the tranquil delights of their solitude! Domestic happiness, the charms of conjugal union, and love itself merged together in my mind with the image of the solitary island where my imagination created a new Eden." Now that he was on the spot, what moved him especially was a vision of untamed nature, bursting with vital energy: "It was as if one could hear a sort of inner sound that revealed the work of creation, and could see the sap and life circulating through channels ever open."

It was just as well he never knew the true story, which scholars have with some difficulty dug up. The Frenchman, whose name was Vatine or Vatines, came to America three years before the Revolution, escaping not politics but enormous debts he had run up. The stay on the island was brief and unsatisfactory, he and his wife soon moved to a large farm on the mainland, and when they eventually came into some money, they returned to France.

At Auburn the young investigators got to see the prison for which the Auburn system of Sing Sing was named, and they met its originator, the formidable Elam Lynds. They found him a hard man, implacable even, and proud of it. "In my opinion," Lynds declared, "a prison director, especially if he's an innovator, needs to be given absolute and assured authority." Warming to the theme, he added that guards as well as convicts must be kept under constant surveillance, and that it was essential to be merciless as well as just. When they asked whether corporal punishment was really necessary, his response was predictable: "I consider punishment by the whip as the most effective and also the most humane, for it never injures the prisoners' health, and it forces them to lead an essentially healthy life." Although he had personally designed Sing Sing, he had been dismissed from the wardenship the previous year. An official report at the time charged him with "doubtful pecuniary transactions," keeping the prisoners on short rations, and excessively ruthless discipline. The report also highlighted an irony that Tocqueville himself had commented on at Sing Sing: "We have, therefore, in the midst of a free country . . . a despotism in comparison with which the government of a camp or a ship of war is mild and free." Lynds's prison still exists as a maximum-security institution, under the name of the Auburn Correctional Facility.

Living on a farm near Auburn was the governor of the state, Enos Throop, whom Tocqueville and Beaumont had met earlier when he was attending the annual Tammany meeting in New York City. On their third day there Tocqueville had jotted in his notebook, "Mr. Morse, a judge at Cherry Valley, introduced us to the governor of New York, who was staying in a *boardinghouse* and who received us in the parlor without the least bit of ceremony. Mr. Morse assured us that everyone could do the same thing at any time." The Frenchmen had been surprised to encounter a high government official in such modest circumstances, and they were equally surprised now to find him living in a single-story house and cultivating his own fields. They heard afterward that his salary was so low that he couldn't survive without farming for half the year. This was one reason, Elam Lynds told them, that men of distinction seldom ran for office, well aware that they could do much better for themselves "in some business." Tocqueville quoted the phrase in English and added, "An idea characteristic of the state of society and the state of mores in the United States." But it was also characteristic that public service was regarded as honorable labor and not as an expression of high-minded generosity. "In aristocratic countries," Tocqueville noted, "there are hardly any public officials who don't claim to serve the state disinterestedly. Their salary is a detail they seldom think about, and they pretend never to think of it at all."

Beaumont, who had a strong anticommercial bias, was amazed that a governor would mention without embarrassment his brother the grocer or his cousin the salesman. He thought Throop at best a mediocre person, and was disgusted to find him a sadly incompetent marksman. "While admiring the lovely trees, we noticed a squirrel. The governor ran as fast as his legs could carry him to get his gun from the house, and soon returned out of breath with the lethal weapon. The little animal had had the patience to wait, but the great man was so inept that he missed it four times in a row."

Far more impressive was John C. Spencer, at whose Canandaigua home they stayed for three days (it still exists, as a nursing home). Spencer was a state representative and a leading legal expert, and he provided a fund of valuable information about American law and politics, much of which ended up in *Democracy in America*. After extensive conversations in Canandaigua, Tocqueville noted admiringly, "His mind is characterized by clarity and perspicacity." Years afterward Spencer contributed a preface and notes to an American edition of Tocqueville's book, declaring that "he has described, or rather defined, our federal government with an accurate precision unsurpassed even by any American pen."

One of the most important insights Tocqueville got from Spencer was that whereas lawyers in France often tended to political radicalism, those in America were generally conservative. Partly this was because

JOHN CANFIELD SPENCER

they dominated the legislatures and already had plenty of power, but it also reflected the assumptions of common law as opposed to the highly rational Code Napoléon. In the Anglo-American tradition, Tocqueville commented drily, "The need for logic is not such a preoccupation as it is with us," and whereas French lawyers competed to out-reason each other, American lawyers built their arguments by amassing precedents. That in itself implied a conservative attitude, and they had a professional stake as well in preserving legal mysteries. If a formal code were ever drawn up, Tocqueville remarked, they would have to begin their studies all over again, and "since the law would become accessible to ordinary people, they would lose some of their importance; they would no longer be like Egyptian priests, sole interpreters of occult knowledge."

More broadly, it seemed to Tocqueville that the legal ethos pervaded society as a whole. When he came to write *Democracy in America*, looking back on his conversations with scores of American lawyers and jurists, he described its influence as subtle but ubiquitous: "It adapts itself flexibly to the exigencies of the times, and yields without resistance to every social movement, but it envelops the entire society, penetrates all of the classes that make it up, shapes it in secret, acts upon it ceaselessly without its knowledge, and ends by shaping it according to its own desires." Tocqueville decided that lawyers as a class formed a sort of unofficial aristocracy, serving as a counterweight to popular passions. "To the democratic instincts of the people, they secretly oppose their aristocratic inclinations; to the people's love of novelty, their superstitious respect for the old; to the vastness of the people's designs, their narrow views; to the people's contempt for rules, their love of forms; and to the people's hotheadedness, their habit of moving slowly."

Beaumont agreed with Tocqueville that Spencer was "the most distinguished man I've yet met in America," but he was more interested in Spencer's family. As he rather archly told his mother:

At his home there are two charming persons, his daughters Mary and Catherine, who would cause us terrible distraction if we hadn't vowed, once and for all, never to permit any. Mary is the prettier of the two; she has that pink and white coloring that's sometimes found among Englishwomen but practically unknown in France. Never yet in the United States have I seen eyes as pretty as hers; they have a velvety sweetness that's indescribable. But why am I telling you so much about her? If I go on, you'll believe I'm in love, and the truth is I'm not. A long stay with her could be hazardous, but in three or four days I'll be leaving Canandaigua never to return.

Beaumont was extremely susceptible to lovely eyes, and during the trip he was always casting lingering looks behind. Even Tocqueville, writing to a sister-in-law on this occasion, was less reticent than usual, though careful to be jocular. "In addition to a very fine library, our host has two charming daughters with whom we get along very well . . . Though they don't know a single word of French, they have among other charms four blue eyes (not the same ones, but two apiece) such as I'm quite sure you've never seen on the other side of the water . . . Suffice it to say that we gazed at them even more willingly than at their father's books."

Evidently, both Tocqueville and Beaumont thought it necessary to make clear that although they might be thinking about sex, they weren't having any. Tocqueville took special care to convey that information to the friend who was his liaison with Marie. "Our virtue is still holding up," he reported. He did admit, however, "We're beginning to stare at women with an impudence that's not appropriate for people studying the penitentiary system."

The Frenchmen could not have guessed that another of Spencer's children, eight-year-old Philip, would one day acquire tragic fame. As a midshipman aboard the USS *Somers* in the Caribbean in 1842, young Spencer was accused of plotting mutiny and was executed without trial, an incident that inspired Melville's *Billy Budd*. He and his boyish co-conspirators allegedly hoped to turn the *Somers* into a pirate ship, but the evidence was sketchy and the necessity of executing the ringleaders far from obvious. Nonetheless, his father, who by then had become Tyler's secretary of war, sought vengeance in vain. A court-martial acquitted the captain.

On July 19, two weeks after leaving Albany, the travelers arrived at Buffalo, which Beaumont described as "a little town on the shores of Lake Erie" (its population at the time was eighty-five hundred). Now at long last they saw Indians in the flesh, and the disappointment was intense. It happened to be the day when Indians came to town to collect an installment of federal payment for their lands. "Unfortunately," Beaumont lamented, "they spend their money on brandy and strong liquor, which is killing them." Tocqueville described coming across a young man, too drunk to move, who was being kicked by his fellows and abused by a woman who seemed to be his companion. "She struck his head, twisted his face in her hands, and trampled on him. While abandoning herself to these ferocious actions, she uttered savage inarticulate cries that still seem to ring in my ears." Back at the hotel they found no one who could be bothered to go and help, even when money was offered, and the condensed comments in Tocqueville's notebook register the intensity of his disgust:

> Arrival in Buffalo. Stroll through the town. A throng of savages in the streets (payday). New idea they give rise to. Their ugliness. Their strange look. Their bronze and oily skin. Their long black straight hair. Their European clothes, worn in a savage way. Scene of a drunken Indian. Brutality of his compatriots and of the Indian woman accompanying him. Population brutalized by our wines and liquors. More horrible than similarly brutalized populations in Europe. Also something of the wild beast. Contrast with the moral and civilized people in whose midst they are.

Pondering this experience later, Tocqueville developed further the analogy with the poorest class at home, "paupers" who were likewise victims of the worst aspects of modern life. "Their features told of the profound depravity that can only be caused by lengthy abuse of the benefits of civilization. One would have said these men belonged to the lowest populace of our great European cities, and yet they were still savages."

Even the most admirable early Americans, when the new nation was getting established, had treated the Indians with casual condescension if not contempt. In his autobiography Benjamin Franklin retailed one of his genial anecdotes, in which some Pennsylvania Indians were rewarded for a successful negotiation with a large quantity of rum, after which they got wildly drunk and had to apologize the next day. "The orator acknowledged the fault, but laid it on the rum, and then endeavored to excuse the rum by saying, 'The Great Spirit who made all things made every thing for some use, and whatever use he designed anything for, that use it should always be put to. Now, when he made rum, he said LET THIS BE FOR INDIANS TO GET DRUNK WITH.'" Genial so far. But then Franklin added blandly, "And indeed if it be the design of Providence to extirpate these savages in order to make room for the cultivators of the earth, it seems not improbable that rum may be the appointed means. It has already annihilated all the tribes who formerly inhabited the seacoast."

In this part of America, indeed, not many Indians were left. Thanks to much-publicized trading and fighting over the years, the Iroquois had always loomed larger in the European imagination than their numbers might have warranted. The Five Nations—Mohawk, Oneida, Onondaga, Cayuga, and Seneca—had about fifteen thousand people all told. And now they were disappearing altogether, as Tocqueville recorded in a melancholy roll call. "All the Indian tribes that once lived in New England, the Narragansett, the Mohican, the Pequot, live now in memory only. The Lenape, who greeted Penn on the banks of the Delaware a century and a half ago, are vanished today. I met the last of the Iroquois; they were begging for money." In similar tones Joseph Story, a Supreme Court justice whose *Commentaries on the Constitution of the United States* would be an essential resource for Tocqueville, wrote elegiacally about the dwindling of the native race: "We hear the rustling of their footsteps, like that of the withered leaves of autumn, and they are gone forever. They pass mournfully by us, and they return no more . . . Braver men never lived; truer men never drew a bow. They had courage, and fortitude, and sagacity, and perseverance, beyond most of the human race." In his notebook Tocqueville wrote, "The Indian races are melting in the presence of European civilization like snow beneath the rays of the sun." It seems not to have been noticed that he must have been recalling the often-quoted words of the Shawnee chief Tecumseh at a grand council of Indians in 1811: "Where today are the Pequot? Where are the Narragansett, the Mohican, the Pokanoket, and many other once powerful tribes of our people? They have vanished before the avarice and the oppression of the white man, as snow before a summer sun."

As for the white settlers, although Tocqueville would make much of American "restlessness" in *Democracy in America*, he was already grasping that there were good economic reasons to keep moving. Land was the way to wealth, not so much for what it could produce as for its appreciation in value when later settlers arrived. A canny farmer would then sell off his holdings, migrate westward, carve a new farm out of the forest, and wait for prices to rise once again. A land agent in Buffalo told Tocqueville that this westward migration was bound to continue for the indefinite future, since it was always possible to buy land more cheaply there; he added, "God be thanked, we have enough of it to extend all the way to the Pacific Ocean." On this Tocqueville commented to one of his friends at home, "Don't you find that a whole big book is contained in that one reply?"

Far more than Tocqueville, Beaumont harbored sentimental feelings about farmers at home, and he rhapsodized with an incredible lack of realism: "Look at the French peasant, with his gay humor, serene brow, and laughing lips, singing beneath the thatched roof that conceals his poverty, and without a care for yesterday or a thought for tomorrow, dancing joyfully in the village square. In America they know nothing of this happy poverty. Absorbed by calculation, the American country dweller loses no time in pleasures. The fields say nothing to his heart, and the sun that brings fertility to his hillsides doesn't warm his soul. He treats the land as industrial material, and lives in his cottage as if in a factory."

In France, land was prohibitively expensive for ordinary workers to buy, and as Tocqueville remarked, "In all the other nations of Europe, it is almost unheard-of for a worker to become a landowner." Very differently, "the Americans never use the word 'peasant,' because they don't have the concept," and even at the frontier a farmer would turn out to be "a very civilized man, who submits to life in the forest for a time, and plunges into the wilds of the New World with a Bible, an ax, and newspapers." The German immigrant Francis Lieber confirmed this view: "The American farmer forms no class by himself. He is a citizen to all intents and purposes, not only as to political rights, but as to his whole standing and social connection. No views of his own, no dress, distinguish him from the inhabitant of the town."

It would be hard to exaggerate the contrast between this style of life and rural existence in France at the time, which has been described as "still recovering from the fall of the Roman Empire." There, regions off the beaten track were effectively isolated, and to get through the winters, the laboring poor often went into a state of near hibernation, eating little and slowing their lives to a torpid pace. No wonder, then, that Tocqueville was astonished at the energy of Americans in the remotest places, and at the regularity of communication with the world back east. He had written to his mother from Canandaigua, "When you've traversed a sort of wilderness on a frightful road and reach a habitation, you're astonished to encounter a more advanced civilization than in any of our villages. The farmer takes pride in his appearance, his dwelling is perfectly clean, and his first concern is to talk to you about politics."

By now Tocqueville and Beaumont had been away from home for three months, and when letters arrived, they were many weeks out of date. Tocqueville's own letters were filled with anxious thoughts about France, and he told his mother that from the sketchy information he was able to gather, it seemed that a civil war was all too likely, "bringing with it so many perils for the very ones who are most dear to me." Yet having sworn an oath of loyalty to the current government, he felt duty-bound to serve it even if its policies were unpalatable. "So long as Louis-Philippe is there," he told his cousin Kergorlay, "my hands are tied; but whoever his successor may be, I'll retire from public life and regain possession of my own conduct and actions." It wouldn't turn out that way.

4

THE ROMANCE OF THE FOREST

Having reached Buffalo, Tocqueville and Beaumont were determined to see the true American wilderness about which they had so often dreamed. In northern France, where they came from, farms and villages were everywhere, and many of the cities went all the way back to Roman times; to see vast tracts of uncultivated land in Europe, they would have had to go as far as Russia. Still more exciting, in the American interior Indians still lived as their ancestors had done, proudly refusing the enticements of civilization that had demoralized their eastern brethren.

On July 19 the travelers boarded the steamboat *Ohio*, bound for Detroit, the seat of government in the Michigan Territory, three hundred miles away at the other end of Lake Erie. Bad weather slowed them down, and they were on the water for the better part of four days. When they finally approached Detroit, Tocqueville was forcibly struck by the contrast between wilderness and civilization. On the Canadian shore the spire of a Catholic church and houses in the French style made him think of home, while a soldier stood guard in the Scottish uniform "made so famous by the field of Waterloo." Then, from the American shore, two Indians, with painted faces and nose rings, set out in a birch-bark canoe. They went off to fish quietly near the soldier, "who, glittering and motionless, seemed placed there to represent the brilliant civilization of Europe in arms." After seeing more canoes, Tocqueville wrote to his father that he would bring home a piece of birch bark, "and you'll think as I do that whoever first got into one was a daring fellow." He also admitted that he found the nose rings "abominable," but to tease a sister-in-law he demanded, "I humbly ask you to explain to me why it's more natural to pierce the ears than the nose."

Detroit at the time was only "a fine American village" with a population of twenty-five hundred; Pontiac was a hamlet of twenty houses. But once again Tocqueville was impressed, as he had been in the Mohawk Valley, by the spectacle of a familiar people in a new land. "The man you left behind in the streets of New York, you will find again in the midst of almost impenetrable solitude, with the same clothing, same mentality, same language, same habits, and same pleasures . . . The people who inhabit these isolated places arrived only yesterday, bringing with them the mores, ideas, customs, and needs of civilization." This was in startling contrast with France, where there were still profound differences between the various regions, and also between city dwellers and peasants. "From New York to the Great Lakes," Beaumont later recalled, "I sought in vain for intermediate degrees in American society. Everywhere the same men, the same passions, the same mores; everywhere the same enlightenment and the same obscurities. How strange! The American nation recruits from all the peoples of the earth, and none of those display such uniformity of traits and characteristics."

In historical hindsight the relative uniformity is not surprising, since the great flood of immigration had scarcely begun, and the settlers Tocqueville and Beaumont were encountering were still representative of what a contemporary editor called "the universal Yankee nation," arriving from New England in search of open spaces and better soil. When Beaumont went into a shop in Detroit to buy mosquito repellent, he found evidence of a civilization even more distant from the north woods: an advertisement offering the latest French fashions. "What do you think of the inhabitants of Michigan," he wrote to a friend, "who devote themselves to Paris style? It's a fact that in the remotest village in America they follow French fashion, and all the *objets de mode* supposedly come from Paris." As Henry Adams later observed, homemade clothes betrayed a rusticity that people in towns were eager to rise above.

Americans back east were beginning to romanticize their hinterland, whose inhabitants had once been dismissed as "backsettlers," "backwoodsmen," and "bushwhackers," but were now being reinvented as folk heroes, inspired by the novels of Cooper and by such celebrities as Daniel Boone and Davy Crockett. The preferred terms now were "frontiersmen," "pathfinders," "pioneers," and "trailblazers." Even the haughty Massachusetts senator Daniel Webster invoked the myth: "It did not happen to me to be born in a log cabin, but my elder brothers and sisters were born in a log cabin, raised amid the snowdrifts of New Hampshire, at a period so early that when the smoke first rose from its rude chimney and curled over the frozen hills, there was no similar evidence of a white man's habitation between it and the settlements on the rivers of Canada."

Tocqueville, however, did not romanticize backwoods heroes. "Two years ago the inhabitants of the district whose capital is Memphis sent to the House of Representatives an individual named David Crockett, who has had no education whatsoever, reads only with difficulty, and has no property or fixed address, but spends his life hunting, selling his game to support himself, and living continually in the forest. His rival, who lost, was a man of some wealth and talent." As for log cabins, what mainly struck Tocqueville was their crudeness and inconvenience, and he rightly understood that their inhabitants hoped to replace them with proper houses as soon as possible.

The real magnet of the frontier was the opportunity to translate land into wealth. The English traveler Harriet Martineau met a farmer in Michigan who had paid $1.25 an acre for his eight hundred acres, and three years later was offered $40 an acre for them. Still more staggering were the profits of speculators who managed to be in the right place at the right time. One man acquired a "preemption claim" to some land in Chicago by living on it, which allowed him to buy it for

$150 when it was authorized for sale. Later the same day he sold it to a friend of Martineau's for $5,000. More than just money, what the frontier offered was scope for rising in the world, as Andrew Jackson and Abraham Lincoln both did, beginning in poverty, largely self-taught, and practicing law with very minimal training before entering politics.

Sixty years after Tocqueville's American trip, Frederick Jackson Turner delivered a lecture that quickly became famous, "The Significance of the Frontier in American History." Arguing that the energy and openness of frontier society had been crucial in the development of the American character, Turner fully acknowledged his debt to Tocqueville. But his 1890s view of the then-closing frontier embodied a romantic image of pioneers that Tocqueville didn't share. Tocqueville definitely recognized that the availability of cheap land provided an outlet for frustrated Easterners, and he grasped that (as Turner put it) "the West was a migrating region, a stage of society rather than a place." But he would not have endorsed Turner's myth of the noble West or his belief in the moral superiority of farming. Tocqueville was greatly interested in political institutions, which Turner wasn't, and he could never have declared as Turner did, "American democracy was born of no theorist's dream; it was not carried in the Susan Constant to Virginia, nor in the Mayflower to Plymouth. It came stark and strong and full of life out of the American forest, and it gained new strength each time it touched a new frontier." Turner himself probably decided that that was a bit excessive; when he reprinted the essay, he omitted the words "stark and strong and full of life."

Tocqueville was indeed a romantic, but not with respect to the settlers. It was Indians and the trackless forest that fired his imagination, and Beaumont was equally enthusiastic. On the steamboat to Detroit they had happened to meet John Tanner, who gave them a copy of his recently published book, *A Narrative of the Captivity and Adventures of John Tanner (U.S. Interpreter at the Saut de Ste. Marie) During Thirty Years Residence Among the Indians in the Interior of North America.* When he was nine years old, Tanner was captured in Kentucky by Shawnee, who sold him to the Ojibwa, with whom he lived for thirty years. Beaumont eagerly drew him out about Indians. "You, who sympathize with their plight," Tanner said, "hasten to get to know them! They will soon have vanished from the earth."

The very idea of plunging into the wilderness for its own sake struck the locals as inexplicable—"You want to see the woods? Go straight ahead, you'll find all you want"—so Tocqueville and Beaumont had to make up a story that they were looking for land to buy. This elicited advice to go to the most developed areas, and after they had been informed which direction was the very worst, that was of course the one they chose. The plan now was to journey on horseback to Saginaw Bay on Lake Huron, nearly a hundred miles away (today an easy two-hour run on the interstate). Hiring a pair of horses and expecting to camp on the ground whenever necessary, they equipped themselves with pillows, a compass, brandy, sugar, and ammunition, and set off on a memorable journey that Tocqueville wrote up afterward as *Quinze jours dans le désert* (*Two Weeks in the Wilderness*). As Beaumont remarked, "We have no word for what the English express so well by 'wilderness.'" *Désert* means "uninhabited place," a very human-centered term. It was likewise hard to name in French the people who were taming the wilderness. Tocqueville called them "'new settlers'—that's the English phrase, we don't have an exact equivalent."

The expedition was an immense success. "We were overcome with joy," Tocqueville reported, "at finally experiencing a place that the torrent of European civilization had not yet reached." The trees were enormous; Beaumont measured an oak eighteen feet in circumference, and a pine that was twenty. It is notable that he and Tocqueville thought in feet, not meters, just as they calculated distances in miles or leagues and not kilometers. The metric system, which had been proclaimed by the French Republic in 1795 with the motto "for all men, for all time," was abolished in 1816 and would not be reinstated until 1837.

Unexpectedly, they were joined by a young Chippewa who spoke neither English nor French, and who perfectly fulfilled their idea of the noble savage. By means of sign language they were able to indicate where they wanted to go, and he agreed to be their guide. "He ran with the agility of a wild animal, without saying a word or seeming to quicken his pace. We stopped, he stopped. We started up again, he started up again . . . I would see him now to the right of my horse, now to the left, leaping over the bushes and landing noiselessly on the ground." When they eventually met other Indians with whom they were able to converse, Tocqueville understood more clearly than ever that their entire way of life was adamantly opposed to assimilation into American society. Echoing the language of Rousseau's great *Discourse on the Origin of Inequality*, he described their system of values with respect: "Lying on his cloak in his smoky hut, the Indian regards the comfortable dwelling of the European with scorn . . . He smiles bitterly as he sees us torment our lives to acquire useless wealth. What we call industriousness, he calls shameful servitude, and he compares the worker to an ox laboriously plowing its furrow."

The expedition was an opportunity to experience the romantic sublimity that Tocqueville's relative the Romantic writer Chateaubriand had recently made popular in novels set in the American interior. Beaumont rejoiced that his countryman had lent his eloquence to prosaic America, and declared extravagantly, "There was no poet among the Americans, but leaping over the Atlantic, the angel of poetry bore the French Homer on wings of flame to the banks of the Mississippi." Whatever the merits of his novels, Chateaubriand's *Voyage en Amérique*, published four years previously, was an extremely unreliable account of a four-month journey taken three decades earlier, with a lot of freewheeling invention and wholesale borrowings from other people's books. Tocqueville had a low opinion of his famous relative's egotism, and no wish to imitate his effusions. "Primitive liberty," Chateaubriand exclaimed, "I have found you at last! . . . Here I am as the Almighty created me, sovereign of nature, borne triumphantly over the waters, while the inhabitants of the rivers accompany me, the peoples of the air sing their hymns to me, the beasts of the earth salute me, and the forests bend their highest branches over my passage . . . I will go wandering in my solitude, not one beat of my heart will be constrained, not a single thought of mine will be enchained; I will be as free as nature."

By contrast, Tocqueville's jottings in his pocket notebook have a terse eloquence. "The wind dies down. Complete calm. Deep darkness. Imposing silence of the forest, disturbed by the sound of our horses and the cries of a solitary bird that seems to follow our steps. Full moon rises." When he elaborated the account in *Two Weeks in the Wilderness*, his theme was not the self-regarding expansiveness of Chateaubriand but a Zen-like fullness of being:

> At midday, when the sun beats down on the forest, you often hear in its depths a sound like a long sigh, a plaintive cry that lingers into the distance. It is the last effort of the dying wind. Then all around you everything subsides into a silence so profound, a stillness so complete, that your soul feels penetrated by a sort of religious terror ... How comes it that human languages, which find words for every sorrow, meet an insuperable obstacle when they try to express the sweetest and most natural emotions of the heart? Who can ever paint a faithful image of those moments, so rare in life, when physical well-being prepares you for mental peace, and before your eyes the universe seems to attain a perfect equilibrium? Then the soul, half asleep, balances between the present and the future, between the real and the possible; enveloped in the beauty of nature, breathing a mild and tranquil air, at peace with yourself in the midst of universal peace, you listen to the steady beating of your arteries, and each pulsation seems to mark the passing of time flowing drop by drop into eternity.

For a young man troubled by volatile emotions and haunted by anxiety that he would fail to make a difference with his life, this was an unforgettable revelation of what Rousseau had called "le sentiment de l'existence," the simple "awareness of being." But Tocqueville added, "One might say that for a moment the Creator had turned his face away, and that nature's forces were paralyzed." André Jardin comments that the religious terror and the God who turns away reflect Tocqueville's early education in the stern theology of Jansenism. There is an evident echo of Pascal's "dieu caché," the "hidden God." In Pascal's words, "Men are in darkness and remote from God, who is hidden from their knowledge; this is the very name which he gives himself in the Scriptures, *deus absconditus*."

The parallels with Rousseau continued in a different way. After a meditation not unlike Tocqueville's, Rousseau had unexpectedly encountered a noisy stocking factory in the depths of what he had taken to be an uninhabited forest. There were no factories yet between Detroit and Saginaw, but Tocqueville experienced a similar ironic reversal. "Suddenly we were startled from our reverie by a gunshot that rang out through the trees. The sound seemed at first to roll crashing along the banks of the river, and then it faded rumbling into the distance until it was entirely lost in the depths of the surrounding forest. One might say that it was a sustained and tremendous war cry uttered by civilization on the march."

Naturally, there were some low points, such as getting alarmingly lost for a while, and merciless mosquitoes that made sleep all but impossible. Tocqueville wrote to his old tutor Lesueur, "You can't imagine what torments these accursed creatures inflict in the depths of the forest." In fact, malaria was a scourge throughout the region, though no one then realized its connection to mosquitoes. As a jingle of the time had it:

> Don't go to Michigan, that land of ills;
> The word means ague, fever and chills.

For the indefatigable hunters, there was plenty of game. They saw partridges, pheasants, grouse, and deer—"but I didn't manage to kill a single one," Beaumont admitted—and they dined regularly on "pigeons," which they found to be excellent. Hummingbirds were a more daunting challenge; "I shot at them, but missed." The pigeons were probably passenger pigeons, in which case the travelers were contributing, in a small way, to their extinction.

In the middle of nowhere they found warm hospitality. Coming upon an isolated log cabin in the dark of night, they advanced with extreme caution, and as Tocqueville described what happened next, just when they started to climb the fence, "the moon revealed, on the other side, a huge black bear. Standing on its hind legs and pulling on its chain, it indicated clearly enough that it intended to give us a fraternal welcome. 'What the devil of a country is this,' I said, 'where they have bears for watchdogs?'" The owner of the cabin told the bear to be quiet, cheerfully took them in as guests, and went out in the moonlight to scythe down grass for their exhausted horses. "There was only one bed in the cabin. Beaumont having won the toss for it, I wrapped myself in my cloak and, lying down on the floor, fell into the deep sleep that befits a man who has just done forty miles on horseback."

In *Two Weeks in the Wilderness*, Tocqueville described a typical log cabin. It was invariably small, no more than twenty feet long and often less, and since it was only temporary, construction was crude. The logs were stacked in dovetailed fashion, with gaps of two or three inches between them stuffed ineffectually with wood chips and clay, and "a resinous fire, crackling on the earthen floor, illuminates the interior better than the daylight can." Doorways were sawed into both sides for ventilation, and there was usually only a single window. The amenities were sure to include a rifle, a Bible, and a few pieces of cracked china, and often there would be a volume of Milton or Shakespeare as well. "In the middle of the room stands a wobbly table whose legs, still wreathed in leaves, seem to have sprouted by themselves from the ground they're standing on."

The jolly hermit they stayed with in the Michigan forest wasn't necessarily typical of backwoodsmen, especially since he had no family. One of Tocqueville's few generalizations about the role of American fathers—it appears in *Two Weeks in the Wilderness*—is suggestive here: "Focused on the single goal of making his fortune, the settler ends up creating a completely individual existence. Family feelings have merged into a vast egotism, and it is doubtful whether he sees anything in his wife and children but a detached portion of himself." Tocqueville was moved by the way pioneer women faced challenges they had never encountered back east:

> I often met, in the farthest wilderness, young women who had been raised among all the refinements of the big cities of New England, and who passed almost without transition from their parents' opulent home to a leaky cabin in the depths of a forest. Neither fever, loneliness, nor boredom had broken the springs of their courage. Their features were

LOG CABIN

This scene shows the windowless design of a typical cabin, and the dead, girdled trees that surround it. Even the smallest children have work to do.

altered and faded, but their gaze remained steady; they seemed at once melancholy and resolute. I don't doubt that these young American women had acquired from early upbringing the inner strength they were now drawing upon.

It is not clear how much Tocqueville ever talked with such women, but he didn't hesitate to attribute to them the noblest self-sacrifice:

On the other side of the hearth a woman sits rocking a young child on her knees; she nods to us without pausing. Like her pioneer husband, this woman is in the prime of life; her appearance seems superior to her condition, and her clothing even betrays an unquenched taste for adornment, but her delicate limbs are weakened, her features are weary, and her gaze is gentle and grave. Her whole face reflects religious resigna-

tion, a profound peace free from passion, and a sort of natural and tranquil firmness that faces all the ills of life without fear or defiance.

It might have given Tocqueville pause to hear the actual feelings of
some of those pioneer wives, like the Massachusetts woman who bitterly told her relatives that her husband had sold their house against

SAGINAW FOREST, BY GUSTAVE DE BEAUMONT

Beaumont has labeled his sketch "25 July 1831. Saginaw Forest (Indian
guide)." This Chippewa, named Sagan-Ruisco (or Kuisco), was one of the
pair who guided the travelers after they left the hermit's cabin; he has
lodged his tomahawk in a tree trunk, while Beaumont reclines wearily on
the ground. In *Two Weeks in the Wilderness*, Tocqueville explains what is
going on: "Civilization has no hold on the Indian; he is unaware of its
pleasures or despises them. I noticed, however, that Sagan-Ruisco paid
particular attention to a little wickerwork bottle that hung at my side. A
bottle that doesn't break! That was a thing whose usefulness appealed to
his senses and excited real admiration. My gun and my bottle were the
only parts of my European equipment that seemed to excite his covetous-
ness. I made signs to him that I would give him my bottle if he would guide
us immediately to Saginaw."

her wishes: "If he can rake and scrape enough after paying his debts to set his family down in Wisconsin he is determined to go. So you wonder that I feel sad. Nothing but poor health and poverty to begin with in a new country looks dark to me. But I can't help it, go we must I suppose if the means can be raised."

The next day the obliging log cabin dweller found them a new pair of Indian guides. Following the Indians as they sprang effortlessly over obstacles, always sure of their way through a forest without landmarks, Tocqueville reflected that the usual power relationship was completely reversed. "Plunged into deep obscurity, reduced to his own forces, the civilized man walked like a blind person, incapable not only of finding his way through the labyrinth he was traversing but even of finding the means to sustain life . . . It was a singular spectacle to see the scornful smile with which they led us by the hand like children until they brought us close to the object they themselves had seen for a long time."

The Indians conducted the travelers to a house where they spent another mosquito-tormented night. "Kept awake by the pain of their bites, we covered our heads with blankets, but their needles went right through them. Thus hunted and pursued, we got up and went outside for some air, until exhaustion finally brought on a painful and fitful slumber." It may have been at this point (the account is in some unused notes for *Democracy in America*) that Tocqueville remarked on a memorable contrast between white and Indian societies:

One night, in the company of several savages, I arrived at the house of an American settler. It was the dwelling of a well-to-do planter and also served as a tavern. They lived in great comfort there, with even a sort of rustic luxury. I entered a well-lit, well-heated room where some neighborhood idlers were already convened around a table, on which were whiskey and water. All of them were more or less inebriated, but their drunkenness had a grave and gloomy quality that struck me. They talked laboriously about public affairs, the price of houses, luck in commerce, and the ups and downs of industry. The Indians remained outside, even though it was a rainy night and they had nothing but scraps of blankets for covering. They had lit a big fire and were sitting around it on the damp ground, chatting cheerfully among themselves. I couldn't understand what they were saying, but their loud bursts of merriment constantly invaded the solemnity of our banquet.

The next day the travelers emerged at last from the labyrinthine forest, and Tocqueville, who appreciated symbolism, was delighted to be granted a symbolic ending. As he prepared to ford a deep stream, a man who looked like an Indian got out of a dugout canoe and surprised him by saying in French, "Don't go too fast, people have drowned here." Tocqueville commented afterward, "If my horse had spoken up I would not have been more surprised." The stranger explained that he was a *bois-brûlé*, "charred wood," the local term for a half-breed métis of mixed French and Indian blood. He invited Tocqueville to share his canoe while Tocqueville's horse swam alongside, and as he paddled, he sang snatches of an old French song:

> Entre Paris et Saint-Denis
> Il était une fille . . .

In his very person this man symbolized the junction of the wild and the civilized. And then, watching him cross the stream again to fetch Beaumont, Tocqueville had a second epiphany. "I will remember for the rest of my life the moment when he approached the bank. The moon, which was full, rose at that very moment above the prairie we had just crossed. Only half of its disk appeared above the horizon, and one might have called it a mysterious portal through which light flowed toward us from another sphere."

The following day they reached Saginaw, a trading post of thirty inhabitants, whose only contact with the outside world was an occasional steamboat delivering supplies and picking up furs. "Saginaw," Beaumont wrote enthusiastically though inaccurately, "is the boundary where civilization ends." He was especially delighted with the métis, who preserved a French liveliness that Tocqueville, too, couldn't help idealizing. The *bois-brûlé*, Tocqueville wrote, "is a tireless hunter, sleeps in his hunting blind, and lives on wild honey and bison flesh. This man, however, is no less a Frenchman still—gay, enterprising, haughty, proud of his origin, a passionate lover of martial glory, vain rather than self-interested, a man of instinct, obeying his first impulse rather than his reason, preferring fame to money." His Anglo-American neighbor, on the other hand, "is cold, tenacious, and relentless in argument. He attaches himself to the land, and seizes from life in the wild all that it can yield to him ... He holds that man comes into the world only to become well-off and to enjoy the conveniences of life." Tocqueville would doubtless have appreciated Thoreau's similar description of an American national type: "Dull but capable, slow but persevering, severe but just, of little humor but genuine." In his own sketch of a typical western settler Tocqueville wrote, with a similar mixture of admiration and distaste, "His features, which are lined by the cares of life, display practical intelligence and a cold, persevering energy that's immediately striking. His gait is slow and formal, his words measured, and his appearance austere."

Later, writing about racial prejudice in *Democracy in America*, Tocqueville would comment that French and Spanish colonists had been far more willing to intermarry with Native Americans than the British ever were. But even in the formerly French north woods, the métis occupied an equivocal position. At one point the travelers heard a psalm of penitence being sung to a haunting Indian melody. They entered a rude cabin and encountered a trapper's wife:

> We asked if she was French. "No," she replied, smiling. "English?" "Not that either," she said, and lowering her eyes, she added, "I am only a savage." Child of two races, brought up speaking two languages, nourished by diverse beliefs, and cradled in contradictory prejudices, the métis is a composite as inexplicable to himself as to others ... Proud of his European origin, he despises the wilderness, and yet he loves the wild freedom that reigns there. He admires civilization but cannot submit completely to its rule. His tastes are in conflict with his

ideas, his opinions with his mores. Not knowing how to find his way by his uncertain lights, his soul struggles painfully in the swaddling clothes of universal doubt.

After some sightseeing and duck hunting around Saginaw, the companions set out to retrace their route back to Detroit. There was a startling incident when they were trudging through high grass and Tocqueville noticed their guide walking with unusual caution. "'Why are you being so careful?' I asked him. 'Are you afraid of getting wet?' 'No,' he replied, 'but I've made it my habit when I cross the prairie to watch where I put my feet, so as not to step on a rattlesnake.' 'What the devil!' I exclaimed, jumping onto the path. 'Are there rattlesnakes here?' 'Oh, yes indeed!' replied my Norman-American with imperturbable sangfroid. 'The place is full of them.'"

The next day their guides left, and they had to press on alone. They had been told which of two paths to take through the forest, but there seemed actually to be three, and it was far from clear which had been meant. After much hesitation, "we did what nearly all great men do, and acted pretty much at random." It was like an allegory of life itself, in which the future can never be clearly foreseen and one must trust to intuition. And so indeed it turned out, because just when the path seemed about to disappear, they recognized a fallen tree they had seen when they were coming the other way, and as night fell they were welcomed again by the hermit in the log cabin. "This time the bear greeted us as old friends, and stood up on his hind legs only to express his joy at our happy return."

It was time to reenter civilization, and Tocqueville concluded his narrative artfully with reflections on the July Revolution in France, just one year before, that had thrown their professional lives into confusion and inspired the American trip:

It was in the midst of that profound solitude that we thought suddenly of the Revolution of 1830, whose first *anniversaire* we had just reached. I cannot express how overwhelmingly the memories of the twenty-ninth of July seized our spirits. The cries and smoke of battle, the noise of cannons, the rattling of musketry, the still more dreadful tolling of the warning bell, that entire day with its inflamed atmosphere, seemed to emerge all at once from the past and appeared before me like a *tableau vivant*. But this was only a sudden vision, a passing dream. When I raised my head and looked around me, the apparition had already vanished; but never had the silence of the forest seemed so chilly, its shadows so deep, or its solitude so complete.

What Tocqueville did not mention was that July 29 had a double significance. It was his own twenty-sixth birthday, for which the French word is likewise *anniversaire*.

In later years Tocqueville declined to publish *Two Weeks in the Wilderness*; as his plans for *Democracy in America* grew, he wanted to leave something for Beaumont to do (Beaumont published *Two Weeks* thirty years later, after his friend's death). In due course Beaumont decided that his own theme would be race relations in America, and he folded a version of the trip into his novel *Marie*, in which a beautiful woman of mixed blood and her lover seek refuge in the forest from the cruelties of civilization in an atmosphere of eroticism virtuously resisted ("the enchantment that comes from her perfumed breath, her flowing hair, and her burning gaze"). There was no woman present when Beaumont and Tocqueville were there, but in the novel his hero, Ludovic, has the beautiful Marie at his side and is sorely tempted to ravish her—"a burning wind passed over my soul and kindled raging desire"—until stern morality intervenes and preserves her honor. Not long afterward, to his great grief, she dies.

This tragedy of self-denial, told in luscious prose, was heavily indebted to Chateaubriand's *Atala*, in which "the moon shone amid a spotless azure, and its pearly light descended upon the indistinct top of the forest. No sound could be heard, apart from a strange distant harmony, and one might have said that the soul of solitude was sighing through the whole length of the wilderness." Beaumont was disgusted, however, to find that the local people noticed no romance in the landscape at all. "Americans consider the forest the symbol of wilderness and therefore of barbarism, so it's against the woods that they mount their attacks. Among ourselves one cuts down only for use; in America they do it to destroy. The country dweller passes half his life in combat against his natural enemy, the forest, and he wages it relentlessly; from an early age his children learn to use the billhook and the ax. The European who admires a lovely forest is greatly surprised to find in Americans a deep hatred of trees."

Beaumont, of course, was an aristocrat who never needed to pick up an ax. Other visitors were more sympathetic to the practical needs of the settlers. A Scotsman was impressed that every American "understands the use of the ax from his infancy." Wood was required not just for houses but also for heating, cooking, fences, and even roads (logs were sometimes laid side by side in a jolting "corduroy" style). It was also the fuel for steamboats, which stopped twice a day at "wooding places," where gangs of men carried the logs aboard, and for light industry. Supplying wood for the boilers of a saltworks near Syracuse meant deforesting three thousand acres a year.

However sad it was that virgin forest was being demolished, few people in those days doubted that to ravish nature was the mission of mankind. In later years, however, it was the vast unpeopled forest that haunted Tocqueville's memory. Indeed, if wilderness was giving way to civilization, in 1831 the process had barely begun. Once started, though, it was irreversible, as a Detroit journalist noted in 1976 in a piece titled "Monsieur Tocqueville! Oh, Get Some Water—He's Fainted!"

> Tocqueville journeyed through a paradise; the traveler today journeys through a junkyard. Tocqueville's trail entered the forest a mile from Detroit. Today that spot marks the beginning of an ugly slum that runs for miles along Woodward Avenue . . . Pontiac today is a depressed industrial town dependent on the General Motors Corporation. Its downtown is gutted by abandonment and urban redevelopment. The stream Tocqueville described as transparent, the Clinton River, is heavily polluted; trees are gone, and its sides have been encased in concrete.

Back in still-rustic Detroit, Tocqueville and Beaumont were expecting to return to the East, but a huge steamboat, the *Superior*, was just then setting out on a sightseeing voyage on Lake Huron and Lake Michigan that happened only once a year. On the spur of the moment they bought tickets and were soon under way. It was a mistake. They had already had their experience of wilderness, and the vast lakes with their uninteresting stopping places were a disappointment, a waste, in fact, of ten precious days. Tocqueville's notebook pretty much dries up at this point, becoming little more than terse annotations:

> August 4. We leave at 6:00 a.m. Absolutely insignificant day. Toward evening we lose all sight of land . . .
> August 8. Insignificant day passed on the water. From time to time, to the right or the left, low ground covered with forest . . .
> August 11. Monotonous day on the lake . . .
> August 13. Departure from Mackinac at 9:00 a.m. Nothing interesting during the return.

At the farthest point in its voyage the steamboat reached Green Bay in the Huron Territory, a subdivision of the immense Michigan Territory, but the Frenchmen found little of interest there. "Village on the bank in the midst of a prairie on the bank of a river," Tocqueville wrote in his notebook. "Iroquois village farther up. Big 'settlement.' We don't know what to do. I go hunting by myself." As for the great cities of the future, they were as yet vestigial. When Harriet Martineau visited Milwaukee, it had been settled less than a year and had a population of four hundred people, only seven of whom were women. Five years later the French economist Michel Chevalier could write that on a map of Lake Michigan "you'll find a little town called Chicago, one of the posts that our French established during their tireless journeys in North America." He added presciently, "Chicago seems destined to have extensive trade at some future time." Settlers were indeed pouring in. A few years later a Detroit writer commented optimistically that the Wisconsin Territory, "washed by Lake Michigan and the upper Mississippi, sweeps forward among the sister States like a young maiden in green and flowing robes, to win the emigrant to her home."

On the *Superior*, as on the *Havre* crossing the Atlantic, the long, idle days were a purgatory of unwelcome socializing. Beaumont wrote that a few young men seemed all right, "forts bons garçons," but no better than that. "They are pretty much nonentities; they seem bored to death, and you can see why." One of these, an Englishman named Godfrey Vigne, in fact went on to write a book about his American travels (not mentioning Tocqueville and Beaumont), which is a travelogue of the most random sort, filled with scorn for American manners. The only subjects about which he was enthusiastic were trout fishing and picturesque views, and in his opinion even the views were deficient by failing to be English: "Where, thought I, are the 'stately homes of England'? Where is the marble-fronted hall and the village church beside it, with its spire pointing to the heavens?"

Tocqueville and Beaumont, bored or not, were unfailingly agreeable to their fellow passengers, as a Detroit journalist confirmed after their return: "We have seldom met with gentlemen better qualified, by their natural temperaments, acquisitions, and habits, for tourists in a foreign land. It was refreshing to hear their expressions of admiration, poured forth with the most winning enthusiasm, as some new scene of beauty opened before them . . . and they looked with curious but kindly eye on the beginnings of improvement in this newly explored region."

Besides, Tocqueville always tried to find something valuable in his experiences, and this one was no exception. After the voyage was over, he wrote to his father:

There was nothing remarkable to look at in the immense stretch of coast we traversed, flat country covered with forests. The whole, however, produces a deep and lasting impression. This lake with no sails, this shore still with no trace at all of the passage of man, the eternal forest that borders it—all of this, I assure you, is not just grand in poetry, it's the most extraordinary spectacle I've ever seen in my life. These regions, which are still an immense forest, will someday become one of the richest and most powerful countries on earth. One can make that assertion without being a prophet. Nature has done everything here: a fertile land, and outlets like no others on earth. All that is lacking is civilized man, and he is at the door.

One evening during the voyage at least was memorable. The passengers had been dancing under the stars to the music of a violin and an English horn, when an unexpected melody suddenly carried the Frenchmen back to the days of revolution in the previous year. The other passengers could not have known with what mixed feelings they listened. Beaumont wrote to his brother, "When the ball was over, the orchestra played us 'The Marseillaise.' I had forgotten what there is of beauty in this air, on account of the memories it recalled. It was just a year ago that I heard it for the first time, sung in Paris in the Place Vendôme and in the courtyard of the Palais Royal. Played like this, it was like an echo of the cannons of July still resounding through the world. But who could have predicted that one year later I would hear it on Lake Huron?" The revolutionary hymn had been illegal after Napoleon's fall and had remained unsung until 1830. Tocqueville, too, was moved. "The warning bell at night, the fusillade in the streets, our sortie from Paris, our armed patrols in Versailles, and the nights passed in the bodyguard, all of that seemed like a dream, the memory of someone else's life and not my own."

As it had during the voyage across the Atlantic, what gave Beaumont particular satisfaction was his own flute. At midnight a few days later, at anchor off Sault Ste. Marie, "I played the variations on 'Di tanti palpiti' on the bridge. The beauty of such a night has no equal. The sky was sparkling with stars, which were all reflected in the depths of the water, and here and there on the shore one could make out the fires of Indians, whose ears were struck with an unfamiliar sound and who were doubtless listening for the first time to the airs of Rossini and Auber." "Di tanti palpiti," from Rossini's *Tancredi*, was enormously popular in Europe at the time.

In Michigan, Beaumont and Tocqueville had finally encountered the noble Indians they longed to know, and now, on the banks of Lake Superior, a memorable meeting took place. A venerable Chippewa chief, adorned with eagle feathers to indicate Sioux he had slain, was deeply impressed by Tocqueville's fine double-barreled shotgun. Learning that Tocqueville came from France, the old man exclaimed, "The fathers of the Canadians are great warriors!" In return Tocqueville ventured to ask through an interpreter, "Would you consent to let me have one of those feathers? I will take it back to my own country, and I will say I got it from a great chief." The Indian solemnly detached a feather and "offered me a huge bony hand, from which I extracted my own with great difficulty after he had grasped it."

A CHIPPEWA CHIEF
This portrait of Shing-Gaa-Ba-Wosin was made by the British artist J. O. Lewis, on assignment for the U.S. government, near Lake Superior in 1826. Lewis notes that part of the chief's face was painted with vermilion and that he is wearing a silver medal with an image of the president (probably Monroe, though it's hard to tell).

To be sure, Indian customs were often disconcerting to Tocqueville, who preferred his savages strong and silent. At one stop along Lake Huron he had, as usual, gone hunting, and was confronted by an unexpected apparition:

In the forest on the way, the sound of a savage drum. Cries. We see eight savages approaching, stark naked except for a small loincloth. Six children, two men. Daubed with colors from head to foot. Bristling hair, the ends falling in a queue at the back. Wooden club in hand, leaping like devils. Handsome men. Dancing to amuse themselves and to get money. We give them a shilling. It is the "war dance." Horrible to see. What degradation!

Yet the more Tocqueville and Beaumont saw of Indians, the more impressed they were. "I sometimes wonder," Beaumont wrote, "whether these Indians, whom Europeans despise, deserve to be called savages. The ones I saw on the way to Saginaw live peacefully in their forest. Everyone who has contact with them agrees in praising their honesty, their good faith, and their magnanimity. The Europeans who trade with them do have one great superiority, it's true, which is to cheat them constantly."

As a lawyer, Beaumont was especially impressed by the difference between the Indian system of justice and the one in which he had been trained. "Practically all of our laws are made for the defense of private property; among the Indians this basis of European societies doesn't exist. They believe the whole of nature belongs to all men, and they don't divide up the forests, which are vast enough for everyone to find a place to dwell. They commit so few crimes that they have no need of courts; they must be just indeed to be able to do without justice." Beaumont had in fact arrived in America already expecting to confirm the superior simplicity of native code. The proposal he and Tocqueville had submitted to justify their trip began with the ominous words: "As with all societies that have attained a high level of civilization, French society is troubled by an inner evil that attacks the very principle of its existence . . . This evil is the progressive increase of crimes and misdemeanors in proportion as society becomes more civilized."

As was inevitable at the time, however, Beaumont also took it for granted that the accomplishments of Western civilization were superior to those of the savage, noble or otherwise. At Green Bay, "I amused myself in the hut of one of my savages by painting a little Indian's face. I gave him a bird on one cheek, a galloping horse on the other, and a cat on his chin. His companions were all admiration at my masterpiece. You know it's the Indians' custom to paint their faces; they do it very crudely, without taste or art." He added complacently, "I learned more about the ways of the Indians by passing half an hour among them than I would have done by reading thousands of books." And he was not exactly reverent during the return voyage, when he discovered a cache of bones on Mackinac Island in Lake Huron. "I found a small piece of these relics, and it is one of the treasures that I'll bring back to my own land."

Tocqueville, with his deep-seated doubts about theology, was especially impressed by Indian religion. "The Lutheran condemns the Calvinist to everlasting fire, the Calvinist the Unitarian, and the Catholic envelops them all in communal damnation. More tolerant in his rude faith, the Indian limits himself to excluding his European brother from the happy hunting ground he reserves for himself . . . He consoles himself easily for the evils of life, and he dies in peace, dreaming of forests forever green which the pioneer's ax will never disturb, and in which deer and beaver will present themselves to be shot during the numberless days of eternity." The only beliefs that Tocqueville himself felt confident in—that God existed and that the soul was immortal—were not very different from those of the Indians.

Tocqueville was struck, furthermore, by the realization that the Indians' martial ethos had much in common with the code of his own ancestors. "There is no Indian so wretched, in his bark hut, that he does not have a haughty notion of his personal value, and regards the tasks of industry as degrading occupations . . . For him hunting and war are the only pursuits worthy of a man. In the depths of his poverty in the forest, the Indian cherishes the same ideas and opinions as a medieval nobleman in his castle." Tocqueville did not discount the Indians' ferocity in war, but he admired the way in which they combined it with an almost mythic generosity. "Mild and hospitable in peace, pitiless in war beyond even the known limits of human ferocity, the Indian would risk starvation to assist a stranger who knocked at the door of his hut at night, and with his own hands would tear apart the palpitating limbs of a prisoner. The most celebrated republics of antiquity never had occasion to admire firmer courage, prouder souls, or more uncompromising love of independence than lay concealed in the wild forests of the New World." In a letter Tocqueville succinctly invoked the language of classical tragedy: "They inspire more pity than fear."

By the time they got back to Buffalo, Tocqueville and Beaumont had covered nearly two thousand miles, and a whole month had slipped by. Nevertheless, one further natural wonder could not be avoided. It was obligatory for travelers to see Niagara Falls and, if possible, to have a life-transforming experience there. Harriet Martineau was exceptional in successfully keeping her head: "A lady asked me many questions about my emotions at Niagara, to which I gave only one answer of which she could make anything. 'Did you not,' was her last inquiry, 'long to throw yourself down, and mingle with your mother earth?'— 'No.'" The Scottish traveler Thomas Hamilton, not normally given to gushing, turned up the volume at Niagara. "The gloom of the abyss, the dark firmament of rock which threatens destruction to the intruder, the terrors of the descending torrent, the deep thunder of its roar, and the fearful convulsion of the waters into which it falls, constitute the features of a scene, the sublimity of which undoubtedly extends to the very verge of horror." Even Dickens, writing when the sublime had already been done to death by his predecessors, chose a note of religious awe, complete with capital letters: "When I felt how near to my Creator I was standing, the first effect, and the enduring one—instant and lasting—of the tremendous spectacle, was Peace: Peace of Mind. Tranquility: Calm Recollections of the Dead; Great Thoughts of Eternal Rest and Happiness."

Local guidebooks were even more over the top. "The august throne upon which Nature sits, clothed in the glorious attributes of power and beauty!—the everlasting altar, at whose cloud-wrapt base the elements pay homage to Omnipotence! . . . The foam of agony thickens upon the face of the dread profound, while far above, upon the verge of the precipice, sits the sweet Iris—like faith upon a dying martyr's brow." Another writer, some years later, could not resist an explicit allegory of national greatness: "There is a certain satisfaction to the imagination in remembering that as the Alps, cold, motionless, and silent, are the great natural features of Europe, and in some sort express the immobility of the European spirit, so Niagara—eternal movement—is the grand, central, characteristic object of American scenery, the majestic symbol of unceasing life and irresistible progress."

NIAGARA FROM BELOW TABLE ROCK

Like everyone who beheld the falls, Tocqueville knew he was expected to describe them, but as he had remarked to Beaumont a few years earlier, "A description of a beautiful thing is always an ugly thing." Rather than report what the eye had seen, he preferred to evoke what the experience felt like. What he remembered most vividly was not the falls seen from a distance but the sensation of crouching against the rock face inside a wall of plunging water. "In that place a profound and terrible obscurity reigns, and when it occasionally brightens, you perceive the entire river that seems to be falling upon your head. It's hard to convey the impression produced by this ray of light, which, after letting you glimpse for a moment the vast chaos that surrounds you, abandons you once more in the midst of the shadows and the roar of the cataract."

Tocqueville clearly relished the meeting of danger and safety, the sensation of enormous power thundering past while he remained a secure observer. It was something of a mirror of his political and historical situation. And the river's placid but irresistible flow up to the headlong plunge resonates with a characteristic metaphor in *Democracy in America*. Right after declaring that "a new political science is needed for a world that is altogether new," Tocqueville added, "But this is what we scarcely think about. In the middle of a rapidly flowing river, we stare obstinately at some scraps of debris that are still visible on the riverbanks, even as the current is pulling us along and forcing us backward toward the abyss."

At this point the travelers were close once more to the Canadian border, and they could not resist a foray into Lower Canada, as Quebec was known, where their former countrymen had been abandoned in 1763 when the humiliating Treaty of Paris surrendered France's North American territory to the British. They had no objection to colonialism—in later years Tocqueville would warmly defend the French annexation of Algeria—but they weren't interested in Anglophone Canada. What they wanted was time travel, back into the French culture of their ancestors. And whether they recognized it or not, they were eager to find evidence that old France was superior not just to modern France but to modern America as well. Tocqueville even fantasized about an alternative eighteenth-century outcome that would have made the United States unnecessary.

Tocqueville and Beaumont stayed briefly in Montreal, making unenthusiastic inquiries about politics and legal procedures, but mainly asking leading questions about the chances of total separation from Britain. Evidently, the discovery of more than half a million colonists of French descent—they had had no idea there were so many—was making them yearn for a French state in North America, but the answers they got were uniformly discouraging. The highlight of the visit came later, when they traveled down the St. Lawrence to the colony's capital at Quebec City. Along the way Beaumont was pleased to discover "a considerable parish" named Beaumont.

After they put ashore, Tocqueville asked a farmer why they retained long, narrow, constricting fields when there was plenty of empty land inland. He replied, "Why do you love your wife best, although your neighbor's has more beautiful eyes?" Tocqueville commented solemnly, "I thought there was genuine and profound feeling in this response." Everything was tinged with romance. "The villages we saw around Quebec City have an extraordinary resemblance to our beautiful villages. Only French is spoken. The population there seems happy and well-off. The stock is remarkably handsomer than in the United States: the race is strong, and the women don't have that delicate, sickly air that characterizes most American women." That last comment is illuminated by Beaumont's later suggestion that an indoor lifestyle was intrinsically unhealthy: "I don't know why these people, who seem so fortunate, are generally of weak and delicate health. The women especially are extremely thin, and almost all seem affected in the chest. I don't know if this state of affairs is due to the climate, which is variable and forever changing from one extreme to the other, or to the way these women live. Here [in Massachusetts] it's completely unheard of for a woman to work on the land and take part in field labor. The result is that her work is all indoors and limited to the cares of the household." Beaumont did not explain why this theory should not apply to the women in the Beaumont and Tocqueville families, who certainly didn't labor in the fields.

FRENCH-STYLE CHURCH ON THE ST. LAWRENCE

In Montreal they had been irritated by provincialism, but here everyone was wonderful. "The people are in general more moral, hospitable, and religious than in France. Only in Canada can one find what in France is called a *bon enfant*, a 'good-natured fellow.' The English and the Americans are either coarse or frigid." Best of all, the commercial spirit had yet to arrive. "This race of men has struck us as inferior to the Americans in knowledge, but superior in qualities of the heart. There is nothing here of that mercantile spirit that shows up in everything the Americans do and say."

In a letter to his old tutor Lesueur, Tocqueville summed up his appreciation of the Canadian non-Americans. "They are as French as you and I," he wrote; "we feel as if we're at home, and they receive us everywhere as compatriots, children of the old France, as they call it. In my opinion the epithet is badly chosen. The old France is Canada, and the new one is *chez nous*. We have found there, especially in the villages away from the towns, the French mores of old." This was Tocqueville's idealized image of feudal France, where peasants were happy to be called peasants, and in Quebec they were prosperous as well.

The peasant is rich and doesn't pay a penny in taxes. At a round table, four times a day, there gathers a family of vigorous parents and sturdy, joyous children. After supper they sing some old French song or recount the prowess of the first Frenchmen in Canada, some great strokes of the sword dealt in Montcalm's day in the wars against the English. On Sundays they play and dance after the service. The curé himself takes part in the communal joy, so long as it doesn't degenerate into license. He is the oracle of the games and the friend and counselor of the people.

Admittedly, this account was calculated to please the old abbé back home, but Tocqueville really did want to believe that the golden age lived on in a chilly northern land. Later, in the American South, he and Beaumont would feel attracted to a temperament that seemed chivalric to them, but southern culture was fatally compromised by slavery. Here it was the merry peasants who were subjected to a foreign conqueror, yet *français* to the core. "Like us, they're lively, alert, intelligent, scoffers, quick-tempered, great talkers, and very hard to handle when their passions are ignited. They are fighters par excellence, and they love fame more than money." Curiously, apart from the intelligence and love of fame, this is hardly a portrait of Tocqueville himself. He was far from being a stereotypical Frenchman, and he knew it.

After two weeks enjoying this survival from the seventeenth century, they knew it was time to return, however reluctantly, to the modern world. A steamboat carried them back to Montreal, and then they headed south to Albany and east to Boston.

5

BOSTON: DEMOCRACY AS A STATE OF MIND

When Tocqueville and Beaumont reached Boston on September 7 and were at last able to catch up with their mail, which they hadn't seen for many weeks, two very unwelcome letters awaited. One was from their superiors in Paris, directing them to come home soon. They had originally planned on eighteen months in America, but maddeningly, that would now be cut in half. They hadn't been sending many reports to the home office, and their superiors may have concluded—with some justification—that the inspection tour was turning into a pleasure jaunt. At any rate, it was high time to renew the penitentiary inquiries, which had been on hold ever since they left Auburn two months earlier. Beaumont acknowledged in a letter to his mother, however, that the chore left him far from enthusiastic. "The prisons have bored us a good deal, since we always see the same thing, and if we do still inspect prisons in the towns we visit, it's only to satisfy a necessary formality. It's important that our mission continue for a while, because the opportune moment for returning to France hasn't yet arrived." To his brother he said more explicitly that he wanted to stay away because he feared some alarming political explosion. "The present state of Europe seems to me like a volcano about to erupt."

The other letter dealt Tocqueville a personal blow. He had been anxious about the failing health of the aged abbé Lesueur, whom Beaumont later described as having been "a second father" to him. When he now learned that Lesueur had died, he poured out his grief in a long letter to his brother. "Opening the packet and not seeing his handwriting, I knew the cruel truth. At that moment, my dear Édouard, I felt the keenest and most heartrending pain that I've ever experienced in my life. It's a sorrow that words can't express . . . There's no use saying, my dear friend, that one should get accustomed in advance to the idea of separation from an old man of eighty. No! One can never get used to the idea of suddenly losing the support of one's childhood, the friend—and what a friend!—of one's entire life." For Tocqueville, the troubled skeptic, the surest evidence for Christianity was the example of his beloved tutor. "I've never been so certain of the eternal happiness of anyone as I am of his. I've read a great deal during my life about the immortality of the soul, and never have I been so completely convinced of it as I am today."

Boston at that time had a population of sixty thousand, barely more than a quarter the size of New York, and European visitors appreciated its Old World charm and cleanliness. One of them remarked that its streets, "unlike the thoroughfares of all the other cities we had visited, were not perambulated day and night by swine." After two months of arduous though exhilarating travel, Tocqueville and Beaumont found urban civilization delightful, though they had arrived without letters of introduction and it took a few days for the local elite to understand who they were. Beaumont wrote to his mother, "We have found here what we never before encountered in America, a superior class with the tone and manners of European society. It's not very numerous in Boston, as you can imagine, but it does exist, and it's curious how it finds itself thrown as if by chance into the midst of a republican society founded on the principle of absolute equality, within which it forms a strange anomaly." However small and anomalous this class may have been, it furnished "a perpetual series of engagements from one day to the next." Tocqueville and Beaumont rose early, since breakfast was served at 7:30 (they started at the Marlboro Hotel and soon moved to the more

BOSTON FROM DORCHESTER HEIGHTS

Sheep graze in the remains of a no-longer-needed fort, while the gilded dome of the State House on Beacon Hill towers over the compact city (which would be greatly enlarged by landfill in later years). To the right, in the distance, are waterfront warehouses accommodating Boston's thriving maritime commerce.

fashionable Tremont), after which they spent some time reading at the Boston Athenaeum or conducting official visits, and then settled down to socializing. Almost every day they were invited to dinner, which began around 2:00 p.m. and continued with drinks and conversation until 6:00. After passing a couple of hours taking tea in a different house, they would return to their hotel to dress for a ball. "We have balls or *soirées dansantes* every day, and sometimes two or three on the same day."

Beaumont kept up his campaign of unremitting flirtation, and hinted that Tocqueville did, too. One evening they dined in the Beacon Hill "palace" of a fabulously rich Bostonian (it was at 42 Beacon Street, now part of the Somerset Club), and what especially interested Beaumont was their host's lovely niece. The ephemeral nature of these encounters, however, was beginning to wear him down. "I chatted a good deal with her, but I don't even know whether I'll ever see her again, so it was completely wasted sentiments. It's exactly the same with all the beauties I meet, and we see a lot of them in society. We get swept away by them three or four times a week, each of us inciting the other, but it's always new faces, and—God forgive me—I believe we always tell them the same things, at the risk of complimenting a brunette on her pale complexion and a blonde on her ebony hair." He added with studied irony, "All of this is a mere bagatelle, and occupies but a tiny place in the life of two men of politics who are devoted entirely to speculations of the highest order." One of the young women they met wrote to her mother that the French visitors were "men of intelligence, information, and highly pleasing manners."

These people represented the type that Oliver Wendell Holmes would later dub the Boston Brahmins, more a caste than a class. John Adams had written a half century before, "Kings we never had among us, nobles we never had. Nothing hereditary ever existed in the country, nor will the country require or admit of any such thing." And the Constitution states explicitly that "no title of nobility shall be granted by the United States." Still, these were self-consciously patrician grandees, and the young Frenchmen were probably not aware how much their own aristocratic status conferred prestige on them. "It seems to us," Beaumont wrote, "that they don't throw themselves so much at strangers here as in New York, but there is more true politesse. There are other people in this society besides businessmen. They occupy themselves here with the fine arts and literature. There is a class of people not engaged in commerce or industry, whose whole way of passing their time is to live with all the amenities that an advanced civilization offers."

Tocqueville's reaction was much the same:

Society, at least the one into which we've been introduced, and I believe it's the highest, is almost exactly like the upper classes of Europe. Luxury and elegance reign. Nearly all the women speak French well, and the men we've seen thus far have all been to Europe. Their manners are distinguished, and their conversation turns on intellectual matters. One feels liberated from the commercial habits and spirit of finance that make New York society so vulgar. In Boston there are already a certain number of people who have nothing to do and who seek out the pleasures of the mind.

In short, they were once again among their own kind, which makes it all the more impressive that, elsewhere in their travels, they were equally sociable and at ease with rural shopkeepers, pioneer farmers, prison guards, state governors, bankers, and Indian chiefs.

Many of the patricians were intellectuals, and that was true of the most distinguished personage they met in America, John Quincy Adams, whose one-term presidency had ended two years before, and who had just been elected to the House of Representatives. Tocqueville was deeply impressed with Adams, who spoke a fluent French that he had used throughout a brilliant diplomatic career. Adams once described himself as "a man of reserved, cold, austere, and forbidding manners," but Tocqueville wasn't put off at all, and drew him out on many topics of history and governance. He was especially impressed by Adams's analysis of slavery. "Slavery has altered the entire state of society in the South," Adams told him. "Every white man in the South is an equally

JOHN QUINCY ADAMS

privileged being, in that his lot is to make the Negroes work without working himself. You cannot conceive to what a degree the idea that it is dishonorable to work has entered into the Southern spirit." When Tocqueville asked where this might lead, Adams's silence was striking. "I spoke to him about the most immediate dangers to the Union and the causes that could lead to its dissolution. Mr. Adams said nothing in reply, but it was easy to see that on this point he had no more confidence in the future than I did." As Tocqueville's biographer comments, "It was hardly a tactful question to raise with a former head of state."

By far the most valuable Boston informant was Jared Sparks, whom Tocqueville had happened to meet in Paris in 1828. A former clergyman, Sparks was editing a literary journal and working on a biography of George Washington. It was he who told Tocqueville, "The political dogma of this country is that the majority is always right. On the whole, we are very satisfied to have adopted it, but it can't be denied that experience often gives the principle the lie. Sometimes the majority wants to oppress the minority." Near the end of his stay in Boston, Tocqueville summarized in his notebook two great principles that he saw as underlying American democracy:

> 1. The majority may be mistaken on some points, but on the whole it is always right, and there is no moral power above it.
>
> 2. Each individual person, society, town, or nation [Tocqueville thought of the states as separate "nations"] is the sole lawful judge of its own interest, and so long as it doesn't harm the interest of others, no one has the right to interfere.
>
> I think I must never lose sight of this note.

As Tocqueville continued to ponder this point in the months and years to come, a dark reverse side came into view: the potential for a stultifying tyranny of the majority. When he later used that phrase in *Democracy in America*, Sparks was indignant, complaining that Tocqueville had completely misunderstood what he meant, which was simply that a majority in the legislature might abuse its power. In Sparks's opinion,

JARED SPARKS

even if it did pass oppressive laws, "that majority will certainly be changed at the next election." As for Tocqueville's wider use of the term, Sparks dismissed it as beside the point. "M. de Tocqueville often confounds the majority with public opinion, which has the same tendency, or nearly so, in all civilized countries."

Only in hindsight could Americans appreciate the real force of Tocqueville's insight: public opinion was indeed the true danger, and prejudices might actually be strongest where expression was free. A self-governing people could internalize rigid attitudes and inhibitions, and in effect police its own behavior. In Europe, where authoritarian control was tight, competing value systems were provoked to argue vehemently with each other, whereas in America there seemed to be an embargo on serious debate. "Once an idea has taken hold of the American people's minds, whether it's a just one or an unreasonable one, nothing is more difficult than to uproot it. The same thing has been observed in England, the European country which for the past century has had the greatest liberty of thought and also the most invincible prejudices."

From this insight follows one of the profoundest and most melancholy passages in *Democracy in America*:

In America the majority erects a formidable barrier around thought. Within its limits a writer is free, but woe to him who dares to go beyond . . . In democratic republics, tyranny leaves the body alone and goes straight for the soul. The master no longer says, "You will think like me or die"; he says, "You are free not to think like me, and you will keep your life and your goods and everything else, but from this day forward you are a stranger among us . . . You will remain among men, but you will lose your rights to humanity. When you approach your fellows, they will shun you as an impure being, and even those who believe in your innocence will abandon you for fear the others will shun them as well. Go in peace, I leave you your life, but the life I leave you is worse than death."

America was thus a nation of paradox, of individualists who were deeply conformist.

From Jared Sparks, Tocqueville got another valuable insight: that even in the old colonial days, New England townships had resembled mini-republics within the larger administrative unit that was controlled by the distant Crown. Massachusetts was thus an exception to the usual way in which a central government would extend its authority into surrounding areas. "On the contrary," Sparks explained, "our forefathers founded the township before the state. Plymouth, Salem, and Charlestown existed before one could say there was a government of Massachusetts; they only became unified later, and by deliberate choice." Tocqueville was so impressed by Sparks's knowledge and acumen that he persuaded him to write a long paper "on the government of towns in Massachusetts," large parts of which were transferred wholesale into *Democracy in America*. "Interests, passions, duties, and rights," as he summarized what he learned from Sparks, "gathered around the separate townships, and within them prevailed a genuine, active political life that was altogether democratic and republican. The colonies still recognized the supremacy of the home country, and monarchy was the law of the state, but the republic was already fully alive in the townships."

The more Tocqueville pursued this theme, the more he found it confirmed. Josiah Quincy, president of Harvard and former mayor of

Boston, declared that each township in Massachusetts was like an independent republic that managed its own affairs, and he argued that the nation thus enjoyed unbroken continuity with its colonial past. "Massachusetts was very nearly as free before the Revolution as it is today," Quincy said. "We have put the name of the people where the king's used to be; apart from that, nothing among us has changed." A planter from Georgia who was visiting Boston pointed out that the very concept of "the people" was ambiguous, depending on whether the government that acted in its name was national or local. "Not only is each state a nation, but each town in the state is a little nation; each *ward* [Tocqueville recorded the English word] in a town is a little nation, with its own particular interests, government, and representation—its political life, in a word. So long as France remains in Paris, you'll have a government of the people, but not by the people."

Quincy also laid stress on a theme that would assume a crucial role in *Democracy in America*, which was the importance of local initiative. "If someone has an idea for any kind of social improvement—a school, a hospital, a road—it never occurs to him to go to the authorities. He announces his plan, offers to carry it out, calls upon other individuals to contribute their strength, and fights hand to hand against every obstacle." It might be true, Quincy acknowledged, that a central authority could have accomplished more, "but the sum total of all of these individual enterprises surpasses by far what any administration could undertake." As mayor, Quincy had promoted improvements on so wide a scale that he became known as "the Great Mayor."

Tocqueville was aware that Quincy was president of "the university of Cambridge," but he didn't bother to visit Harvard, or indeed any other American university. Of course he had gone to no university himself, and anyway the Harvard of that time was hardly prepossessing. With a few hundred students and twenty-five faculty members, most of whom were more interested in discipline than instruction, it was more like an old-fashioned boarding school than a modern college. Far from being a national university, it was hardly even a state one; people in western Massachusetts called it "the college of Boston and Salem, and not of the commonwealth." (George Wilson Pierson, however, who wrote a history of Yale, was scandalized: "The conduct of Tocqueville and Beaumont in the matter of higher education appears extraordinary. They met the presidents of Harvard and Columbia, but, so far as can be ascertained, they neither visited nor studied a single college in the United States!") Years later, when Sparks was president of Harvard, he offered Tocqueville an honorary degree. Tocqueville declined the distinction but added politely that he considered Harvard "a great and fine institution."

At one point Sparks showed Tocqueville a collection of Washington's letters that he was editing, many of which he had rescued from almost certain loss (he also found bundles of letters by Franklin being cut up for patterns in a London tailor's shop). Admittedly, he liked to alter the texts when the great men seemed too informal; Washington called a sum of money a mere "flea-bite," and Sparks rewrote it to say that it was "totally inadequate to our demands." Tocqueville was completely taken aback by the physical appearance of the letters. "The whole thing is done with a care, neatness, precision, and detail that would do credit to an office clerk." The thought seems to have been that a great man shouldn't stoop to writing beautifully: "It's hard to conceive how a man whose ideas were so wide-ranging could submit himself to such details." In keeping with this principle, Tocqueville's own handwriting was awful, a barely legible scrawl that he himself ruefully called *crottes de lapin*, "rabbit turds."

Nearly all of his distinguished informants assured Tocqueville that too much democracy was a bad thing. That was the opinion not just of students of public affairs like Sparks and Quincy but of the distinguished preacher William Ellery Channing, too. Expecting the people to judge accurately in the complex tariff controversy that was then raging, Channing remarked, would be like asking his ten-year-old son to do it. "No, I cannot believe that civil society was made to be controlled directly by the masses, who are always comparatively ignorant. I think we are going too far."

What Tocqueville found most interesting about Channing was that he was the leading figure in the Unitarian movement, which rejected the grim Calvinist theology of the Puritans but kept their stern morality. Unitarianism was especially popular among the elite, and by mid-century two-thirds of the wealthiest Bostonians would be members of a Unitarian church. Beaumont, more conventional than Tocqueville in many ways, was scandalized to learn that the Unitarians denied the Trinity and the divinity of Christ and refused to believe in eternal damnation for sinners. In his opinion, "Unitarianism is in general the religion of those who don't have any. In France, the philosophy of the eighteenth century attacked religion and its ministers with its mask off. In America, it's working on the same thing, but it's obliged to conceal its leanings under a veil of religion." Tocqueville agreed that this lukewarm faith was the logical outcome of Protestantism. "I have always thought that constitutional monarchies end up as republics, and in the same way I'm convinced that Protestantism will soon end up as natural religion."

Tocqueville feared a slackening of belief because as he understood American history, it had been the Puritan contribution that was crucial, with its paradoxical combination of moral repression and political freedom. "When democracy arrives along with mores and beliefs," Tocqueville wrote in the margin of his manuscript, "it leads to liberty. When it arrives along with moral and religious anarchy, it leads to despotism." And although Puritanism was "as much a political theory as a religious doctrine," its religious element was absolutely essential in providing a sense of mission, "a great people placed in a predestined land by the hand of God."

In addition to blue-blooded Bostonians, Tocqueville and Beaumont met an immigrant who, like Sparks, remained a favorite correspondent for years to come. Francis (originally Franz) Lieber had fought in the Prussian army against the French when he was sixteen, and at Waterloo he was shot through the neck and chest. After recovering from his wounds, he succumbed to a typhoid fever that nearly killed him. When he finally got back to Berlin, he was imprisoned for political radicalism; after his release he left Germany and lived in various places in Europe, ending up in Boston in 1827, where he quickly gained a reputation as an indefatigable writer and editor. Eventually he would become a law professor at Columbia and a pioneering political scientist, and during the Lincoln administration he would develop a code of conduct for soldiers that was an important forebear of the Geneva Convention. He was thirty-three years old when Tocqueville and Beaumont met him.

FRANCIS LIEBER
The portrait was made in later years, when Lieber had become a leading political scientist and in his own mind (if nobody else's) the equal of Tocqueville.

Lieber stressed an idea that would become central to *Democracy in America*: democracy was as much a state of mind as a political system. "The republic is everywhere," he said, "in the streets as much as in Congress . . . The people have the republic in the marrow of their bones." Lieber had especially illuminating things to say about the Constitution. "Every day," he told Tocqueville, "I'm more inclined to think that constitutions and political legislation are nothing in themselves. They are the superstructure, to which only the mores and social condition of the people can give life." The expression translated here as "superstructure," incidentally, illustrates the ambiguity of idioms. Lieber, who was speaking French, was making an analogy to *oeuvres mortes*, the upper parts of a ship, which by themselves would be useless unless the great submerged hull—the *oeuvres vives* alive in the sea—bore them onward. Two of Tocqueville's translators, not realizing this, both give "dead creations," but neither Lieber nor Tocqueville was likely to think of the Constitution as dead.

Trained as a lawyer, Tocqueville filled whole notebooks with American legal minutiae, but he came to see that far from defining a society, its legal code reflected the deep assumptions that gave it coherence. *The Federalist Papers* had been conceived in the tradition of John Locke, for whom the social compact was a voluntary agreement negotiated by independent individuals, much like a business contract in the economic realm. But there was also a very different line of thinking that derived from Jean-Jacques Rousseau, who saw modern individualism as a disturbing challenge. The goal of Rousseau's *Social Contract* was to create a shared community that could be called a *moi commun*, a "common self," "in which each person, uniting himself with the rest, still obeys only himself and remains as free as he was before." Rousseau was one of the three writers whom Tocqueville honored most deeply (the others were Pascal and Montesquieu), although his radical reputation made it unwise to invoke him explicitly. According to Rousseau, "The most important law of all is engraved not on marble or brass but in the hearts of the citizens . . . It preserves a people in the spirit of their founding, and it imperceptibly substitutes the force of habit for that of authority. I am speaking of mores and customs, and above all of opinion, a subject which is unknown to our political theorists, but on which the success of all the other laws depends." In just this way Tocqueville, in *Democracy in America*, invoked "what one might call the habits of the heart."

The phrase "habits of the heart" has furnished the title of a widely read book by Robert Bellah and colleagues, with the subtitle *Individualism and Commitment in American Life.* As Bellah notes, more was meant than emotional commitment alone. "I intend the expression *moeurs*," Tocqueville explained, "in the sense that the ancients gave to the word *mores*, and I apply it not only to mores proper, which might be called habits of the heart, but also to the various notions men have, the diverse opinions that circulate among them, and the whole ensemble of ideas that shape the habits of the mind." Ideas are at least as important as feelings, for without them "there is no action in common, and without action in common there are only people, not a social body. For there to be a society, and still more for that society to prosper, the minds of its citizens must be brought together and held together by certain leading ideas."

There were plenty of intellectuals in Boston, and plenty of publications—ten daily papers, thirty-four weeklies, twenty-five magazines—but one thing that was missing was truly accomplished writers. In *Democracy in America*, Tocqueville would describe America as unintellectual, with no literature to speak of and hardly any philosophy. Americans not surprisingly took offense, but he saw it as the corollary of a spirit of pragmatic enterprise and openness to the future. "They all consider society as a body in progress, and humanity as a changing tableau where nothing is or should be fixed forever. They acknowledge that what seems good to them today may be replaced tomorrow by something better that as yet is hidden." In a manuscript note Tocqueville suggested further that the reason the Americans weren't philosophical was that they didn't need to be. "I doubt that More would have written his *Utopia* if he had been able to realize some of his dreams in English government, and I think the Germans of our own day wouldn't philosophize so passionately about universal truth if they could put some of their ideas into political practice."

Indeed, the blossoming that would become known as the American Renaissance was still just beyond the horizon. In 1831, Emerson was twenty-eight and Hawthorne twenty-seven, both still unknown; Longfellow was twenty-four, Poe twenty-two, Stowe twenty, Thoreau fourteen, Melville and Whitman twelve, and Dickinson a toddler. Apart from Cooper, whom Tocqueville didn't see, because he was living abroad, the "living American writers" he listed in his notebook were "Verplanck, Paulding, Hall, Stone, Neal, Barker, Willis, Miss Sedgwick." (The list implies no special research on Tocqueville's part, since he found them all in an anthology.) Of the lot, Catharine Maria Sedgwick is perhaps the only one whose name might be recognized today. Her bestseller *Hope Leslie* was a historical novel set in the early Puritan days. More memorably, responding to a nation in need of traditions, a story of hers introduced the German custom of the Christmas tree (while Washington Irving and Clement Moore, at about the same time, were inventing the story of Santa Claus with his reindeer on the roof).

Tocqueville did try to see her when he visited her Stockbridge residence on the way to Boston, but she was away from home. Other members of the family, however, proved to be interesting acquaintances—it was said that the Sedgwicks pervaded the Berkshires, and that even the grasshoppers chirped "Sedgwick! Sedgwick!"—and Catharine Maria's nephew Theodore would later be an indispensable research assistant for *Democracy in America*.

In a note that never got published, Tocqueville proposed a striking insight into the nature of publication in a mass commercial culture. "Democracy doesn't just spread a taste for literature among the industrial classes; it introduces the industrial spirit into letters. Since readers are very numerous and very easy to please, due to the absolute need for novelty that they feel, one can make a fortune by endlessly turning out a mass of new but imperfect books. In this way it's easy to acquire a modest fame and a big fortune." At another point he remarked, "The Americans don't have a literature, but they do have books."

Meanwhile, it was high time for Tocqueville and Beaumont to remember the official reason for their visit, and they accordingly inspected the Massachusetts State Penitentiary in Charlestown, across the river from Boston. This was a new facility with three hundred cells on the Auburn plan, and it was something of a tourist attraction. According to a guidebook, "White persons of respectability are admitted to visit the prison at any time except on Fast Day and the Sabbath, by paying 25 cents each." The French visitors did their best to seem interested; Beaumont wrote sardonically to his brother, "We are incontestably the *premiers pénitentiers* of the universe."

Tocqueville got an unexpected insight into another aspect of the justice system. When he and Beaumont were out walking, Francis Lieber pointed out the sheriff, whom they had met the day before at a fashionable dinner, and remarked that he had recently hanged two men. As Lieber later recalled: "'*Ma foi*, that is rather too much!' exclaimed my friend, in whom, though a gentleman of clear mind, all the European prejudices against every person who has anything to do with the administering of capital punishments were excited." After Tocqueville calmed down, though, "he was struck with the rationality of this state of things. The more civilized a nation, the fewer are the prejudices against professions and classes." In Tocqueville's own record of the conversation with Lieber, what he learned was that "the sheriff executing a criminal is simply obeying the law, just as the magistrate does who condemns him to death. No hatred or contempt attaches to his profession. It is this respect for agents of the law, deriving from the extreme respect people have for the law itself (since it's they who have made it), that causes them to feel no animosity toward police officers, tax collectors, and customs officials. All of those employments are held in honor."

One popular destination for foreign visitors was the newly founded town of Lowell, where farm girls seeking to save money lived in well-supervised dormitories and put in long days in a textile factory. Tocqueville didn't bother to go there, although in *Democracy in America* he would acknowledge that advances in technology definitely improved the quality of life: "Every innovation that leads to wealth by a more direct path, every laborsaving machine, every instrument that lowers the cost of production, every discovery that facilitates and increases pleasures—they all seem the finest achievement of human intelligence." But in this area Tocqueville's sympathies were with the populists who yearned for the simpler economy of the past, not with the grandees he was spending time with in Boston, who had established the lucrative Lowell mills. In his usage the word *industrie* often means "industriousness" rather than factories, and it could apply to skilled trades of all kinds, just as *manufacture* still had its root meaning of making things by hand. Nobody at the time foresaw the immense increase in industrialization that lay in the future, made possible by the transportation revolution that was just taking off.

By the time he finished *Democracy in America*, however, Tocqueville had indeed seen factories in England and had been appalled by the filth, degradation, and poverty. He described Manchester as if it were Tolkien's Mordor: "All around this place you'll see the immense palaces of industry. You'll hear the noise of furnaces, the hissing of steam. These vast buildings prevent light and air from reaching the human dwellings that they dominate, and envelop them in perpetual fog; here is the slave, there the master . . . A thick black smoke covers the city, and the sun appears through it like a disk without rays. In the midst of this half-light 300,000 human creatures labor unceasingly."

Even if conditions had been less horrible, Tocqueville saw clearly that division of labor was dehumanizing in itself. "Each day the worker becomes more skillful and less industrious, and one may say that the man in him is degraded as the worker improves. What should one expect of someone who has spent twenty years putting heads on pins?" The example was not chosen at random. Adam Smith had used it in *The Wealth of Nations* to show that if each of "eighteen distinct operations" was assigned to a different worker, a pin factory could produce tens of thousands of pins per day. And whereas Smith had lived in the age of small workshops, the modern factory system was extracting enormous profits from the most abject poverty. "In the midst of this infected cesspool," Tocqueville commented trenchantly, "the greatest river of human industry has its source and goes forth to enrich the universe. Out of this vile sewer flows pure gold. There the human spirit both perfects itself and brutalizes itself; civilization produces its marvels, and civilized man becomes virtually savage once more."

It was now the enterprising settlers of the American West that Tocqueville held up as an inspiring contrast. "It sometimes happens that the same man will plow his field, build his dwelling, fabricate his tools, make his shoes, and with his own hands weave the coarse cloth that clothes him. This detracts from the excellence of the work, but it serves powerfully to develop the intelligence of the worker. Nothing tends so much to materialize man and to eliminate every trace of soul from his work than great division of labor."

What preoccupied Tocqueville most during all this time was the accumulating evidence that decentralized government could work really well. It is common for his modern interpreters to lament what one of them calls his "habitually inexact use of key words." But no one could have tried harder than he did to be precise and clear. It was a time when new words were being invented and old words given new meanings, because Western societies were experiencing unprecedented change. Tocqueville's manuscripts are filled with questioning notes to himself on this score, and when he was pondering what would become a crucial term in his thinking, he wrote from Hartford to ask his father to clarify "centralization": "I know that in general *chez nous* the government involves itself in almost everything; people have shouted the word at me a hundred times without explaining what it means . . . If, my dear Papa, you could dissect this word 'centralization' for me, you would be doing me an immense service, not just for the present, but for the future as well."

For good measure he also wrote to ask his magistrate friend Ernest de Chabrol for information. "Our stay in Boston was very useful; we found a throng of distinguished men and valuable documents there. But we realize constantly that the biggest obstacle to learning is the lack of knowledge. On a multitude of points we don't know what to ask, because we don't know what exists in France, and without comparisons to make, the mind doesn't know how to proceed." In particular, what baffled Tocqueville was understanding how American independence and individualism, with no central direction such as dominated French life, could manage to coalesce into a unity. "What is most striking to anyone who travels in this country, whether or not he tries to reflect on it, is the spectacle of a society going forward all by itself, without guide or support, by the single fact of the concurrence of individual wills."

As he continued to ponder this issue, Tocqueville came to believe that he had been given the key to it in Massachusetts. There were actually two very different kinds of centralization, and the difference was all-important. In France even the most minor local decisions were made in Paris. In the United States, on the other hand, the federal government legislated for the whole country but left administration and enforcement to the states and localities. The implications were far from merely procedural, as Tocqueville's Boston acquaintances had helped him to understand. French *communes* or townships, he said, kept superb records but vegetated in "invincible apathy," whereas in America townships were "enlightened, active, and enterprising, and I see there a society always at work."

Meanwhile, Tocqueville's notebooks continued to fill up with re-corded conversations and with observations of his own, and he was in-creasingly sure that producing a report on penitentiaries was far too modest a goal. Before leaving France, he had talked grandly about illuminating the new nation for European readers, but how to do that still remained a perplexing question. "Will I ever write anything about this country?" he wrote to his mother. "In truth, that's what I absolutely don't know. Everything I see, everything I hear, everything I still see from far away, forms a confused mass in my mind that I may never have the time or ability to disentangle. It would be an enormous labor to pre-sent a tableau of a society as vast and un-homogeneous as this one."

6

PHILADELPHIA: TOLERATION, ASSOCIATION, AND INCARCERATION

After nearly a month in Boston, Tocqueville and Beaumont were on the road again, heading for Philadelphia after a rather perfunctory pause in Hartford. Philadelphia was at first a letdown. Even its physical layout was disconcerting to European visitors, who hated the rectangular grid of streets, a scheme that had yet to be introduced in Manhattan. "The city is built with extreme and almost wearisome regularity," Frances Trollope complained, and Dickens exclaimed, "I would have given the world for a crooked street." To some travelers—Thomas Hamilton, for instance—the grid even suggested a moral failing: "Philadelphia is mediocrity personified in brick and mortar. It is a city laid down by square and rule, a sort of habitable problem, a mathematical infringement on the rights of individual eccentricity." Tocqueville felt much the same way. "I believe Philadelphia is the only city in the world," he complained, "where they've had the idea of identifying the streets by numbers and not names . . . I'm living in street number three. Europeans never fail to join an idea to every exterior object—a saint, a famous man, an event—but these people know nothing but arithmetic."

The trouble was partly simple burnout. "I have nothing new to tell concerning myself," Tocqueville wrote to his mother. "Nothing in my situation has changed since my last letter. Prisons, learned societies, drawing-room parties in the evenings—that's our life." But soon he was getting interested in an important subject he thought he had already understood, the role of religion in American society. With its Quaker tradition of toleration, Philadelphia had every possible shade of belief on view. One visitor counted thirty-two churches representing seventeen different sects, as well as two synagogues. Back in Boston, Tocqueville had assumed that absence of dogma was evidence of spiritual laxness, and he thought of Protestantism in general as watered-down Christianity. The Quakers, who had hardly any dogma at all, might have been expected to disappoint him completely, but the very opposite happened. At some point (recorded in a note that has never been quoted in English) he attended a Quaker meeting and was deeply impressed. Not realizing that an ordinary-looking house was the place of worship, he asked directions from a soberly dressed man who showed him the way.

I stayed for an hour and forty minutes in continuous silence and immobility. Finally I turned to the man who had brought me there and said, "Sir, I wanted to attend a divine service, but you seem to have conducted me to an assembly of deaf-mutes." My guide, showing no offense at my question, gazed at me with the same benevolence as before and said, "Dost thou not see that each one of us is waiting for the Holy Spirit to illuminate him? Learn to moderate thy impatience in a holy place." I kept quiet, and soon one of those present did stand up and begin to speak. His tone was plaintive, and every word he uttered was as if isolated between two long silences. In tones of lamentation he declared highly consoling things, for he spoke of the inexhaustible goodness of God and of the obligation of all men to help each other, whatever might be their beliefs or the color of their skin. After he fell silent, the assembly began quietly filing out. As I was departing, still moved by the words I had just heard, I found myself next to the man who had brought me there, and I said to him, "It seems to me that I have just heard the language of the Gospel spoken here."

The Quaker city had long encouraged cooperation in public affairs as well as toleration in religion; Benjamin Franklin had been a tireless promoter of voluntary associations for civic improvements of all kinds. In this area, too, Tocqueville found his understanding of American society deepening, and the importance of associations would become a major theme in *Democracy in America*. It happened that a free-trade convention, opposed to the protective tariff that was highly controversial at the time, was about to meet in Philadelphia, while the tariff's supporters, the Friends of Domestic Industry, would be meeting simultaneously in New York. Neither assembly would have had the slightest chance of happening in France. Tocqueville was impressed that the First Amendment to the Constitution expressly guaranteed "the right of the people peaceably to assemble, and to petition the government for a redress of grievances." It is not easy today to appreciate how radical that right once was. French law prohibited any assembly of more than twenty people unless they had obtained official permission, and Tocqueville lamented, "What can public opinion itself do when *twenty* people may not assemble in one place, and when there is no man, family, group, class, or free association that can declare its views and act upon them?"

When Tocqueville wondered aloud whether unpoliced assemblies might have dangerous consequences, a Philadelphia lawyer responded, "When men can speak freely, the chances are that they won't act," adding that the majority could never change its opinions if minority groups didn't have means of persuasion. As Tocqueville later formulated it, "The object of associations is to put ideas into competition in order to find the ones most likely to impress the majority, because they are always hoping to win over enough of the majority to gain power themselves." Even though their agendas might make them seem sometimes "like separate nations within the nation," they were no threat to established order because they remained members of the community as a whole.

Anyway, it was not pressure groups with national agendas but ad hoc local involvement in the Franklin tradition that struck Tocqueville as most significant. In *Democracy in America* he would write,

> No sooner do you set foot on American soil than you find yourself in a sort of tumult. A confused clamor rises up on all sides, and a thousand voices reach your ears, each expressing some social need. Everything is in motion around you. The people of one district have come together to decide whether to build a church; in another they're working to elect a representative. Farther off, delegates from the countryside are hurrying into town to advise on certain local improvements; in another village the farmers have left their fields to debate plans for a road or a school. Some citizens assemble for the sole purpose of declaring their disapproval of the government's policies, while others proclaim that the men holding office are fathers of their country.

In France most of these measures would have been dictated from above, and the rest would have been forbidden. "Democracy doesn't give people the most competent government," Tocqueville acknowledged, "but it does what the most competent government is often powerless to do. It spreads throughout the entire social body a restless activity, a superabundant strength, an energy that never exists without it."

More important even than the shared agendas of associations was emotional bonding. "The heart expands," Tocqueville wrote optimistically, "and the human spirit develops simply by the reciprocal action of men upon each other." Loner and outsider as he was, he couldn't help idealizing the mutual reinforcement he believed Americans were giving each other. But with his ability to take a historical long view, he also anticipated the swelling of central power and the decline of community that so many later writers have lamented. As always, he saw the causes as deeply rooted in the nature of American society, and indeed of democracy in general. The communal efforts that were necessary in a primitive subsistence economy would inevitably lose their relevance, except as nostalgic myth, in an industrial age. "It is easy to foresee the time when men will be less and less able to produce, by themselves, the commonest necessities of life. The task of the social power will therefore increase endlessly, and its very efforts will make that task bigger every day. The more it takes the place of associations, the more individuals will lose the idea of associating and will need its assistance. These causes and effects engender each other without end."

There was one area, however, in which Quaker thought inspired paradoxically repressive practice, and that was the treatment of prisoners. Just two years previously the first convicts had been admitted to the Eastern State Penitentiary, popularly known as Cherry Hill, two miles from downtown Philadelphia. Unlike the Auburn system in New York, in which prisoners worked in groups under the supervision of guards, Eastern State was based on a principle of total, round-the-clock isolation. The rationale for this was grounded in Quaker thought; as Michel Foucault has observed, solitude was intended to encourage the offender to discover "what may enlighten him from within." A board of prison inspectors therefore decreed, "Cut them off from all intercourse with men; let not the voice or face of a friend ever cheer them; let them walk their gloomy abodes and commune with their corrupt hearts and guilty consciences in silence, and brood over the horrors of their solitude and the enormity of their crimes, without the hope of executive pardon." A historian of prisons observes that this was "a profession of penological faith which for deliberate elimination of hope can scarcely be equaled."

The system of total isolation had been given a trial run in a wing of an older Walnut Street prison, but the results were not encouraging. Whether or not the prisoners communed with their consciences, they showed an alarming tendency to go mad. The solution at Eastern State was to keep them in solitude but give them useful work to do, permit visits by a chaplain, and allow them a Bible as their single book (which, as a later critic commented, "however good, would sometimes pall"). Published images of the vast Gothic structure were usually exterior views, emphasizing its resemblance to an impregnable castle, though of course it was designed to keep people in, not out. What the pictures didn't reveal was the system of surveillance, based once again on Ben-

EASTERN STATE PENITENTIARY

The artist has evoked a romantic castle out of the novels of Walter Scott. A guidebook of the time said approvingly, in the florid style that Mark Twain loved to parody, "This penitentiary is the only edifice in this country which is calculated to convey to our citizens the external appearance of those magnificent and picturesque castles of the middle ages, which contribute so eminently to embellish the scenery of Europe."

tham's panopticon principle, with an all-seeing warden at the center of the web.

On arrival each prisoner had a black hood pulled over his head, and when he was next permitted to see, he found himself in a small cell with no idea what the surrounding building was like or what other inmates might be nearby. At Sing Sing he would have encountered them whenever he went to work; at Eastern State he never saw anyone at all except the chaplain. Food was passed in through a folding door that concealed the guard, who knew his charges by number; names were recorded in a book that only the warden could consult. Misbehavior of any kind, including masturbation, was severely punished whenever the guards detected it through a spy hole, the various penalties being star-

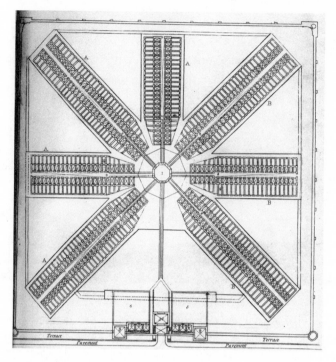

PLAN OF THE EASTERN STATE PENITENTIARY
An illustration from an official government report showing the rigid layout
of the Benthamite panopticon

vation diet, withholding of work, and total darkness. Especially recalcitrant prisoners had metal gags agonizingly clamped into their mouths, and were sometimes drenched from a height with frigid water.

Official reports during the first few years claimed excellent moral results, even though funds were as yet lacking for a full-time chaplain. The year before Tocqueville was there, a clergyman had volunteered to counsel the prisoners, one of whom insisted that he had been wrongly convicted of murder. According to the report, "After the Rev. Mr. Demme had visited him in his cell, he was reduced to tears, fully confessed his guilt, subsequently became very industrious and a good prisoner, and has continued to exhibit every appearance of penitence." Demme himself explained that the inmates were very appropriately condemned "not to a momentary pain but to a protracted monotony of joyless existence, having no other companion but a wounded heart, and being left to themselves, to be forced to commune with that heart."

Tocqueville and Beaumont made repeated visits to the penitentiary, whose records show that eighty-seven prisoners were there at the time, the majority serving long sentences for burglary or horse stealing (only eight for murder). Fully half were employed in weaving and dyeing, with shoe making the next largest trade. Two were locksmiths—not that it did them much good.

In search as always of precise information, Tocqueville wrote to the head of prisons in charmingly Gallic English, "In thus addressing ourselves to you without the honour of your personal acquaintance, we should greatly fear trespassing too much upon your indulgence, were we not convinced that the object of our mission is one of so general and vital importance as to excuse the trouble which we are about to take the liberty of giving you." Once he gained admission, he was allowed to interview prisoners individually with no one else present. This privilege may seem surprising, but it was very much in the spirit of "correction" as then understood, with a goal of understanding the particular history that had brought each culprit to transgress. A contemporary French penologist wrote that it was essential to identify "not only the circumstances, but also the causes of his crime; they must be sought in the story of his life, from the triple point of view of psychology, social position, and upbringing." That is exactly what Tocqueville's questions were intended to elicit.

The notebook he compiled during two weeks of extended interviews is exceptionally interesting, and often moving. It survives on little sheets folded in half, on which he scribbled rapidly while the lonely and depressed informants told him their stories. There were forty-four entries in all, some brief, some quite lengthy. Without exception the prisoners assured him that far from resenting having to work, they couldn't have endured their solitary existence without it. They also appreciated the little outdoor enclosure attached to each cell, where they could breathe fresh air, and many were grateful for the Bible and the chaplain's visits. Some even claimed to have been completely transformed by religion, including a murderer who said he longed to give his family a Christian education, and added poignantly, "This summer a cricket got into my courtyard, and I felt like I'd gained a companion. When a butterfly or some other creature comes into my cell, I never harm it."

Tocqueville tried to put a positive spin on what he heard, stressing the salutary effects of religion and hard work, but it was impossible to ignore the underlying despair. This comes through clearly in a brief exchange with a thief who had been incarcerated for five months: "His health seems very good, but his spirit is greatly oppressed. 'I don't believe,' he says, 'that I'll ever get out of here alive. This solitude is disastrous for the human constitution, and it's going to kill me.'" Another prisoner, who had been there for only three weeks, was "plunged in absolute despair," and he, too, thought that the solitary confinement would be fatal.

> Q. Don't you at least find consolation in your work?
> A. Yes, sir; solitude without work is a thousand times more dreadful. But work doesn't keep me from thinking and being truly miserable. Here, I assure you, the soul is very sick.
>
> This poor man sobbed when he spoke of his wife and children, whom he expected never to see again. When we entered his cell, we found him weeping and working at the same time.

The conclusion Tocqueville drew from these encounters was not what might be expected today. In his view, the prisoners' emotional distress was completely desirable. At Sing Sing he had been shocked by the physical anguish caused by the lash, and mental suffering seemed far better:

> The interior of the Philadelphia cells presented us with a sight that was altogether new and full of interest. The prisoner who is confined there generally enjoys good health and is well dressed, fed, and accommodated. These physical advantages that he never had in the outside world are within his reach, and it pleases him to recognize that. Nonetheless, he is profoundly unhappy. The mental punishment that is in-

flicted on him strikes a far deeper terror into his soul than chains or blows ever could. Is this not how an enlightened and humane society should wish to punish? The punishment here is at once the mildest and the most terrible ever invented. It addresses itself to a man's mind only, but it exerts an incredible hold over him.

The tone of approval does not mean, however, that Tocqueville wasn't strongly affected. As Beaumont related, "He devoted two weeks to this detailed inquiry, begun at first out of duty but continued with great interest, struck by the singular effects of isolation on the human soul and moved by the moral miseries whose secrets were being unveiled before his eyes. Often he was detained beyond the appointed time by the interest these solitary interviews had, and also by the poor prisoners themselves, who sought to prolong this rare opportunity to converse with a man. Little did they suspect what man!"

The English liberal Harriet Martineau likewise interviewed a number of prisoners at Eastern State, and she, too, approved of solitary confinement. She told a number of highly positive stories about prisoners who responded with heartfelt gratitude to enlightened wardens—"'God bless you, Sir!' replied the regenerated man. Such is the power of faith in man!" Just as at Sing Sing, Dickens seems to have been the only visitor who empathized totally: "The prisoner is a man buried alive, to be dug out in the slow round of years, and in the meantime dead to everything but torturing anxieties and horrible despair."

The optimism of the early visitors and inspectors was not borne out by time. According to a Supreme Court justice who investigated conditions there in 1890, "A considerable number of the prisoners fell, after even a short confinement, into a semi-fatuous condition, from which it was next to impossible to arouse them, and others became violently insane; others still, committed suicide; while those who stood the ordeal better were not generally reformed, and in most cases did not recover sufficient mental activity to be of any subsequent service to the community." No longer a prison, Eastern State Penitentiary is today a popular tourist attraction that features haunted-house tours, known as Terror Behind the Walls, in the month leading up to Halloween.

A PHILADELPHIA PRISONER

This illustration was prepared for a Boston edition of Dickens's *American Notes*. Of his visit to the penitentiary Dickens wrote, "On the haggard face of every man among these prisoners, the same expression sat. I know not what to liken it to. It had something of that strained attention which we see upon the faces of the blind and deaf, mingled with a kind of horror, as though they had all been secretly terrified."

A mishap at this time gave evidence of Tocqueville's impressive ability to reproduce conversations. After fifteen hours of prison interviews he mislaid his notebook, and when he gave up searching, he concluded it was lost forever. He then wrote up the whole thing a second time. As Beaumont later recalled, "These conversations in solitude had made such a deep impression on his soul that in a few hours he recreated them all on paper without any confusion, and without omitting a single one. The next day, no longer looking for his notes, he found them. One could see by comparing them with his recollections how precise they were, and with what incredible fidelity his memory had reproduced everything . . . Alexis de Tocqueville didn't have a memory for words or numbers, but he possessed in the highest degree a memory for ideas. Once those entered his mind, they never left it." Of course, what this actually confirms is Tocqueville's ability to reconstruct his own account, written down in French rather than English, which is not the same thing as the exact words of the prisoners.

By the middle of November the tedium of daily life was beginning to tell on the always restless Tocqueville. "When I'm active and wandering," he wrote to a friend, "the idea of inner tranquillity charms my imagination. But when I return to my regular habits, the uniformity of existence is the death of me, and I feel seized by an indescribable restlessness at heart. I must have either moral or physical agitation, even at the risk of my life." What he and Beaumont needed now was adventure, and with time running out, they were determined not to miss what was still known as the West.

7

DEMOCRACY IN "THE WEST"

It was late November and the weather was turning cold. Beaumont
wrote home:

> The trip from Philadelphia to Pittsburgh was one of the most difficult
> I've ever made. The roads are detestable and the carriages even worse.
> We traveled night and day for three days, and eighty miles out from
> Philadelphia we reached the Allegheny Mountains, where we were as-
> saulted by dreadful cold. Nearly the whole way after that we pressed
> on through a perpetual hurricane of snow, such as had not been seen
> here for a very long time, certainly not in the autumn. The Alleghenies
> aren't very high but they go on forever. They're not mountains so much
> as an interminable series of hills cut up by a thousand valleys, all ex-
> tremely picturesque. I admit however that I didn't much admire the
> beauties of the country—it was too cold. There is no such thing as
> beautiful countryside without verdure, and one is necessarily a cold
> admirer when freezing.

This would indeed turn out to be the most brutal fall and winter for at
least fifty years.

The travelers stayed only one day in Pittsburgh, described unenthusiastically by Beaumont as "the most industrial town of Pennsylvania, the Birmingham of America, where the air is continually obscured by the multitude of steam engines that keep the factories going," and then they boarded a steamboat named the *Fourth of July* to go down the Ohio River to Cincinnati. Today America is a land of highways; a few generations ago it was railroads. In Tocqueville's day it was the network of navigable rivers that carried commerce into remote areas that were all but unreachable by land. One writer at the time called rivers "the great turnpikes of the West," and another extolled the Ohio for "rolling its volumed floods through half a continent."

Tocqueville wrote optimistically to his brother Édouard that they expected to leave the snow behind before long, "and in a week we'll have nothing more to fear." What would mainly interest his soldier brother, he knew, was a vision of the martial past, and recalling that Pittsburgh had once been Fort Duquesne, he indulged in a fantasy of the brilliant French empire that never came to be. "Had we succeeded, the English colonies would have been hemmed in by a huge crescent, with Quebec and New Orleans at its extremities. Pressed from behind by the French and their Indian allies, the Americans in the United States would not have rebelled against their mother country. They all acknowledge this. There would have been no American Revolution, and perhaps no French Revolution either, at least not in the form it took."

Four days after writing this, Tocqueville ended with a terse postscript: "We have arrived at Cincinnati, after a voyage made rather difficult by the snow and the cold." That was a colossal understatement, as was Beaumont's carefully offhand remark to his sister-in-law, "After voyaging for a day, we reached a small town called Wheeling, and we had a most amusing and singular adventure there, but there's no way to recount it in a letter. Just remember this, and when I get home, I'll tell you a story that will make you laugh."

This is what actually happened. During the night of December 6 Tocqueville was seated more or less at ease in the *Fourth of July*, beginning a letter to his friend Chabrol and complaining of appalling cold, as the boat struggled to push through heavy ice floes. "Your ears freeze

WHEELING

According to the original caption, "The view shows Wheeling as it appears from an eminence on the Ohio side of the river, about a mile and a half below the central part of the town. Wheeling Island is seen at the left, and above it, on the hills in the distance, the National Road." The road ran all the way from Baltimore to Wheeling, and would soon be extended farther westward.

the moment you put your head outside. It's a Russian cold; nobody in this country can remember its like." For a couple of pages Tocqueville scribbled routine remarks about the American spirit of enterprise—"they throw themselves boldly and unhesitatingly into the limitless field of innovation, accepting no rules except their own reason and whim"—and then the letter breaks off startlingly, "At this moment the vessel is cracking from poop to prow." The boat had struck a submerged rock and was sinking rapidly.

To their families both Tocqueville and Beaumont avoided any mention of the disaster at the time, but Beaumont kept a journal, now lost, from which he later transcribed the notes he made soon afterward:

Toward midnight a cry of alarm—"All is lost!" It's the voice of the captain; we have struck an obstruction (Burlington Bar). Our boat is shattered; it's sinking before our eyes. Solemn impression: two hundred passengers on board, and only two lifeboats that might hold ten or twelve people apiece. The water rises, rises; already it's filling the cabins. Admirable sangfroid of the American women, there are fifty of them, not one outcry at the sight of approaching death. Tocqueville and I look out at the Ohio, which in that place is more than a mile wide and filled with huge blocks of ice; we shake hands as a gesture of farewell. Suddenly the boat stops sinking. Its hull is perched on the same obstruction that broke it, and what saves it is the very depth of the injury, and the rapidity with which the invading water makes it settle down on the rock.

Fortunately, another steamboat came along and everyone was saved.

It was only at the end of the American stay, and then in the context of assuring his family loftily that he would be perfectly safe crossing the Atlantic, that Tocqueville proudly recalled, "We ran a hundred times more risk on steamboats, but you never suspected it. Thirty of them exploded or sank during the first six weeks we were in the United States. We got out of one of them three hours before that happened to it, and another time we were crushed like a nutshell against a rock." Tocqueville may well have heard that in 1825 a steamboat bearing Lafayette on his farewell tour had likewise foundered in the Ohio, though less dangerously. It was very common, especially in bad weather, for boats to strike submerged logs, sandbars, or rocky shoals, and loss of life depended mainly on whether the river at that point happened to be deep or shallow. Less frequent, but regarded by the public with morbid fascination, were the horrific explosions caused by excessive steam pressure, mechanical failures, and carelessness of the engineers whose sole mission was to make the vessel go fast.

Except when accidents struck, steamboats offered comfortable accommodations—Frances Trollope called them "grand floating hotels"—and Tocqueville and Beaumont were at least insulated from the rougher side of backwoods life. A Scotsman who chose to float down the river in a flimsy skiff reported, "The river Ohio is considered the greatest thoroughfare of banditti in the Union. Here the thief, in addition to the cause of his flight, has only to steal a skiff and sail down the river in the night. Horse stealing is notorious in the western country, and also escapes from prison."

CINCINNATI LANDING

From Wheeling (still in Virginia in those days, of course), Tocqueville and Beaumont continued on the steamboat *William Parsons* to Cincinnati. Cincinnati was a thriving meatpacking and flour-milling city of twenty-five thousand that aspired to become the metropolis of the region. Pork was the principal export, and European visitors were appalled to find the streets infested by even more pigs than the cities of the East, but they had to concede their usefulness. "Without them," Frances Trollope observed, "the streets would soon be choked up with all sorts of substances in every stage of decomposition." She knew Cincinnati well, having lived there for two unhappy years, and in *Domestic Manners of the Americans* she described the city as crass and provincial. What she neglected to mention was that she had invested a large sum in a disastrous commercial failure, a "bazaar," or department store, that offered inferior goods in a grotesque building of exotic design. "A large Greco-Moresco-Gothic-Chinese-looking building," Thomas Hamilton called it, "which could scarcely have been more out of place had it been tossed on the earth by some volcano in the moon."

Trollope sailed home to England in July 1831, a few weeks after Tocqueville and Beaumont arrived, and soon afterward published *Domestic Manners*, which concludes majestically, "I suspect that what I have written will make it evident that I do not like America . . . I do not like their principles, I do not like their manners, I do not like their opinions." She was especially disgusted by the "coarse familiarity, untempered by any shadow of respect, which is assumed by the grossest and lowest in their intercourse with the highest and most refined," as illustrated by the "violent intimacy" of a Cincinnati neighbor who freely used first names with her children and even addressed them as "honey." (Thirty years later, her son the novelist Anthony Trollope was similarly outraged that in America "the man to whose service one is entitled answers one with determined insolence.") An American reviewer was only partly exaggerating when he said bitterly that Frances Trollope portrayed "a nation of spitters, and chewers, and smokers, and dram-drinkers, and majors, and colonels, and generals, and pigs, all alike swaggering republicans, boasting, bullying, bellowing, roaring, and squealing for liberty and equality under a government of tinkers and tailors."

Like so many visitors to America in this period, Trollope had her own reasons to be critical. She had been hoping to bolster the conservative cause in the great Reform Bill debate, which would end in 1832 with the first significant extension of voting rights in English history, and she therefore declared that in America "the great experiment, as it has been called," was a complete disaster, producing "the jarring tumult and universal degradation which invariably follow the wild scheme of placing all the power of the state in the hands of the populace." In Ohio, she reported, there was actually a law forbidding fathers to beat their children. And the widespread consumption of newspapers offended her for the same reason that it would impress Tocqueville: it fed a preoccupation with public affairs. She expected her readers to share her disapproval when her milkman said, "How should freemen spend their time, but looking after their government, and watching that them fellers as we gives offices to, doos their duty, and gives themselves no airs?"

English visitors to America, conditioned to pay attention to subtle nuances of expression, were regularly offended by American colloquial speech. Trollope complained that she hardly ever heard "a sentence elegantly turned, and correctly pronounced," and she entertained her readers with little dialogues in which Americans exclaimed, "Well! if that don't beat creation!" "Now go the whole hog." "Well now, if that don't make me crawl all over to think of it!" "Keep cool, mother, I know a thing or two." Any variation from standard British usage was enough to give offense. She thought it bizarre that Americans would say "crackers" when they meant dry biscuits and "creek" when they meant a stream. More archly, Thomas Hamilton reported that "the term 'dry goods' is not, as might be supposed, generally applicable to merchandise devoid of moisture," and other writers complained that Americans said they were sick when they meant unwell, buried their dead in graveyards rather than churchyards, and drank in bars rather than pubs. Far less common were travelers who actually relished the tangy quality of American speech. Harriet Martineau was amused when a companion on the road was asked if someone was "a smart fellow" and replied, "He! he can't see through a ladder."

Interestingly, a principal reason for Tocqueville's apparent lack of snobbery was that his command of English, fluent enough for lively conversation, was not so perfect as to register nuances. He was quite capable of being offended in French, and when he was in Quebec, the speech of the lawyers there grated on his ear: "They are notably lacking in distinction, speaking French with a middle-class Norman accent [he came from Normandy himself]. Their style is vulgar, and mixed with oddities and English expressions." But there was a deeper reason as well for the respect Tocqueville showed to American speech. He thought that when new words got adopted in Europe, it was because pedants had exhumed them from dead languages. Here, very differently, "the perpetual change at the heart of a democracy tends to reshape the face of language endlessly, just as it reshapes the face of business . . . Democratic nations love change for its own sake. This is apparent in language as much as in politics." As the dictionary maker Noah Webster told an English visitor, "It is quite impossible to stop the progress of language—it is like the course of the Mississippi."

To the French visitors, the still provisional nature of Cincinnati was obvious. Tocqueville wrote to his mother, "Everything good and bad in

American society appears there in such relief that it's like those books printed in big letters to teach children to read. Everything there is jostling and extreme. Nothing is yet in its right place, and society is growing faster than man does. The place where Cincinnati is situated was still covered by forest thirty years ago. The spectacle it presents today is like nothing I'm familiar with. Everything reflects precipitous growth: fine houses and shacks; streets scarcely paved, imperfectly aligned, and encumbered with construction materials; places without names and houses without numbers—in a word, it's the sketch for a city rather than the city itself." The pace of growth was indeed staggering. Ohio as a whole had had fifty thousand people in 1803 and by now almost a million. With its farms and cities, its mingled influx of Northerners and Southerners, and its location on the Ohio River, it has been aptly called "a microcosm of nineteenth-century America."

This was what Tocqueville had been waiting for: a region with hardly any past, in dizzying transition, inventing itself with ferocious energy. There was a heady spirit of optimism, too. As the author of *A Statistical and Chronological View of the United States* proudly declared two years later, "The state of Ohio is said to resemble a gigantic youth, who having passed his teens with hurried pace, is rapidly striding on to vigorous manhood of commanding stature." But it was also a staging area for further migration as the frontier continued to recede. A guidebook for settlers published in 1836 noted that "hundreds of men can be found, not fifty years of age, who have settled for the fourth, fifth, or sixth time on a new spot. To sell out and remove only a few hundred miles makes up a portion of the variety of backwoods life and manners." One Illinois woman had twelve children, every one of whom had been born in a different house.

In Cincinnati, Tocqueville soon made contact with a number of impressive young professionals who were energetically building a civilization. Mostly they had brought conservative opinions with them from the East, but they all agreed that popular democracy was irreversible. A twenty-three-year-old lawyer who had recently arrived from New Hampshire spoke earnestly about the crudeness of American politics. When Tocqueville asked how inferior candidates kept getting elected, he replied, "By flattering everyone, which distinguished men would never do; by mingling with the populace and basely flattering their passions; by drinking with them." He added, however, that things were worst at the local level, and that in higher office "in spite of everything, it's still the influence of men of talent that governs us." He would live, indeed, to see his confidence rewarded, for this was Salmon P. Chase, subsequently senator from Ohio on the antislavery Free Soil ticket, first Republican governor of his state, treasury secretary under Lincoln, and, finally, chief justice of the U.S. Supreme Court. Lincoln himself, aged twenty-two, was only three hundred miles away at the time, reading Shakespeare and teaching himself mathematics in New Salem, Illinois.

There were extensive discussions of politics with John McLean, an associate justice of the Supreme Court, who emphasized the virtues of the decentralized government that Tocqueville had already admired in Massachusetts. "What seems most favorable with us for establishing and maintaining republican institutions," McLean said (no doubt more informally than in Tocqueville's French rendition), "is our division into states. I do not believe that with our democracy we could govern the whole Union for long if it formed but a single people. That is still more true of the great nations of Europe. I would add that the federal system is singularly favorable to the happiness of peoples. The legislature of a large nation can never enter in detail into local interests in the way a small nation's legislature can. With our federal organization, we have the happiness of a small nation and also the strength of a large one." Both in his origins and in his subsequent career, Justice McLean epitomized much that impressed Tocqueville in America. The son of an Irish immigrant who had been raised on a farm in Kentucky, he rose to great eminence, and in the celebrated *Dred Scott* case would deliver a dissenting opinion condemning slavery.

As it happened, the river voyage itself opened Tocqueville's eyes to the social and economic implications of slavery. He was struck all along the way by the fact that the "free soil" Ohio side was well cultivated and prosperous, while the Kentucky side was unkempt and poor. A young Cincinnati lawyer, Timothy Walker, confirmed the distinction and offered an explanation: "The only reason one can give for this difference is that slavery rules in Kentucky and not in Ohio. Work there is dishonorable; here, it is honored. There, idleness; here, ceaseless activity." In *Democracy in America*, Tocqueville would generalize: "The traveler on the Ohio River who lets the current carry him as far as the junction with the Mississippi is navigating, so to speak, between freedom and bondage. He has only to look around him to see at once which is more favorable for humanity." In the weeks ahead he would have a number of further experiences that would inspire a brilliant chapter on race relations in *Democracy in America*, and he wrote in his notebook, "Man is not made for servitude; this truth is perhaps proved even better by the master than by the slave."

But even though Ohio was a free state, Timothy Walker confirmed that it shared the prejudices that Tocqueville had encountered in the East. "You have passed some very severe laws against the blacks," Tocqueville ventured. Walker replied:

> Not only have we passed laws that permit expelling them at will, but we hamper them in a thousand ways. A Negro has no political rights; he cannot serve on a jury or give evidence against a white. That last law leads sometimes to the most revolting injustices. I was recently consulted by a Negro who had supplied the captain of a steamboat with a large amount of foodstuff. The white man denied the debt. Since the creditor was black, as were his workers who would have testified on his behalf but could not appear in court, there was no way even to open a case.

As Tocqueville and Beaumont journeyed onward into the South, their understanding of slavery and its threat to the Union would continue to deepen.

What impressed Tocqueville most in Ohio was the open-ended opportunities it offered to the democratic impulse. Several of his informants used the expression "democracy without limit," or perhaps it was he himself who prompted them with leading questions. Timothy Walker testified, "It seems to me that the United States is in crisis. At this time we are making an experiment in democracy without limit.

Everything is tending that way, but will we be able to sustain it? No one can yet say." Even Salmon Chase, the future ally of Lincoln's, struck the same note: "We have pushed democracy here to its ultimate limit . . . I am convinced there is no man of distinction in the Union who doesn't believe that full suffrage is a fatal thing, but it's impossible to resist the flood tide of public opinion that runs continually in that direction."

In a letter home a few days later, Tocqueville made clear why he was so interested. In Ohio he was encountering a population altogether different from the established culture of the East, "absolutely without precedents, without traditions, without customs, without even prevailing ideas." This was in effect a laboratory experiment in unalloyed democracy, liberated from the patrician traditions that still modified it in the East. "This is a society that as yet has no bonds, political, hierarchical, social, or religious, in which each individual is on his own because it suits him to be, without concerning himself with his neighbor—a democracy without limit or moderation." In his notebook Tocqueville expressed the same idea still more strongly: "No one yet knows what such a thing as an upper class might be. The hodgepodge is total. The entire society is a factory! More than anywhere else, in Ohio there are no general ideas, social ranks are intermingled, and the very rules of behavior are still unclear. No one has had time to establish a political and social position; the people escape all influences. Democracy there is without limit."

Like much else in Tocqueville's notes and letters, all of this would bear memorable fruit. "It is in the West," he would write in *Democracy in America*, "that one can observe democracy attaining its furthest limit. In those states, which were in a sense improvised by chance, the inhabitants arrived only yesterday on the land they occupy. They barely knew one another, and each was ignorant of his closest neighbor's past. In that part of the American continent, therefore, the people escape the influence not only of great names and wealth but also of that natural aristocracy that derives from wisdom and virtue." A natural aristocracy of virtue and talent had been an ideal of Thomas Jefferson's, and the promising young professionals of Cincinnati might seem to have embodied it, but Tocqueville was struck instead by the universal equality that he saw as the essence of democracy. As a settler in the region later recalled, "Dependence upon one another caused differences of education and station to disappear, and almost absolute social equality prevailed; hence every person felt that he or she was the social equal of every other person."

Whether equality was good or bad in itself depended, of course, on the perspective of the viewer. A Cincinnati author wrote at the time, "The Puritan and the planter, the German and the Irishman, the Briton and the Frenchman, each with their peculiar prejudice and local attachments, have here set down beside each other . . . The society, thus newly organized and constituted, is more liberal, enlarged, unprejudiced, and of course more affectionate and pleasant, than a society of people of *unique* birth and character, who bring all their early prejudices, as a common stock, to be transmitted as an inheritance in perpetuity." But the German immigrant Francis Grund was more equivocal about the implications of erasing the past. "They do not love the land of their fathers, but they are sincerely attached to that which their children are destined to inherit. They live in the future, and *make* their country as they go on." That might sound hopeful, but it was inseparable from a predatory attitude toward the land: "They treated nature as a conquered subject, not as a mother who gave them birth. They were the children of another world, who came thither to burn, ransack and destroy, and not to preserve what they had found." As Tocqueville and Beaumont had seen in the wilds of Michigan, Americans regarded the land as theirs for limitless exploitation, and the western half of the continent still beckoned them on.

Tocqueville naturally identified with the ancestral estate from which his surname came, and he wrote feelingly that for an aristocrat, "the family represents the land and the land represents the family, perpetuating its name, origins, fame, power, and virtues. It is an imperishable witness to the past and a precious pledge for future." But he also knew that his aristocratic yearnings were antithetical to the American spirit. "To flee the paternal hearth and fields where one's ancestors rest, abandoning the living and the dead to chase after fortune—nothing, in their eyes, is more praiseworthy." And he was willing to acknowledge that this spirit of enterprise deserved praise; he well knew that rural France was backward and stagnant by comparison. An economist who had recently traveled through provincial France found life there "languishing for lack of momentum or actually going backward . . . The result is monotony such as anyone accustomed to life in Paris can scarcely comprehend."

Creating a new life attracted a type of ambitious, take-charge personality that fascinated Tocqueville. "An American taken at random," he observed, "will be ardent in his desires, enterprising, adventurous, and above all an innovator." In the margin of his manuscript he kept turning the point over: "Nothing prevents him from *innovating*. Everything leads him to *innovate*. He has the energy that it takes to *innovate*." The typical American in the West was therefore a jack-of-all-trades. No one was obliged to spend a lifetime in a single occupation or career; "you meet Americans who have successively been lawyers, farmers, businessmen, ministers of the Gospel, and physicians." Achille Murat, who had lived for years in America, confirmed this perception. "You may have known a man as a lawyer," Murat wrote, "and then you see him again a few years later at the other end of the Union as captain of a ship, or a planter, or an officer, or a merchant, or even a preacher. In some instances he will have run the circle of all these."

Back in Connecticut, Tocqueville had found a perfect illustration of this openness to opportunity. No fewer than thirty-six current members of Congress, he was told, had been born in that state, which had only five congressmen of its own. "If the other thirty-one had stayed in Connecticut," he speculated, "it is likely that instead of becoming well-to-do landowners, they would have remained humble laborers, living in obscurity with no chance of a career in politics, and far from becoming useful legislators, they would have been dangerous citizens."

For people starting from scratch, the West thus offered an opening to infinite possibilities. The term "manifest destiny" didn't appear until the 1840s, when the Democrats invoked it as justification for annexing Texas and the Oregon Territory, but Tocqueville was impressed by something much like it. In *Democracy in America* he would write, "In this gradual and continuous advance of the European race toward the Rocky Mountains, there is something providential; it's like a flood of men ceaselessly swelling, drawn on each day by the hand of God." At various times he chose to invoke providence in this way, not out of piety, but in the hope of persuading readers that it would be foolish to resist the irresistible current of history.

Beaumont, whose liberal sympathies were always more mixed, took a less tolerant view:

> In the most recent Ohio elections the people sent to the legislature a petty lawyer whose entire merit was to have sold little cakes in the streets of Cincinnati three years previously. They have confidence in him because he came from their ranks. To win an election, candidates have to enter into very intimate relations with the citizens (and that's everyone). They must drink with them in taverns and beg them for their votes. These are things that a man who is at all distinguished by education and social position will never do. Consequently, all the men whom the people elect to public office in Ohio are more or less mediocre. It is nonetheless true that this society is full of life and prosperity, but the source of its strength is not its extreme democracy, as our demagogues in Europe claim. To anyone who is willing to see things as they are, it is obvious that their prosperity has material causes completely independent of this extreme democracy, *in spite of which* it prospers.

Beaumont was disgusted to learn that Henry Clay had campaigned for the presidency "in an old hat and clothes full of holes; he was paying court to the people."

Tocqueville, however, came to a very different conclusion. Politicians might be mediocre, and yet competent in the ways that really mattered. "America demonstrates irrefutably one thing I had doubted until now, that the middle classes can govern a state. I don't know whether they could do it creditably in truly difficult political situations, but they're adequate for the ordinary pace of society. Notwithstanding their petty passions, incomplete education, and vulgar manners, they do definitely supply practical intelligence, and that turns out to be enough."

Crucially, elementary education was available to an ever-growing segment of the population, enabling a sophisticated political consciousness that was still unimaginable in France. "Americans are hardly more virtuous than others, but they are infinitely more enlightened (I speak of the masses) than any other people I know . . . The mass of those with a grasp of public affairs, a knowledge of laws and precedents, a feeling for the well-understood interests of the nation, and an ability to understand them, is greater there than in any other place on earth." For as Tocqueville said in a manuscript note, "The hardest task for governments is not to govern, but to teach men how to govern themselves."

Still more important, Tocqueville was arriving at a penetrating explanation of the way in which American individualism contributed to the common good instead of opposing it. "In France, say what you will," he wrote in his notebook, "the prejudice of birth still has great power, and it still forms an almost insurmountable barrier between individuals." It had always been perfectly obvious that some Americans had more money than others, and that the rich naturally associated with their own kind. But when two Americans from different economic strata happened to meet in public, Tocqueville said, "they regard each other without pride on the one side and without envy on the other. At bottom they feel themselves equal, and they are."

As he later put it in *Democracy in America*, what made America different was that the inequalities it did have were constantly shifting, rather than assigned at birth. Since in principle anybody might someday rise to the top, "a sort of imaginary equality" was understood to exist. In his last work, *The Ancien Régime and the Revolution*, he gave a telling example:

> Let us trace the development of the word "gentleman," whose ancestor is our word *gentilhomme*, in time and space. You will see its connotations widening in England as social conditions approach each other and merge. Century by century it was applied to men who were a little lower in the social scale. Next it went over to America with the English, and there they use it to indicate all citizens indiscriminately. Its history is the very history of democracy. In France the word *gentilhomme* has

always been restricted to its original sense; it has virtually fallen out of use since the Revolution, but it has never changed. It still designates the members of a caste, because we have retained the caste itself, which is as separate from the other castes as it ever was.

All of this equality might sound admirable, but for Tocqueville it raised a warning flag. The French Revolution had rejoiced in liberty, equality, and fraternity, but since its outcome was the Terror and then Napoleon's empire, was it not possible that too much equality could result in suppression of liberty? In the 1830s that was the fear of many liberal thinkers in Europe, as well as of conservatives. Mill warned that democracy was all too capable of "degenerating into the only despotism of which in the modern world there is real danger—the absolute rule of the head of the executive over a congregation of isolated individuals, all equals but all slaves."

The theorists of the eighteenth-century Enlightenment, and their heirs who drafted the U.S. Constitution, had relied on a classical ideal of disinterested civic virtue to make society work. "Political virtue," Montesquieu wrote, "is a renunciation of oneself, which is always very painful." That was the code Hervé de Tocqueville lived by, and it had been the code of Alexis's ancestor Malesherbes, who went to the guillotine for honorably defending his king. Yet America was replacing the civic virtue of its patrician founders with what might seem its very opposite. In a letter written back in New York, Tocqueville had defined the problem he needed to solve in this way:

Imagine if you can, my friend, a society formed from all the nations of the world—English, French, Germans... All of these peoples have different languages, beliefs, and opinions. In a word, it's a society without roots, memories, biases, routines, shared ideas, or national character, and yet it's a hundred times more fortunate than our own. More virtuous? I doubt it. So there's the point of departure: What serves to bond such diverse elements? What makes a people out of all of this? *L'intérêt!* That's the secret: the interest of individuals that comes through at every moment, and declares itself openly as a social theory.

Or, as Tocqueville posed the problem in his notebook, "The principle of the republics of antiquity was to sacrifice individual interest to the common good, and in that sense one could say they were virtuous. But it seems to me that the principle of this republic is to make individual interest merge with the common interest. A sort of refined and intelligent egotism is apparently the pivot on which the whole machine turns." In short, whereas traditionalists lamented that old ideals were being trampled on, Tocqueville realized that self-interest could do the same work that disinterested virtue formerly did.

In *Democracy in America* he hit on a phrase that crystallized this insight, "l'intérêt bien entendu," "interest well or properly understood." (As Arthur Goldhammer notes, the French word *intérêt* has a broader range of meaning than "self-interest," and can extend to everything that matters to a person.) Tocqueville's idea was that modern capitalism rewards foresight and cooperation, so that society as a whole prospers if its individual members do. "The doctrine of interest properly understood," he concluded, "does not produce great sacrifices, but day by day it prompts little ones. By itself it cannot make a man virtuous, but it shapes a multitude of citizens who are orderly, temperate, moderate, foresighted, and masters of themselves. And if it doesn't lead directly to virtue through the will, it advances gradually closer to virtue through the habits." Interest, in effect, could serve as a pragmatic equivalent of morality. In his notes for *Democracy in America*, Tocqueville commented, "If morality were strong enough by itself, I wouldn't regard it as so important to rely on utility. If the idea of what is just were more powerful, I wouldn't say so much about utility . . . It's because I see that morality is weak that I want to place it under the protection of interest."

In a society based on "interest" in this sense, the pursuit of happiness was virtually synonymous with the pursuit of material gain. In France it was dishonorable for a well-born *gentilhomme* to go into commerce; in America making money was precisely what conferred honor. Tocqueville wrote in Ohio, "Given the total absence of material and external distinctions, wealth presents itself as the natural scale by which to measure men's merit." His respect for this ethos is the more impressive since it ran counter to his instinctive values. According to Beaumont, "Alexis de Tocqueville, even though his reason embraced democratic ideas, retained the aristocracy of feelings; now, there's nothing so aristocratic as contempt of money." But with characteristic open-mindedness Tocqueville set prejudice aside, and he developed real admiration for risk-taking entrepreneurship. "The Americans bring a sort of heroism to the way they conduct commerce."

But if Ohio seemed to embody the essence of the new America, there was still the South to see, where very different conditions awaited. Tocqueville and Beaumont would soon get acquainted with the quasi-aristocratic culture of the slave states, and they would see slavery itself far more intimately than before. In addition, a chance meeting would bring aboard their steamboat a melancholy band of Indians expelled from their ancestral lands by official U.S. policy, setting out upon what would soon become known as the infamous Trail of Tears.

8

DOWNRIVER TO NEW ORLEANS

With only the South left to explore, Tocqueville and Beaumont had originally planned to trek overland from Cincinnati to Charleston, and after that to visit Washington on the way back to New York and home. But since the winter was shockingly severe, there was real danger of getting trapped indefinitely in the Appalachians. The friends decided to go instead down the Ohio and Mississippi rivers to New Orleans, continuing afterward to Washington through the Deep South. Beaumont admitted that romantic associations, including their fascination with Native Americans, encouraged the change of itinerary:

> We're curious to see the Great River, as M. de Chateaubriand calls the Mississippi, not that we expect to see blue herons, red flamingos, monkeys, and parakeets assembled on the bank to watch us go by, as one might anticipate after reading the fine description of the "Meschacébé River" at the beginning of *Atala*. But without indulging in imaginative flights, it's unquestionably one of the most magnificent rivers on earth, and for that reason well worth going hundreds of miles to see. Besides, our interest is piqued by New Orleans, the former French colony to

which our ancestors gave the beautiful name of Louisiana. And a final reason for extending our tour is that to reach Charleston from New Orleans, we'll need to cross the states of Alabama and Georgia, where the Creeks, Cherokee, and Choctaw are to be found.

They didn't get trapped in the mountains, but they did get trapped. When their steamboat was within a couple of hours of Louisville, the Ohio River froze solid, and there was no alternative but to disembark at the village of Westport. As Tocqueville later related,

> A big strapping pioneer in the neighborhood offered to transport our luggage to Louisville in his wagon. Ten fellow travelers joined the party, and we went forward on foot through the woods and mountains of Kentucky, where no loaded wagon had passed since the beginning of the world. We managed to get through, thanks to plenty of shoulder shoves and the bold spirit of our driver, but we were trudging through snow that was up to our knees. Eventually this mode of travel fatigued our companions so much that they began to abandon us, one after another. But we stuck to our resolution, and we did reach Louisville at last, around nine at night.

They had covered twenty-five exhausting miles, only to learn they were no better off than before, since at Louisville the river was just as impassable as at Westport.

There was nothing for it but to hit the road again. Everybody said that if only they could reach Memphis, the Mississippi there was sure to be free from ice, so they set off by way of Nashville, 170 miles to the south. This time they were able to go by stagecoach, but conditions were still terrible. "We had to travel over abominable roads," Tocqueville recalled, "in the most infernal carriages, and still worse, in the most incredible cold you can imagine. The natural order of things seemed to have been turned upside down just for us. Tennessee is almost below the latitude of the Sahara desert in Africa, and they raise cotton and exotic plants there, but when we were traversing it, it was freezing at fifteen degrees [Fahrenheit]. No one had ever seen anything like it." In the East that winter the Hudson froze at Albany, and people crossed from Manhattan to Brooklyn on the ice.

Nashville detained the Frenchmen only briefly. It was a smallish town of five thousand inhabitants, with ambitious residents who were necessarily jacks-of-all-trades. One man who was there at the time not only was a prosperous merchant but had served as a town alderman, trustee of the University of Nashville, treasurer of the thespian and antiquarian societies and of the Presbyterian church, editorial writer for the *Nashville Whig*, and grand mason of the Masonic lodge. The town's most famous citizen had pursued a similarly varied career. When Andrew Jackson was in his early thirties, he gave up his seat on the Tennessee Supreme Court in order to run a combined store and tavern and to open a racetrack, at which he gambled heavily. He did retain his position as major general of the state militia, in which capacity he became the hero of the Battle of New Orleans. It might have been possible to visit Jackson's estate, the Hermitage, but the friends showed no interest in Jackson then or later.

They pressed on toward Memphis, another two hundred miles away, in an open wagon this time. Beaumont later transcribed the account from his (now lost) diary: "Frightful roads. Precipitous drops. No defined roadway; the route is nothing but a hole through the forest. Trunks of badly felled trees are like posts that we bang into constantly." Not surprisingly, the wagon began to break down. "Tocqueville and I found ourselves advancing night and day along with several other travelers, each more frozen than the others. To warm us up, however, fortune bestowed three little accidents that forced us to pause along the way. First a suspension strap broke, then a wheel, and finally the axle of our conveyance. With the help of some oaks cut down in the forest, which was continuous the entire way, we succeeded in partially repairing our poor cart. It was in fragments and limping on all four feet when we reached the place where we are now."

They had covered ninety grueling miles in four days, and were resting at a humble tavern in a hamlet called Sandy Bridge (known today as Hollow Rock). As Beaumont described it,

In the room where I'm writing, there are three beds on which travelers have flung themselves, regardless of their number or sex. An immense fire is burning in a chimney that's the size of the ones in the old châteaus; it's big enough to hold ten logs, each three feet in circumference. But in spite of this fire that could roast an ox, the room is freezing. Just now I was going to drink a glass of water they had brought me, but having carelessly left it for five minutes, I found it was frozen right through. This can be explained by two reasons: it's eight or ten degrees outside, and there are large gaps that allow air to circulate freely between the logs that form the walls.

All this was unpleasant enough, but it was far from the whole story: Tocqueville had come down with an alarming fever. From Beaumont's diary again:

13 December. What a day! What a night! Tocqueville's bed is in a room whose walls are made of unsquared oak logs piled on top of each other. It's cold enough to crack stone. I light a monstrous fire; the flame crackles on the hearth, stirred up by wind that blows in on us from all sides. The moon sheds its light through the gaps in the logs. Tocqueville can get warm only by suffocating under his blanket and the multitude of coverings I pile on him. No help to be obtained from our hosts. Depth of our isolation and abandonment. What to do? What will happen if the illness gets worse? What *is* this illness? And where to find a doctor? The nearest one is more than thirty miles away; it would take two days or more to get there and back, and what would I find on my return?

Beaumont later wondered whether this was an early premonition of the tuberculosis that would eventually kill his friend. Indeed, alarming bouts of illness had plagued Tocqueville for a long time. The year before their trip he complained on one occasion, "It's only a cold, you say; very well, but it's such a cold that I'm reduced to near helplessness by it."

In his letters Tocqueville made no mention of his illness, but he did comment on a rare opportunity to experience the daily life of settlers in the backwoods, including the lordly way in which even the humblest southern whites treated their slaves:

> In the evening we discovered a log cabin through whose badly joined sides we could see a big fire crackling inside . . . By the fire sat the mistress of the abode, with the tranquil and modest air that distinguishes American women, while four or five big children rolled around on the floor, dressed as lightly as in the month of July. Crouching beneath the mantelpiece, two or three Negroes seemed to find it less warm there than in Africa. In the midst of this scene of poverty, *mon gentilhomme* did the honors of his home with ease and courtesy. Not that he made the slightest movement of his own; as soon as the poor Negroes noticed a stranger, one of them brought us a glass of whiskey at his master's command, and another a corn cake or a plate of venison; a third was dispatched to get wood. The first time I saw this order given, I expected him to go to a cellar or woodshed, but the ax I heard ringing in the woods soon informed me that he was cutting down the requisite tree, and that's how it's always done. While the slaves were thus busy, their master, tranquilly seated before a fire that would have roasted an ox right down to the marrow, enveloped himself majestically in a cloud of smoke and, to make the time pass more quickly, regaled his guests between puffs with all the great deeds that his hunter's memory could furnish him.

In effect, a white man in the South, however impoverished, could comport himself like a medieval seigneur. "To ride on horseback, to hunt, and to smoke like a Turk in the sunshine—that's the destiny of a white. To work with his hands would be to act like a slave." It isn't clear whether Tocqueville had any conversation with the slaves themselves, and it might not have done much good if he did; travelers testified that they were understandably guarded in talking with strangers.

Fortunately, Tocqueville began to recover, and in a few days he was ready to travel again. A stagecoach turned up and took them aboard, and they resumed their laborious progress. At the Tennessee River the ice was broken enough to allow crossing by ferry, and at that point there was an incident that gave further disturbing evidence of racial attitudes.

Tocqueville wrote to his father, "I must tell you a little anecdote that will let you judge the value they attach to a man's life here when he has the misfortune to have black skin. To reach the other side, there was nothing but a paddle-wheel boat managed by a horse and two slaves. We got ourselves across well enough, but since the river was rushing fast, the owner of the boat was afraid to take the stagecoach across. 'Don't worry,' said one of our companions, 'we'll make up the value of the horse and the slaves.'" In effect, men and horses alike were nothing more than property to be sacrificed freely as long as financial compensation could be assured. "This argument was decisive," Tocqueville reported. "The coach was embarked, and it did get across."

After two more exasperating days on the road they reached Memphis at last. The town was disappointing. "Memphis!!! the size of Beaumont-la-Chartre!" exclaimed Beaumont. "What a letdown! Nothing to see, neither people nor things." Still more disconcerting was the discovery that despite repeated assurances that the Mississippi could never freeze, it had. "A number of steamboats were locked in the ice," Tocqueville recounted later. "We could see them there, but they were as immobile as stones." There was not even any possibility of returning the way they had come, because word reached them that the Tennessee, too, had become impassable. "We thus found ourselves in the middle of a triangle formed by the Mississippi, the Tennessee, and an impenetrable wilderness to the south, as isolated as on a rock in the ocean, living in a tiny world made expressly for us with no newspapers, no news from outside, and the prospect of a long winter."

To kill time, the friends got some local Chickasaw to take them hunting. Big game had long since been driven away, "but on the other hand," Tocqueville reported cheerfully, "we killed a flock of pretty birds that are unknown in France. That didn't raise us much in the esteem of our companions, but it did have the merit of keeping us amused. It was thus that I killed red, blue, and yellow birds, not forgetting the most brilliant parrots I've ever seen." Shooting them was all too easy. "We killed four during a single hunt," Beaumont reported; "the only difficulty is to kill just a single one. The death of the first brings all the others; they perch on the hunter's head and let themselves be shot like boobies." Another traveler described the same phenomenon: "At each successive discharge, though showers of them fell, yet the affection of the survivors seemed rather to increase; for, after a few circuits round the place, they again alighted near me, looking down on their slaughtered companions with such manifest symptoms of sympathy and concern as entirely disarmed me."

CAROLINA PARROT OR PARAKEET, BY JOHN JAMES AUDUBON

In the original the birds have green bodies, yellow heads, and red masks between their eyes. Audubon has shown them feeding on cockleburs, but in a caption remarks that farmers hated them because they stripped orchards bare and would cover a field of grain in such numbers that it looked "as if a brilliantly coloured carpet had been thrown over them."

These were the celebrated Carolina parakeets, the only species of parrot native to the eastern United States, and the Frenchmen were doing their small part to hasten their extinction. The last wild parakeet was killed in Florida in 1904, and the last captive died in the Cincinnati Zoo in 1918. Of course in those days the supply of wildfowl seemed inexhaustible. The great Audubon, who had made his first trip down the Mississippi a few years earlier, routinely shot a couple of dozen birds as models for a single picture, and boasted that he customarily killed at least a hundred per day.

One other incident of interest happened near Memphis. Beaumont recorded tersely, "We found Shakespeare and Milton in a log cabin," and as an example of rustic literacy Tocqueville later mentioned in *Democracy in America* that he first read *Henry V* in that cabin. But he also wrote down a more extended recollection, which has never been published except as a footnote to a French scholarly text:

While I was reading [Shakespeare], I soon lost any sense of my surroundings, and the poet's great characters all rose up gradually around me. I felt as if I were seeing them with their language, beliefs, passions, prejudices, virtues, and vices. Memories of the heroic era of our history poured in upon me, my imagination was suddenly filled with the pomp of feudal society, I beheld high turrets and a thousand banners floating in the air; I heard the clang of armor, the sound of trumpets, and the heavy tread of caparisoned warhorses. I contemplated for a while this mingling of poverty and riches, strength and weakness, inequality and grandeur that characterized the Middle Ages, and I then opened my eyes and found myself in my little log cabin, built only yesterday in the midst of a flourishing wilderness that recalled the first days of the earth, and inhabited by descendants of those same Europeans who were now obscure and peaceable citizens of a democratic republic . . . Do you wish to behold the impetuous and irresistible stream of time flowing before your eyes? Seat yourself in the home of an American pioneer and read Shakespeare there, in the shadow of the virgin forest.

Clearly Tocqueville had taken to heart the prologue to *Henry V*:

> Think when we talk of horses that you see them
> Printing their proud hoofs in the receiving earth;
> For 'tis your thoughts that now must deck our kings,
> Carry them here and there; jumping o'er times,
> Turning the accomplishment of many years
> Into an hour-glass.

After a week of enforced idleness, hope suddenly revived. As Tocqueville described it, "At last, one fine day, a plume of smoke could be seen above the Mississippi at the farthest horizon. Gradually the cloud approached, and out of it emerged not a giant or dwarf as in a fairy tale but a big steamboat coming up from New Orleans. After parading before us for a quarter of an hour, as if to leave us in doubt whether it would stop or keep going, and after blowing like a whale, it finally approached, broke through the ice with its heavy prow, and tied up at the bank."

Actually, there was no danger that the boat (it was called the *Louisville*) wouldn't stop, since Memphis was a regular station for picking up firewood, but it was true that the captain expected to continue northward. The stranded travelers assured him that he would be prevented by ice, and their pleas were reinforced by a totally unexpected arrival. Out of the forest, with loud drums and barking dogs, emerged a bedraggled band of Choctaw Indians. In pursuance of the infamous Indian Removal Act of 1830, they were in the charge of a federal agent who planned to set them ashore in Arkansas for the long trek westward to Indian Territory, in today's Oklahoma. After the agent offered the captain a handsome sum to transport his sixty charges, the trip south was no longer in doubt.

Beaumont and Tocqueville were both moved by the spectacle. In Beaumont's account, written on board just before the tribe was to be set ashore:

> Their property consists of very little: a horse, a hunting dog, a gun, a
> blanket—and that's the fortune of the wealthiest. Old people aren't

spared any more than the rest. I've just seen on deck an old woman more than 120 years of age; she is almost entirely naked, wearing nothing but a shabby blanket that can hardly protect her shoulders from the cold, the very image of dilapidation and decrepitude. This unfortunate woman is obviously at death's door, leaving the land where she has lived for 120 years to go to another country and begin a new life there.

That was written on Christmas Day, as was Tocqueville's account, framed with studied irony:

You must know that the Americans of the United States, who are unprejudiced, good reasoners, and great philanthropists, have imagined as the Spanish did that God gave them full ownership of the New World and its inhabitants. They discovered moreover that since it was proved—listen carefully—that a square mile could nourish ten times as many civilized men as savages, it followed that wherever civilized men were able to establish themselves, the savages had to turn the land over to them. See how beautiful logic is!

The Indians coming aboard moved Tocqueville to a memorably elegiac vision:

In the whole of this spectacle there was an air of ruin and destruction, something that felt like a final farewell with no returning. One couldn't look on without a pang at the heart. The Indians were calm, but somber and silent. One of them knew English, and I asked him why the Choctaw were leaving their country. "To be free," he replied. I couldn't get him to say any more. We'll deposit them tomorrow in the emptiness of Arkansas. You must admit it was a singular coincidence that brought us to Memphis to witness the expulsion—one might say dissolution— of the last remnants of one of the most celebrated and ancient American nations.

In *Democracy in America*, Tocqueville added a last, haunting memory: "In this great throng no sobs or cries were heard; they were silent. Their misfortunes were long-standing, and they felt them to be irremediable. All of the Indians were already in the vessel that was going to carry them, but their dogs still remained on the bank. When the creatures understood at last that they were going to be left behind forever, they burst all together into a terrible howl, and plunging into the icy Mississippi, they swam after their masters." That makes it sound as if the dogs were left behind, but in his letter at the time Tocqueville said their masters pulled them aboard. At White River, Arkansas, the Indians were put ashore and began their weary journey into the West.

Tocqueville's solemn, measured account is characteristic of the style he polished so carefully, aspiring to the open-eyed clarity of the seventeenth-century classics. His younger contemporary Sainte-Beuve, though his own preference was for colorful description, caught its tone well: "This is a very French way—the French way of the old school— of seeing things and displaying them. Nothing is granted for curiosity or amusement. We don't see the feathers, weapons, and tattoos of the Choctaw, the kinds of striking details that would add depth and liveliness. One might say that Chateaubriand had never existed. But on the other hand, nothing is lacking to make one feel the profound sorrow."

No flamingos or monkeys were to be seen along the shores of the Mississippi, and the scenery was bland, but the friends enjoyed themselves thoroughly. Tocqueville knew that the river's Indian name meant "Father of Waters," and he was later inspired to personify it himself: "The valley watered by the Mississippi seems to have been created for it alone; there it dispenses good and ill at its own will, like a god." After the snow and bad roads, he wrote to a friend, "Traveling in this country is so expeditious, since one can make use of the steamboats, that one forgets all about distances." The author of a guidebook to the region was still more enthusiastic: "Distance is no longer thought of in this region; it is almost annihilated by steam!" The same writer worked out that in 1831 no fewer than 348 steamboats were plying the western waterways. The fourteen hundred miles from New Orleans to Louisville used to take nine months when boats had to be rowed or poled upstream, and could now be accomplished in nine days.

These were impressive vessels, specialized for their purpose with shallow draft and wide superstructures. A typical riverboat, a historian says, "looked like a cheaply constructed, ornate, white wooden castle floating on a raft." Some were only seventy feet long, some twice that, with paddle wheels enclosed in round boxes (on the sides, for agile maneuvering). The boilers were on the lowest deck, stoked with firewood by slaves. The middle deck held the main salon, ladies' cabin, staterooms, and—at the bow—the bar where men drank and gambled. The top deck, known as the hurricane deck because it was open to the elements, held the pilothouse and chimneys, from which sparks and soot poured forth.

The Scottish naval officer Basil Hall was greatly impressed by the skill with which the pilots negotiated the bends and kept clear of shoals. Piloting was crucial since hazards abounded, in particular "planters," submerged tree trunks stuck in the river bottom, and logs called "sawyers" that bobbed up and down with the current; either could easily drive a hole into the hull. Mark Twain, who became a skilled river pilot twenty-five years later, perhaps had them in mind when he named Tom Sawyer.

As was their habit, most British travelers were censorious. Frances Trollope deplored "the sameness of the thousand miles of vegetable wall"; Dickens called the river "an enormous ditch, sometimes two or three miles wide, running liquid mud"; and the dashing Captain Marryat expressed revulsion "at the idea of perishing in such a vile sewer, to be buried in mud, and perhaps to be rooted out again by some pig-nosed alligator." Life aboard was apparently no better. "The people are all alike," Dickens complained. "There is no diversity of character. They travel about on the same errands, say and do the same things in exactly the same manner, and follow in the same dull cheerless round." To be sure, he was recalling table conversation, where strangers would naturally make routine small talk.

The conversation, though, was the least of the offenses at meals, which featured gargantuan helpings of meat. In the early 1830s all three daily meals on a typical trip upriver from New Orleans included beefsteaks, ham, duck and other fowl, and various ragouts and fricassees. Passengers had to grab what they could the moment they reached the long tables, which resulted in a feeding frenzy that appalled foreigners. "The table was cleared in an amazing short space of time," an English bishop recalled, "and food was *bolted* as I have never seen before." Thomas Hamilton complained that the passengers devoured their food like zoo animals, and Frances Trollope deplored "the frightful manner of feeding with their knives, till the whole blade seemed to enter the mouth, and the still more frightful manner of cleaning the teeth afterwards with a pocket knife." Few stopped to reflect that, as Harriet Martineau pointed out, stagecoach travelers in England behaved in exactly the same way; she added that "in private houses I was never aware of being hurried." Tocqueville, as usual, registered no complaints, and Beaumont's comments were mild and diplomatic. "The cooking is bad," Beaumont observed, "because in America it's never good, except in some of the private houses." But he added charitably, "As American cuisine goes, it's excellent."

Traveling by steamboat actually meant consorting with a relatively genteel class of passenger. There was plenty of other river traffic, composed of keelboats, which could be sailed very slowly upstream, and flatboats, which could only drift downstream and were sold off as lumber in New Orleans. A clergyman who traveled throughout the West on behalf of the American Sunday School Union commented that the boatmen were characterized by "boldness, readiness to encounter almost any danger, recklessness of consequences, and indifference to the wants of the future, amid the enjoyments, noise, whiskey, and fun of the present." With a similar mixture of amusement and disapproval, he called them "half-horse, half-alligator." The epithet had been around for years; a traveler in Natchez in 1808 heard a boatman proclaiming, "I am an alligator, half man, half horse; can whip any man on the Mississippi, by God!" Eventually, Samuel Woodworth, best known for the sentimental ballad "The Old Oaken Bucket," invoked the phrase to celebrate the Battle of New Orleans in a song called "The Hunters of Kentucky" that was immensely popular during Jackson's 1828 election campaign:

> Behind it stood our little force,
> None wished it to be greater,
> For every man was half a horse
> And half an alligator.

BACKWOODSMEN AND STEAMBOAT PILOT

In the original caption the artist explains that the figure on the left is "a regular backwoodsman" who had made his fortune trading in slaves and was now settling down as a farmer. On the right is one of the pilots who took turns steering the vessel during an eleven-day journey from New Orleans to Louisville. The man in the middle, "who looks so well pleased with himself," is one of a hundred or so deck passengers who had floated a cargo downriver on a flatboat and is now returning home.

Tocqueville and Beaumont had a gift for bumping into people who were famous at the time or destined to be later, and when the Indians went ashore, a remarkable passenger came aboard. Arriving on "a superb stallion that had been caught on the prairie that divides Mexico from the United States" was Sam Houston, a handsome and strapping six-footer. His victory over Santa Anna and his presidency of the Republic of Texas were still four years in the future, but at a well-worn thirty-eight (Tocqueville thought he might be forty-five), he was already an exceptionally colorful character. Houston had spent his teenage years in Tennessee living with Cherokee, one of whose chiefs adopted him as a son and named him Colonneh, "the Raven." At twenty-one he was gravely wounded by an arrow and two rifle balls at the Battle of Horseshoe Bend, in which his friend Andrew Jackson put down a

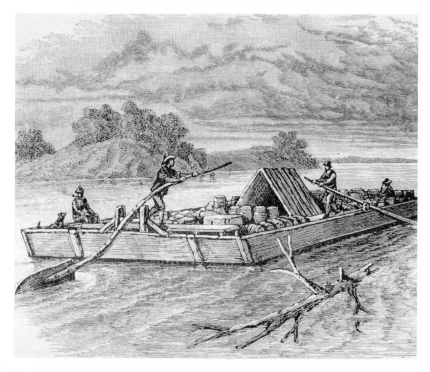

A FLATBOAT

Creek Indian uprising. More recently he had served as governor of Tennessee, until a scandal ended his marriage and impelled him to resign. He left a grimly sarcastic declaration behind him: "Know all men by these presents that I, Sam Houston, late governor of the State of Tennessee, do hereby declare to all scoundrels whomsoever . . . that they are authorized to accuse, defame, calumniate, slander, vilify, and libel me to any extent." He then moved in with his Cherokee friends in Arkansas, adopted their garb, and took one of them as a common-law wife.

Houston was bitter about the white man's treatment of the Indians, which he had described the previous year in a contribution to *The Arkansas Gazette*: "A succession of injuries has broken his proud spirit, and taught him to kiss the hand which inflicts upon him stripes—to cringe, and ask favors of the wretch, who violates his oath by defrauding him money promised by treaties." He boasted that he had always done his best to keep alcohol from reaching the susceptible Indians, but admitted that he had no objection to using it himself, and in fact the Cherokee had renamed him Ootsetee Ardeetahskee, "Big Drunk."

SAM HOUSTON

Tocqueville was a bit disdainful of Houston at first, astonished that this raffish character could ever have been governor of a state. Houston's conversation, however, proved to be intelligent and thought provoking, especially on the subject of Indians: "The Indian is born free, and he makes use of this freedom from his very first steps in life. From the moment he is able to take action, he is left to himself, and even the authority of his father is a tenuous bond. Surrounded by dangers, pressed by wants, and able to rely on nobody, he must keep his mind constantly active to foresee these cares and to sustain his life. This necessity gives his intelligence a development and keenness that are often wonderful."

At this moment Houston was en route to Washington to present a petition on behalf of the Indians to his old friend Jackson, who during years of fighting them had formed a fixed impression of their recalcitrance and cruelty. Davy Crockett, who had fought with him at Horseshoe Bend, recalled with satisfaction, "We shot them like dogs." The body count was established by slicing off the noses of the Indian dead. Yet there was mutual respect between Jackson and many Indians, and he genuinely believed that their best hope of survival was to move far to the west. He and his wife even adopted two Indian orphans and raised them as their own.

The Indian Removal Act of 1830—"removal" was the euphemism then, as "ethnic cleansing" is today—gave Jackson no qualms of conscience at all. He considered the Indians a childlike race that was refusing to grow up and should be grateful for the opportunity to make a fresh start. Not coincidentally, he and his cronies got rich buying up thousands of acres of Indian land at ridiculously low prices. The Choctaw whom Tocqueville encountered on the Mississippi were there in accordance with the 1831 Treaty of Dancing Rabbit Creek, by which they had agreed to move by stages to Oklahoma. As Tocqueville saw firsthand, and as a historian otherwise sympathetic to Jackson sums it up, "The entire operation was marked by inefficiency, confusion, stupidity, and criminal disregard of the rights of the Indians." But at the time the policy did not lack for apologists. The German immigrant Francis Grund, a fervent Jackson supporter, wholeheartedly approved of Indian removal in terms that contrast strikingly with Tocqueville's generosity of spirit. According to Grund, "the quiet progress of civilization" was destined to displace barbarism. "Is it cruel," he asked rhetorically, "to civilize and improve a country, and to open a new road to wealth and comfort to thousands of intelligent beings from all parts of the world who would otherwise starve or be reduced to poverty, because in so doing they cannot avoid intruding on the favorite hunting-grounds of some wandering tribes?"

In *Democracy in America*, Tocqueville declared that cultural murder was being committed, even when Indians were permitted to live. "The social bond, long weakened, has broken down. There was no longer any fatherland for them, and soon they will no longer be a people. At most, some families will survive. The common name is lost, the language is forgotten, the traces of their origin vanish. The nation has ceased to exist." Tocqueville's indignation swelled as he pursued the topic. In a footnote he quoted Jackson's proclamation granting a western homeland as long as the grass should grow and the water run, and commented bitterly, "The Spanish, with unparalleled atrocities, have covered themselves with indelible shame, but they haven't succeeded in exterminating the Indian race or even preventing it from sharing their rights. The Americans of the United States have achieved this double result with marvelous ease, quietly, legally, and philanthropically, without shedding blood, and without violating a single one of the great principles of morality in the eyes of the world. It would be impossible to destroy men with greater respect for the laws of humanity."

A few hours before the end of the journey down the Mississippi, the boat stopped to refuel, and Tocqueville and Beaumont went ashore for a few minutes at a big cotton plantation. Unfortunately, this seems to be the only plantation they ever visited in what would prove to be a hasty rush through the South. They had a strong sense of the evils of slavery, but firsthand inspection might have made it even more vivid. The Scotsman Thomas Hamilton did visit Louisiana plantations, and was horrified at the backbreaking labor of the sugarcane harvest: "The fatigue is so great that nothing but the severest application of the lash can stimulate the human frame to endure it." His friendly host admitted that to make sure the work was done before the first frosts, "the slaves are taxed beyond their strength, and goaded to labor until nature absolutely sinks under the effort." A fellow Scot told Hamilton in Mobile that "men are treated in this country far worse than brute beasts in Scotland." The expression "sold down the river," indeed, originated as a threat to slaves in the upper states, who could expect brutal treatment if they were sold to plantations in Louisiana and Mississippi.

On New Year's Day 1832 the *Louisville* docked in New Orleans, having endured yet another delay of two days before it could free itself from a sandbar. Tocqueville and Beaumont had hoped to spend at least a week in the city, but after so many delays they could only afford three days. Still, New Orleans made a deep impression. With a population of nearly fifty thousand, it was the fifth-largest city in the United States, and since the entire traffic of the Mississippi River system funneled through New Orleans, it was second only to New York among American ports. Throughout the western part of his journey, Tocqueville kept hearing that the Mississippi Valley was certain to become the power center of the country.

Here, as in Canada, was a bilingual city with strong memories of the lost French empire, but its ethos was startlingly different from Montreal's and Quebec's. Pondering the huge cultural differences, Tocqueville fell back rather weakly on a climate theory that had been around for a century. He wrote to a friend, "When people tell you that climate makes no difference in a people's makeup, you may assure them that they're mistaken. We've seen the French in Canada, and they are tranquil, moral, and religious. In Louisiana we're about to leave another French people who are restless, dissolute, and slack in every way. There are fifteen degrees of latitude between them, and really that's the best reason I can give for the difference." New Orleans was indeed well on its way to being the Big Easy. "If there is no conversation," Achille Murat said, "there are eating, playing, dancing, and making love in abundance . . . The gaming houses are also very numerous in New Orleans, and have ruined many of the young people of Kentucky, come to pass their carnival in this Babylon of the West." As Tocqueville noted, the French-descended Creoles were very different from the people of Quebec, but an Irish traveler was struck all the same by their Gallic demeanor: "The Creole of Louisiana invariably conserves much of the air and appearance of *la belle France*, offering according to his disposition all the varieties of his original stock, from the amiable deportment and companionable *bonhommie* of the well-bred Frenchman, to the fierce *brusquerie* and swaggering sneer of the gallant."

Tocqueville and Beaumont took in as many of the sights of New Orleans as they could, and made a point of calling on the most distinguished French lawyer there. When he received them in a flowered dressing gown and they saw his entire family assembled, they recalled with much embarrassment that New Year's Day was an important gift-giving holiday at home. Hurrying awkwardly forward, Tocqueville managed to trample some of the new toys. "Alas!" he wrote afterward. "Where is the happy time when I would rather have forgotten my name than the arrival of the first of January?"

With little time for business, Tocqueville and Beaumont did ask their usual questions about politics and the law, and they did visit a prison, where the barbarity appalled them. "In locking people up," they reported, "there is no thought of making them better, only of controlling their wickedness. They are chained like wild beasts; they are not corrected, they are turned into brutes."

One thing they learned was that no one stayed in New Orleans in the summer if he could avoid it. Disease was rampant, especially where swampy land bred malaria and yellow fever, and there were frightening epidemics of smallpox, typhoid fever, and cholera. Yellow fever was especially horrible—it was known as "the black vomit"—and Tocqueville was told that during an epidemic as many as eight out of ten fieldworkers might die. It would be another fifty years before the link with mosquitoes would be understood. One guidebook gave the typical explanation that malaria, as its name, "bad air," implies, was "the offspring of the combined action of intense heat and marsh exhalation." Beaumont found the explanation convincing. "In the American South," he wrote in his novel *Marie*, "a cold and penetrating humidity always follows the last light of dusk. This sudden moisture, exhaled from the earth, is pernicious." What no one could have suspected was that malaria and yellow fever were by-products of the slave trade, since the mosquitoes that carried them arrived in that way from Africa. The slaves themselves had partial immunity to malaria (paying for it with susceptibility to sickle-cell anemia) and were better able to survive in swamps and rice fields than whites were.

What most distressed Tocqueville and Beaumont—especially Beaumont, who built his novel on it—was the rigid ranking of racial status. One evening they went to the opera and were startled at the way the audience was stratified by gender and race, with white men in front, mulatto women ("very pretty") behind them, and black women in the balcony. "Strange sight," Tocqueville wrote in his notebook, "all the men white, all the women colored, or at least with African blood." The racial makeup of quadroons and octoroons was strictly computed, and it was understood that white men might have mulatto mistresses but never wives. Beaumont made his heroine, Marie, a New Orleans mulatto who appears white but is treated nevertheless as a pariah, even when she moves to Baltimore, as soon as her ancestry is known. The anomaly of deep racial prejudice in the land of the free preoccupied Tocqueville as well as Beaumont, and it would inspire one of the most powerful sections of *Democracy in America*.

A German traveler gave fuller details of the unwritten racial code. Noting that "many quadroons have skin whiter than many proud Creoles," he commented that white men's sexual relationships with mixed-race women were regularized by formal contract and payment of money to the women's fathers, but that white women still treated them with contempt and could have them whipped like slaves. He witnessed a scene at his boardinghouse when a quiet, polite colored maid was delayed bringing water to a Frenchman, who struck her in the face and drew blood. When she hit back, he was enraged and began to pack his bags. "When Mrs. Herries, our innkeeper, found out about this, in order to satisfy this fellow, she initiated the infamy of having the poor girl whipped with twenty-six strokes of the bullwhip, and drove the cruelty to the extent of forcing the girl's lover, a Negro slave serving in the house, to count out the twenty-six strokes." Not content with this retribution, the Frenchman went down to city hall, had her arrested, and watched the police whip her all over again.

The deadline for returning to France was approaching all too rapidly, and with great reluctance Tocqueville and Beaumont decided they had to leave. They mapped out a route by stagecoach that would take them through Mississippi, Alabama, Georgia, the Carolinas, and Virginia. In this way they would see something of the South. Their destination would be the nation's capital, which they hoped to reach in time to see the opening of the new Congress.

9

ROAD TRIP THROUGH THE SOUTH

On January 4, Tocqueville and Beaumont were on the road again, heading through the Deep South, which Tocqueville liked to call "le Midi," the French term for the south of France. Their destination was Norfolk, from which they would continue by water to Washington. They had very little to say about their itinerary, but it was a standard stagecoach route and can be confidently traced, passing through Mobile, Montgomery, Knoxville, Macon, Milledgeville, Augusta, and Fayetteville. They reached Norfolk on January 15, having covered a little over a thousand miles in twelve days, and this time there were no major disasters, though Beaumont reported the by now familiar catalog of "bridges out, impassable roads, and carriages broken down." The region was still very thinly inhabited; Mississippi and Alabama had been states of the Union for less than fifteen years. When Harriet Martineau traveled through South Carolina, she encountered only one other vehicle during the course of several days, so that "our meeting in the forest was like the meeting of ships at sea."

By now Tocqueville was sure that he wanted to write a big book on American politics and culture, and he was uneasily aware that this scramble through the South was no way to get to know a region. In his notebook along the way he conceded frankly, "It would be absurd to want to judge an entire people after living among them for a week or ten days. I can only rely, therefore, on *on-dit*, hearsay." At least the frightening bout of illness was past, and he wrote proudly to his sister-in-law that he was now the strongest member of the party. He even added that it might be good to think less and simply to exist in the present moment, as Rousseau had believed:

> If ever I write a book on medicine, I can tell you it won't be like the ones that usually get published. I'll maintain and prove that in order to be well, you must first of all eat maize and pork, consume a little or a lot or nothing at all according to circumstances, sleep on the floor fully dressed, pass in a single week from icy cold to heat and from heat to icy cold, put your shoulder to a wheel or wake up in a ditch, and, above all, never *think*. That's the essential point: plunge yourself into *matter* as much as you can, and if possible be like an oyster. I think it was Rousseau who said that a man who thinks is a depraved animal. For myself, I would have said that a man who thinks is an animal with poor digestion.

Tocqueville could certainly live rough when necessary, but his actual values were much closer to those of Rousseau's friend Diderot, who commented sarcastically, "He who meditates may not be a depraved animal, but I'm sure he won't take long to become an unhealthy animal . . . I don't care for acorns and dens and hollow oaks. I require a carriage, a convenient apartment, fine linen, and a perfumed girl, and after that I would gladly accommodate myself to all the other curses of our civilized state. I go very well on my two hind feet." As for the claim that it was not natural for man to think, Diderot's view would normally have appealed to Tocqueville: "Whoever does not want to reason is renouncing the status of being human, and should be treated as unnatural."

With racial prejudice and slavery in his thoughts, Tocqueville witnessed a memorably symbolic scene in Alabama. As he recorded it soon afterward, they encountered a young Creek Indian woman caressing "a charming little white girl," evidently the daughter of a nearby planter, while a black woman crouched alongside. The little girl accepted the attentions "with a sort of feudal condescension." What especially struck Tocqueville was the difference in demeanor between the enslaved woman and the free Indian. "Watching the girl's slightest gestures, the Negro seemed singularly torn between the affection and the respectful fear that her young mistress inspired, while in the Indian's outpouring of tenderness there was something free and even a bit savage that contrasted strikingly with the slave's submissive posture and humility." The little tableau was short-lived, for something startled the Indian "and she rose abruptly, pushed the child aside rather roughly, and without a word plunged into the foliage." When Tocqueville retold the story in *Democracy in America*, he admitted that his own curiosity might well have been what made the Indian woman leave, since she shot an angry glance at him before disappearing into the trees. In the margin of the manuscript he asked, "Why is it that of these three races, one was born to perish, one to rule, and one to serve?"

From fellow stagecoach passengers it was possible to get some insight into southern culture, which was radically different from that in either the North or the West. The so-called southern way of life was actually a quite recent development, stimulated by the cotton gin, whose invention in the 1790s had made large-scale cotton farming profitable. This in turn was a potent incentive to expand the use of slave labor. Slaves themselves went up in price and were seen as essential assets, representing over 40 percent of the wealth of the five chief cotton-producing states. The result was a de facto aristocracy of whites, who haughtily refused to work with their hands.

It has been suggested that Tocqueville might have formed a more nuanced view if, as one critic rather severely suggests, he had met "more of the established gentry to set off the impressions gained from the many yahoos he interviewed." In any event, he believed that his sketchy understanding of the South would not be a significant handicap for the book he intended to write, since his principal theme was to be the essential nature of democracy, not its regional differences. When he came to argue that commercial success was the source of "honor" in America, he acknowledged frankly, "I am speaking here of the Americans who inhabit areas where slavery does not exist. They are the only ones who can show the complete picture of a democratic society."

Besides, if Tocqueville saw Southerners as aristocrats, that didn't mean he found them unsympathetic. In his summary of regional temperaments in *Democracy in America*, they certainly seem more appealing than Northerners: "The Southerner is wittier, more spontaneous, more open and generous, more intellectual, and more brilliant. The Northerner is more active, a better reasoner, better educated, and better skilled. The former has the tastes, prejudices, weaknesses, and grandeur of all aristocracies. The latter has the qualities and defects that characterize the middle class." A lawyer in Baltimore, which Tocqueville had visited briefly when he was staying in Philadelphia, offered a similar evaluation: "What distinguishes the North is the spirit of enterprise, and what distinguishes the South is the spirit of chivalry. A Southerner's manners are frank and open; he is excitable, irritable even, and extremely touchy on points of honor. A New Englander is cold, calculating, and patient. When you stay with a Southerner, he makes you welcome and shares all the pleasures of his home with you. As soon as the Northerner has received you, he starts to consider whether he might be able to do business with you." In the stagecoach Tocqueville jotted down an even harsher description of the northern temperament: "Coldly burning spirit, serious, tenacious, egoistic, cold, frozen imagination, respectful of money, industrious, proud, a reasoner."

Northerners, of course, took a different view. John Quincy Adams had said disparagingly that cotton planters "devote themselves to physical exercise, hunting, and horse racing," and after the Civil War his grandson Henry would declare that from them "one could learn nothing but bad temper, bad manners, poker, and treason." Their ways could indeed be high-handed. In 1836, James Henry Hammond, a South Carolina planter and apologist for slavery, declared in the House of Representatives that slavery had produced "the highest toned, the purest, best organization of society that has ever existed on the face of the earth . . . an aristocracy of talents, of virtues, of generosity and courage." The following year Hammond was traveling in Belgium, quarreled with the management of a hotel, and left without paying; when an employee tried to restrain his horses, Hammond gave him a bloody thrashing with his stick, and was astonished to find himself the next day "in the midst of all the felons" in the local jail.

Inseparable from the code of honor, apparently, was a proclivity to violence. For a couple of days on the road, a fellow passenger was a young lawyer who impressed Tocqueville as having "plenty of practical good sense," and who took part in a memorable exchange:

> Q. Is it true, then, that people in Alabama are as accustomed to violence as is said?
>
> A. Yes, there's no one here who doesn't carry weapons under his clothes. At the slightest quarrel he'll have a knife or a pistol in his hand. These things happen constantly, the state of society is half barbarous.
>
> Q. But when a man is killed like that, isn't his murderer punished?
>
> A. He's always brought to trial, and the jury always acquits, unless there are extremely aggravating circumstances. I don't remember a single man who was at all well-known having to pay for such a crime with his life . . . Besides, I've been no better than anyone else in my time— look at these scars all over my head (we saw, indeed, the traces of four or five deep wounds). That's how many knife blows I've received.
>
> Q. But you lodged a complaint?
>
> A. My God, no! I tried to give back as good as I got.

A lady in Montgomery told Martineau that during the four years she lived there, "no day had passed without someone's life having been attempted, either by dueling or assassination."

Having grown up in a culture in which dueling was still an accepted way of vindicating honor, Tocqueville had no trouble understanding why it was so prevalent in the South. It was a highly ritualized performance that ratified both parties' status as gentlemen; Andrew Jackson, like Hammond, merely caned offenders whom he considered social inferiors. In most cases, moreover, no shots were actually exchanged, since the principals' seconds would negotiate face-saving reconciliations. It has been suggested also that the willingness to fight was an essential component of the slave owners' ethos. They considered their slaves contemptible for preferring bondage to death, and as duelists, by showing that they were unafraid of death, they confirmed their status as masters. Still, mortality was much higher in American duels than in European ones, and Tocqueville commented, "In Europe they seldom fight a duel just to say that they've fought one. The offense is a sort of mental stain that they want to wash away, and that usually happens at small cost. In America they fight to kill."

Maryland in those days was very much a southern state, and when Tocqueville and Beaumont visited Baltimore, they encountered the old planter aristocracy at its best, but also racial prejudice at its most ominous. They were profoundly impressed by an aged patriarch, Charles Carroll of Carrollton, whom Tocqueville described as "a little old man of ninety-five, straight as the letter I." Carroll had inherited a gigantic thirteen-thousand-acre estate and a patrician tradition; the planters of the Chesapeake have been called "the strongest aristocracy America has ever had." He was still "very well preserved," Beaumont noted, and justly proud of being the last surviving signer of the Declaration of Independence. Another visitor found him "gay, cheerful, polite, and talkative," preserving his health by plunging into cold water every morning and riding eight miles a day.

CHARLES CARROLL OF CARROLLTON

"This race of men is vanishing today," Tocqueville commented, "after having provided America with its greatest men, and with them is perishing the tradition of lofty manners. The people are growing enlightened, knowledge is spreading, and average abilities are becoming common, while outstanding talents and great characters are becoming rare." Even Jefferson, that most active and curious of men, had felt out of place by the end of his life. "All, all dead!" he wrote to a friend in 1825, "and ourselves left alone midst a new generation whom we know not, and who know not us." Not that Carroll was living in the past. He had recently dug the first shovelful of dirt for the Baltimore & Ohio Railroad, and had said, "I consider this among the most important acts of my life, second only to my signing the Declaration of Independence, if even it be second to that." Still, he and his patrician friends were deeply resentful at having to compromise with egalitarianism; he told Tocqueville (who recorded the comment in English), "A mere democracy is but a mob."

As for race, signs of vicious prejudice were everywhere. Carroll had tried to get the Maryland legislature to pass an emancipation bill and had set some of his own slaves free, but he still had two hundred of them—which put him in the top one-tenth of 1 percent of slave owners—and the economy still rested on the backs of slaves. In cities, to encourage hard work, owners often allowed slaves to save money and eventually buy their freedom, and at that time four-fifths of the black people in Baltimore were legally free. But it made no difference to the way whites treated them. At a horse race Tocqueville and Beaumont attended, "when a Negro took the liberty to enter the grounds with some whites, one of them gave him a volley of blows with his cane, without any surprise on the part of the crowd or even of the Negro himself." They were told that there were no black children in the public schools, and when they asked why, the answer was: "It would degrade the white children to have them associate with beings who are condemned to public contempt." It is fascinating to realize that at the very time they were in Baltimore, a thirteen-year-old slave named Frederick Bailey was teaching himself to read there. Seven years later he would escape to Massachusetts and change his name to Frederick Douglass.

A deeply disturbing encounter at that time gave the Frenchmen further insight into the cruelties of slavery:

Today we saw in the almshouse a Negro whose insanity is extraordinary. There is a famous slave trader in Baltimore who, it seems, is much feared by the black population. Day and night the Negro I'm speaking of sees this man dogging his steps and tearing off bits of his flesh. When we entered his cell, he was lying on the floor in a blanket that was his only garment. His eyes rolled in their sockets, and his face expressed both terror and fury. From time to time he threw off his covering, raised himself up on his hands, and cried, "Get out! Get out! Don't come near me!" It was an appalling sight. This man is one of the handsomest Negroes I've ever seen, and in the prime of life.

Beaumont took an intense interest in race relations and eventually decided to make them his specialty, leaving to Tocqueville the bigger project on American institutions and culture. "There was something extremely interesting to investigate in Baltimore," he wrote to his brother, "and that's slavery, which is still legal there. I've made a great many observations on it, which to my mind are not very favorable to the people concerned. But all of this will probably be published in the great work that is to immortalize me, and I'll refer you to that to find out more." The great work ended up being the not very satisfactory novel *Marie*. If anything has immortalized Beaumont, it is not his writings but his friendship with Tocqueville.

The Civil War was still thirty years in the future, but many people were deeply concerned about the crisis that seemed fated to come. Nobody Tocqueville met believed that integration could ever be possible, and there were grim predictions of a racial Armageddon. Just three months before, Nat Turner's rebellion in Virginia had terrified planter society. It lasted only two days, but left sixty dead and was followed by savage reprisals; the heads of several dozen slaves were displayed on poles. Nobody knew when the same kind of thing might flare up again.

JOEL POINSETT
Poinsett had served as ambassador to Mexico and brought
back ("for good or ill," the
Tocqueville biographer Hugh
Brogan comments) the poin-
settia that bears his name.

At a tavern in South Carolina, Joel Poinsett, a former ambassador to Mexico whom they had previously met in Philadelphia, turned up. He was there on a mission from President Jackson, trying to shore up pro-Union sentiment at a time when the planter oligarchy was fiercely asserting states' rights. The pressing issue was the nullification controversy, in which South Carolina asserted the right to nullify or override the so-called tariff of abominations that imposed heavy duties on imports. New England manufacturers were thus enabled to sell their products at high prices without fear of foreign competition, while the southern planters, who had no factories, had to sell their cotton cheaply in an unprotected world market and to buy manufactured goods at artificially high prices. The mastermind of the nullification movement was John C. Calhoun of South Carolina, who as Jackson's vice president was obliged to work behind the scenes; his argument was that since the Constitution was originally ratified by independent states, they retained the right to ignore any federal laws they found unacceptable.

The vehemence of southern antagonism to the North was startling to foreigners. "Many a time in America," Martineau said, "have I been conscious of that pang and shudder which are felt only in the presence of hatred," and she saw the nullifiers as prisoners of a rigid ideology. When she met Calhoun, she called him "the cast-iron man who looks as if he had never been born, and never could be extinguished," and she was struck by his total imperviousness to anyone else's thinking. "His mind has long lost all power of communicating with any other. I know no man who lives in such utter intellectual solitude."

The tariff crisis would subside after a while, thanks to a compromise that satisfied both sides, but it was obvious that the issue of states' autonomy would continue to fester. On the road Tocqueville asked Poinsett whether he feared for the stability of the Union, and got a reassuring answer: "No, the nullifiers form a party only in South Carolina, and even there it's doubtful that they're a majority. And even if the entire state was with them, what could the 700,000 whites who live there do against the forces of the Union?" Other informants were less optimistic, and in *Democracy in America* Tocqueville would make explicit reference to the South's resentment and its tendency to dwell in the past. Why would the region ever consider secession, when with its overspecialized economy it would have the most to lose? "The answer is easy: the South has given the confederation four presidents, but it now sees federal power slipping away, and the number of its congressmen shrinking year by year while those of the North and West increase. Peopled by fiery and irascible men, the South is growing worried and angry. It turns its gaze despondently on itself, and interrogating the past, it wonders every day whether it's not being oppressed."

Tocqueville also understood clearly the constitutional issue at stake, and the specific way it might be challenged. The crucial innovation in the federal system of the United States, as contrasted with weaker federations, including an American one that had preceded it briefly, was that the central government had the power to enforce its laws throughout the entire nation. Its authority could only be resisted, therefore, if a state took the extreme step of "openly violating the laws of the Union, interrupting the usual course of justice, and raising the flag of rebellion." In 1860 that would indeed happen, and Tocqueville foresaw exactly what would make it possible. "The only case in which a civil war could break out would be if the army was divided, one part raising the flag of rebellion and the other remaining loyal."

As he did so often, Tocqueville took the occasion to question Poinsett about sexual mores, and invited him to compare attitudes in the American South with what he had seen in Latin America. It turned out not to be a comparison so much as a spectacular contrast. In the southern states, Poinsett declared, a man who slept with a married woman would be branded with dishonor, blocked from advancement and wealth, and lucky if the woman's family didn't kill him. South of the U.S. border, on the other hand, "I can say that from Cape Horn to the thirty-fifth parallel I have never known a single woman who was faithful to her husband. Ideas of right and wrong are so reversed on this point that a woman there regards it as shameful not to have a lover." (Poinsett must have said, or at least meant, the thirtieth parallel, since the thirty-fifth forms the northern boundary of Mississippi, Alabama, and Georgia; most of South Carolina and all of Louisiana and Florida are also below it.)

Tocqueville of course tended to idealize the domestic role of American women, and here Martineau provides a much-needed counterbalance. In a chapter titled "Political Non-existence of Women," she lays out a catalog of civil and property rights denied by law to American women, and briskly dismisses the usual counterargument: "I cannot enter upon the commonest order of pleas of all—those which relate to the virtual influence of woman, her swaying the judgment and will of man through the heart, and so forth. One might as well try to dissect the morning mist." Worst of all, she thought, was the lot of southern women, whose husbands treated them with chivalrous condescension while sleeping with slaves (and callously putting their own mulatto children up for sale). "Where the busiest and more engrossing concerns of life must wear one aspect to the one sex, and another to the other, there is an end to all wholesome confidence and sympathy, and woman sinks to be the ornament of her husband's house." A planter's wife bitterly told Martineau that she was nothing more than "the chief slave of the harem." Martineau was especially angered by attempts to treat these issues as merely social rather than political. "The principle of the equal rights of both halves of the human race is all we have to do with here. It is the true democratic principle which can never be seriously controverted, and only for a short time evaded. Governments can derive their just powers only from the consent of the governed."

Tocqueville did understand that although racial intermarriage was strictly prohibited, slave owners routinely slept with slaves and sired offspring who could not be openly acknowledged. In *Democracy in America* he described a memorable encounter (he didn't mention where it occurred):

> In the South of the Union I met an old man who had formerly had illicit relations with one of his Negro women. He had had several children by her, who, as they came into the world, became their father's slaves. Several times he had thought of at least granting them freedom in his will, but as the years slid by, he was unable to overcome the obstacles to emancipation imposed by the legislature. By now old age had overtaken him and he was about to die. He imagined his sons being dragged from market to market, passing from their father's authority to a stranger's whip. These horrible images threw his expiring imagination into delirium. I saw him prey to all the anguish of despair, and I understood then how nature can avenge wounds that are inflicted on her by the laws.

On the question of emancipation Poinsett took a hard line, even while acknowledging (perhaps perfunctorily) that slavery was "a great evil." Like all the Southerners Tocqueville talked with, and like many Northerners, too, Poinsett was convinced that it was now economically impossible to set the slaves free. For one thing, intensive single-crop agriculture in cotton and tobacco was dependent on them; for another, they represented valuable property whose loss would bankrupt their masters. Not only did Poinsett oppose emancipation in general; he even opposed it for individuals. "The most dangerous men are the emancipated blacks. Their presence spreads unrest among the slaves and makes them want to be free. I believe it's indispensable to take away the right of masters to grant freedom, above all in their wills. Washington gave a very bad example when he liberated his slaves at his death."

It would in fact have been hard to find any Southerner in the 1830s who thought that slavery could conceivably be abolished, even though its economic contribution was unclear (and is still being debated today). Many of Tocqueville's informants thought that paid labor might actually have been cheaper in the long run, since children and elderly slaves who couldn't work still had to be supported, but they also said that slavery had become a huge capital investment that had to be respected. This was a very strange variant of capitalism, in which slave owners traded and speculated in a market economy, while the labor force was utterly excluded from participation.

The Scottish traveler Basil Hall heard the tired excuse that "the climate of a great part of the Carolinas renders it nearly impossible for white men to work in the fields," and was surprised that many planters were willing to admit "that there was not naturally and essentially any intellectual difference between the two races." Their preferred rationalization was that American slaves were actually more comfortable and secure than farmworkers in Europe. Martineau was told that they were "the most contented, happy, industrious peasantry in the world." She noticed that the word "slaves" was strictly avoided; planters referred to them as their "force," "hands," "Negroes," or "people." Another favorite argument of apologists was that classical civilization had likewise been founded on slavery, and that Greek and Roman masters were often outrageously harsh. Beaumont, noting that Jefferson cited a Roman who killed his slave for breaking a goblet, denied that this proved anything. If ancient masters did sometimes indulge in capricious violence, the southern planter had good economic reasons for treating his human property more prudently.

When southern politicians talked about equality, they meant white equality sustained by racial inequality. A Mississippi senator declared, "All men are equal; I mean of course white men. Negroes are not men, within the meaning of the Declaration." Since it seemed likely that if slavery were abolished, many whites would slide into poverty and be forced to do menial work, a startling degree of doublethink was freely practiced. "Break down slavery," a congressman from Virginia declared, "and you would with the same blow destroy the great democratic principle of equality among men."

In Britain and France there were by this time no more slaves, and campaigns were well under way for emancipation in the overseas colonies, where a relatively small number of slave owners would need to be given financial compensation. Just two years after Tocqueville's American visit, the British Emancipation Act freed the slaves in the West Indies, and he himself would work energetically on behalf of French emancipation there. But if British visitors were full of moral superiority, many were also full of prejudice. Dickens called slavery "that most hideous blot and foul disgrace," but his criticism owed as much to dislike of America as to sympathy with slaves. When the Civil War came, Dickens strongly supported the Southern side, and after emancipation he revisited America and remarked with obvious contempt that in Baltimore, "the ghost of slavery haunts the houses, and the old untidy, incapable, lounging, shambling black serves you as a free man. Free, of course he ought to be; but the stupendous absurdity of making him a voter glares out of every roll of his eye, stretch of his mouth, and bump of his head. I have a strong impression that the race must fade out of the States very fast." Marryat thought it droll that a museum in St. Louis exhibited a huge stuffed alligator "and to make him more poetical, he has a stuffed Negro in his mouth." Still more telling was his contemptuous comment that while he was waiting to be served at a Lexington restaurant, "three Negro lads, about twelve or fourteen years old, came in and, in a most authoritative tone, ordered three glasses of soda water."

When Sam Houston, back on the Mississippi, had described the extreme independence of Indian life, he added that the institution of slavery produced a diametrically opposite result: "The ordinary Negro has been a slave since before he was born. Without pleasures and without needs, he's useless to himself. His first conception of life makes him understand that he's someone else's property, that any care for his future isn't up to him, and that for him the very act of thinking is a useless gift of providence." Tocqueville was struck by this insight, commenting in a note that the subjected races were polar opposites. "The Negro, as a result of being a slave, loses his liking for freedom and the very possibility of it; the Indian, as a result of being free, grows incapable of civilizing himself. The one cannot learn to be free; the other cannot learn to set boundaries to his freedom." In *Democracy in America* he would declare with epigrammatic concision, "The Negro is placed at the furthest boundary of servitude, the Indian at the extreme limit of liberty." And he would describe, with impressive sympathy, the ways in which slaves had been robbed of their identity. "At one blow oppression took almost all the privileges of humanity from the descendants of Africans. The Negro of the United States has lost even the memory of his homeland. He no longer understands the language his forefathers spoke, he has abjured their religion, and he has forgotten their mores. While thus ceasing to belong to Africa, he has, however, acquired no right to the good things of Europe. He remains trapped between two societies, isolated between two peoples, sold by one and rejected by the other, and in the entire universe there is only the home of his master to give him the incomplete image of a fatherland."

Tocqueville was uncompromising about the immorality of slavery: "It is impossible to imagine anything more contrary to nature and to the secret instincts of the human heart than this kind of subjugation." But he came to the grim conclusion that the South would never change unless overwhelming force were brought to bear. In the ancient world, he observed, slaves were acquired in war, were of the same race as their masters, and were symbols of luxury who were often better educated than their owners. When given freedom, as often happened, they could quickly merge with the population at large. But in America the slaves were members of a visibly different race. Furthermore, they were forbidden education; Beaumont noted that in South Carolina the penalty was as severe for educating a slave as for killing him. And black people continued to be segregated in essential ways even when they were set free. Tocqueville thought it a shameful irony that Christian nations, in defiance of their own religious teachings, had not only instituted modern slavery but had also given it a racial basis unknown in the ancient world. "Christianity had abolished slavery; the Christians of the six-teenth century reestablished it. But they admitted it only as an exception to their social system, and they took pains to confine it to a single one of the races of man. They have thus dealt a wound to humanity that is smaller, but infinitely more difficult to heal." James Madison, living in retirement in rural Virginia, told Martineau that if he had the power to work a miracle, "he would make all the blacks white, and then he could do away with slavery in twenty-four hours."

Tocqueville was aware that the American Colonization Society had bought land in Africa that would become the Republic of Liberia, and there was a lot of talk about repatriating blacks there, but he could see that it was only talk. Quite apart from the enormous numbers that would need to move, there were no funds to buy slaves their freedom, with the result that the only colonists were freemen, and few freemen had any wish to leave their country for a strange land. As for the abolitionist movement, it was only just getting under way. At the beginning of 1831, William Lloyd Garrison launched his weekly *Liberator* in Boston with the manifesto "I am in earnest—I will not equivocate—I will not excuse—AND I WILL BE HEARD," but it is not clear that Tocqueville did hear of it. Martineau noted that the South was the great exception to freedom of publication, and that racial incidents went totally unreported there because "the laws against the press are as peremptory as in the most despotic countries of Europe." Southern apologists for slavery, of course, were free to say anything they liked.

Like most of his informants, Tocqueville feared that a horrific racial war would someday break out, a bloodbath in which there could be no winners. "The threat of a conflict, more or less distant but inevitable, between blacks and southern whites haunts the American imagination continually, like a bad dream." He concluded soberly, "God forbid that I should try to justify the principle of Negro slavery, as some American authors do. I only say that those who accepted this dreadful principle in the past are not equally free to abandon it today." If the slaves ever did win their freedom, he predicted, discrimination would persist, and they would resent it so bitterly that it would lead to "the most horrible of all civil wars, and perhaps the destruction of one of the two races." In his manuscript notes he admitted with distress, "I avow that if I had the misfortune to live in a country where slavery had been introduced, and if I held in my hand the power to free the Negroes, I would be wary of opening it."

Just as Tocqueville's lack of prejudice was remarkable, so also his treatment of the underlying issues was extraordinary in its depth and clarity. When his Canandaigua host, John C. Spencer, came to introduce the first American edition of *Democracy in America*, he wrote admiringly, "His remarks on slavery will not be found to coincide throughout either with abolitionists or with slaveholders, but they will be found to present a masterly view of a most perplexing and interesting subject, which seems to cover the whole ground and to lead to the melancholy conclusion of the utter impotency of human effort to eradicate this acknowledged evil."

On January 15, Tocqueville and Beaumont reached Norfolk, after averaging better than eighty miles a day and seeing all too little of the South. They never got to the old city of Charleston, the headquarters of the nullification movement, and in Virginia they never saw the still-vigorous eighty-year-old James Madison, whose *Federalist Papers* Tocqueville had been studying assiduously. "I have only a superficial idea of the South of the Union," Tocqueville admitted in a letter, "but to know it as well as the North, I would have had to stay there six months." There was still a month to go, but it would quickly slip away: two weeks in Washington, two more in New York, where they had already spent a total of two months, and finally to sea.

10

THE NATION'S DISAPPOINTING CAPITAL

From Norfolk the travelers took one final steamboat—there had been at least a dozen—and on January 18 they were in Washington at last. This was to have been the culmination of the whole trip, but the city was an anticlimax. Like other foreigners, they were amused by a plan that laid out a hundred square miles and anticipated a population of a million but as yet had only thirty thousand. Beaumont commented, "Take away from America their Capitol, the poetic expression of their national pride, and the Bank of the United States, the poetic expression of their passion for money, and there won't be a single edifice left in the country that looks like a monument."

To classically trained Europeans, it seemed presumptuous to name the Capitol, still surrounded by ignoble shacks and mud, after the noblest building of ancient Rome. "In the center of the city," Tocqueville observed, "they have erected a magnificent palace to serve as the seat of Congress, and they have given it the pompous name of the Capitol." In fairness, however, he added that if the Romans had understood the science of hydraulics as well as the Americans did, they could have built pumps instead of colossal aqueducts, and if they had had steam engines, they would not have needed to cover Europe laboriously with paved roads. And in a way, he thought, the disproportionate grandeur of the Capitol was an apt reflection of the culture it symbolized. "Nowhere do citizens seem smaller than in a democracy, and nowhere does the nation itself seem greater . . . Thus it happens that the same people who inhabit cramped dwellings often aim at the gigantic in their public monuments."

Washington in those days also illustrated the impossibility of foretelling the future. Anticipating a populous city with a busy maritime trade, the planners had cut down trees as far as the eye could see to make room for the opulent buildings that would soon arise. But alas, "the population never arrived, and the shipping never came up the Potomac. Washington today presents the image of an arid plain scorched by the sun, on which are dispersed two or three sumptuous edifices and the five or six villages that make up the town." Two decades later it would still be much the same, as Henry Adams testified in recalling his own first impressions. Outside his grandmother's town house "he found himself on an earth-road, or village street, with wheel-tracks meandering from the colonnade of the Treasury hard by, to the white marble columns and fronts of the Post Office and Patent Office which faced each other in the distance, like white Greek temples in the abandoned gravel-pits of a deserted Syrian city."

Back in Philadelphia, Beaumont had confidently predicted that they would spend a full month in Washington, going deeply into the mysteries of government. In Norfolk he had reiterated, "During our stay in Washington, which can't be less than three weeks, we're going to complete the labors we've begun. We'll find all the political notables of the United States collected there, and we know enough people in this country already to be sure of finding a warm welcome." In the end the three weeks shrank to two, and all they wanted was to go home. "This letter, my dear father," Tocqueville wrote after a week in Washington, "will perhaps be the last that I'll write to you from America— God be praised!"

He did know by now what kind of book he wanted to write: not a comprehensive survey of the United States, for which even a nine-month acquaintance would have been too brief, but a focused study of

PRESIDENT'S HOUSE, WASHINGTON

Not yet known familiarly as the White House, it stands all alone with open country just beyond and with cows and sheep grazing on the grounds. There was no running water inside.

society and government with "more or less direct connections to our own social and political condition; a work of that kind could have both permanent interest and an interest for the present moment." He was right on both counts. To his brother Édouard he went into more detail: "I've talked a lot and thought a lot about what I've been seeing, and I believe that if I have enough time after I get home, I might write something quite tolerable about the United States. To try to cover everything would be crazy. I can't aim at complete exactitude, I haven't seen enough for that, but I think I already know much more about this country than we've ever heard of in France, and some parts of the picture could be of great interest, timely interest even."

Because there were so many foreign diplomats in Washington, French was widely understood, and Beaumont cheerfully reported that "you'd think you were in a Paris salon." There were plenty of old acquaintances whom it was a pleasure to meet again. Edward Livingston and his beautiful wife from New York were there, as was the ubiquitous Poinsett, whom they had met in Philadelphia and again on the road. Beaumont commented, "I've never known anyone who keeps rolling along like him; he has made the crossing from America to Europe and back again twenty-two times." The French ambassador gave a dinner party for Representative Edward Everett, at whose Boston home they had first met John Quincy Adams, and Adams himself, who was now taking his seat in the House of Representatives, invited them to dine. But no matter how many prominent people were on hand, Tocqueville was no longer interested in pumping them for information. He remarked complacently, "It's not a matter of getting ideas from them about things we're unfamiliar with. In our conversations we review everything we already more or less knew, and we settle any doubtful points."

The reason for bypassing Charleston and hurrying to Washington had been to see the new Congress in session, and Tocqueville and Beaumont did go there a number of times, but it made little impression. The only reaction either of them recorded was Beaumont's vague comment: "The debates are serious and imposing, and only rarely do political passions get involved and make them disorderly." They were probably unaware of the ritual nature of the long vapid speeches, or of the serious negotiations that went on behind the scenes. Also, then as now, Congress was a club in which even the most heated debate was a kind of game. "You may see senators and representatives in Washington fighting deadly battles," Francis Lieber remarked, "and an hour later walking and joking together." What other foreign visitors usually emphasized was the coarseness of American manners. Frances Trollope was revolted to see congressmen sitting "in the most unseemly attitudes, a large majority with their hats on, and nearly all spitting to an excess that decency forbids me to describe." Dickens did describe the "incessant, remorseless spitting," and called Washington "the headquarters of tobacco-tinctured saliva." Characteristically, the aristocratic Tocqueville and Beaumont were more tolerant of this kind of thing than the middle-class Dickens and Trollope.

What might have been a high point of the visit, but sadly failed to be, was a meeting at the White House with Andrew Jackson himself.

Unfortunately, numerous anti-Jackson informants had given the Frenchmen a low opinion of him, and Jackson was just being polite to a couple of young foreigners, never suspecting that his image in a classic work of political theory was at stake. "He is not a man of genius," Beaumont said; "he was formerly celebrated as a duelist and hothead." He and Tocqueville could not get used to the idea that a head of state would allow himself to be addressed as "sir" rather than "Your Highness," and would receive visitors all by himself rather than amid a brilliant entourage. In those days it was easy for total strangers to get into the White House. When John Quincy Adams was president, a conversation with Henry Clay was interrupted by an unannounced visitor who turned out to be a dentist, whereupon Adams excused Clay and (as he recorded in his diary) "took the opportunity to have a decayed tooth drawn."

ANDREW JACKSON

In *Democracy in America*, Tocqueville would write dismissively that Jackson was "a man of violent temperament and mediocre abilities" who had gained prominence solely by virtue of his victory at New Orleans twenty years before, an achievement "that wouldn't be noticed for long except in a country that never has any battles." In his notebook before meeting Jackson, he was still more contemptuous. "How could one doubt the pernicious influence of military glory in a republic? What prompted the people to choose General Jackson, who, it seems, is a very mediocre man? What continues to assure him their votes in spite of opposition by the enlightened classes? The Battle of New Orleans. And yet that battle was a very ordinary feat of arms, and the people who allow themselves to be thus captivated are the most antimilitary, prosaic, and chilly that exist on earth."

Tocqueville himself, who had once dreamed of following his brothers into the army—until the abbé Lesueur protested that it would be a waste of his fine mind—was certainly not antimilitary. He declared in *Democracy in America*, "I do not wish to speak ill of war; it nearly always enlarges a people's thinking and elevates its heart." The trouble with the New Orleans engagement was that it seemed both provincial and irrelevant, having been fought two weeks after the Treaty of Ghent, unbeknownst to anyone in America, had already ended the war. Tocqueville believed that only great generals, like the Waterloo rivals Napoleon and Wellington, deserved political eminence. In fact, he was quite starstruck by the memory of Napoleon, much though he deplored his imperial rule, and when he had an opportunity to hear Wellington speak in the House of Lords—even though the great man was awkward and ill at ease—he reported, "*La gloire* is invested with such extraordinary prestige that when I saw him take off his hat and begin to speak, I felt a shudder run through my veins." Tocqueville's attitude reflected an aristocratic blind spot, which had perhaps been reinforced by seeing earnest but amateurish militiamen at the Fourth of July celebration in Albany. Achille Murat, son of a French general and himself a colonel in the Florida militia, could have explained that those unprepossessing characters were far from typical of the nation as a whole, and that it had been backwoods militiamen who destroyed the cream of the

British army at New Orleans. In his book on America Murat mentioned that the three public holidays observed throughout the land were Independence Day, Washington's Birthday, and the anniversary of the Battle of New Orleans.

More surprising is Tocqueville's reluctance to recognize the Tennessean's charisma as a political leader. When he had been traveling in the West, he was much taken with the region's energy and independence, but now he was being recaptured by the eastern gravity field. When he asked Adams why the western states seemed so different from New England, the ex-president dourly replied, "That's due almost entirely to the point of departure. New England was populated by a well-educated and deeply religious race. The West is being populated by all the adventurers to be found in the Union, people for the most part without principles or morality, who have been driven out of the older states by poverty or bad behavior, or who have no other passion than to get rich."

Jackson once commented sardonically that his opponents thought him a savage "who always carried a scalping knife in one hand and a tomahawk in the other," and his supporters relished that image. To celebrate his first inaugural, his admirers in Philadelphia bought a buffalo, tied it to a tree, and pumped it full of bullets. When the animal failed to die, they finished it off with an ax. Jackson was, indeed, a complex and paradoxical figure. A nineteenth-century biographer concluded, "He was the most candid of men, and was capable of the profoundest dissimulation. A most law-defying, law-obeying citizen . . . A democratic autocrat. An urbane savage. An atrocious saint."

In addition to personal feelings, however, Tocqueville had intellectual reasons to depreciate the first populist presidency. Adams stood as an exemplar of the old ideal of civic virtue, willing to lose an election rather than pander to the people's wishes. Thinking about the Jackson phenomenon, Tocqueville came up with two rather contradictory opinions. On the one hand, he believed that the executive was the weakest branch of government, but on the other hand he thought Jackson's relationship with the electorate empowered him to "trample his personal enemies underfoot wherever he finds them more easily than any other president," and to treat Congress "with almost insulting disdain."

It was true in a way, as Tocqueville disapprovingly said, that "the desire to be reelected dominates the president's thoughts, and the entire policy of his administration is directed toward that goal." But it need not follow that "the president of the United States is merely a docile tool in the hands of the majority. He likes what they like and hates what they hate, anticipates their wishes and their complaints, and bends to their least desires." By the time Tocqueville finished writing his book, it was almost quixotic to assert that the executive was weak, for by then Jackson was vetoing bills with unprecedented frequency and sternly imposing his will in several major controversies. Tocqueville's conclusion was that he had learned to exploit popularity in a totally new way, with potentially ominous implications for the future of democracy. "After having thus bowed before the majority in order to win its favor, General Jackson rises up again and advances toward those goals which the majority itself pursues, or those which it does not see with a jealous eye, overturning all obstacles before him."

One reason why Tocqueville undervalued Jackson was that in Philadelphia he had been greatly impressed by one of the president's most able opponents, Nicholas Biddle, the head of the Second Bank of the United States, who exerted extraordinary power over the American financial system. Since the federal government printed no paper money, notes issued by individual banks had long served as the principal means of exchange. But bank failures often rendered such notes worthless, and in a crisis known as the Panic of 1819, a period of wild speculation had been followed by a crash that brought massive unemployment and foreclosures, impoverishing the wealthy as well as everyone else. Thomas Jefferson and Andrew Jackson were among those it took down, and Jackson never forgave or forgot. The Second Bank was intended to stabilize the system by acting, in effect, as a modern central bank, expanding or contracting the money supply as the business cycle seemed to dictate, but it was still a private corporation whose avowed purpose was to enrich its stockholders.

NICHOLAS BIDDLE

By the time of Tocqueville's arrival, the Second Bank and its provincial satellites had become the focus of bitter populist resentment; a senator from Ohio charged that they did their work "not in the light of day, but in darkness and in secret, between the walls of subterraneous caverns." The banks' powers and procedures were indeed bafflingly complicated, and as a historian says, "One of the important functions of Jacksonian rhetoric was to help individuals order their world. It made the unseen visible, the complex simple, the confused orderly, and the impersonal personal." In particular, the impersonal was made personal in the form of Nicholas Biddle, whose enemies called him Czar Nicholas the First. Senator Thomas Hart Benton of Missouri proclaimed, in the bombastic rhetoric of the day, "All the flourishing cities of the West are mortgaged to this money power . . . They are in the jaws of the monster! A lump of butter in the mouth of a dog! One gulp, one swallow, and all is gone!" All of this would come to a head just a year later, when Jackson vetoed a bill renewing the Second Bank's charter, asserting— as was then almost unprecedented—his right to reject a bill on the simple grounds that he disapproved of it. In the years that followed, he pursued a campaign of open warfare against the Second Bank, which he succeeded in destroying in 1836, a Pyrrhic victory that has been blamed for provoking another financial crash.

It is fair to say that here, as in so many other ways, the tide of modernization was creating new puzzles that few people at the time were in any position to solve. For all its populism, the Jacksonian program promoted economic laissez-faire, as the result of a conviction that Whigs controlled banking and commerce and would use a strong central government to keep ordinary people down. What was happening, really, was an imperfectly understood collision of value systems that were often incompatible and sometimes contradictory. Historians have described them in various ways: as a tension between the ethical principle of equality and the competitive model of society; or as a gap between the model of economic individualism and a developing corporate reality; or as the process by which "history's most revolutionary force, the capitalist market, was wresting the American future from history's most conservative force, the land."

Tocqueville needed, in fact, to postulate a president who was strong and weak at the same time—not so much a characterization of the actual person as a feature of the theory he was developing. Jackson was strong because he had a forceful personality, was unafraid of picking fights and vetoing bills he didn't like, and enjoyed the support of an unprecedented populist majority. On the other hand, the checks and balances that the founders had built into the Constitution were an effective defense against authoritarian rule. What impressed Tocqueville most of all as he studied *The Federalist Papers* was how abstract ideas could be given life in practical institutions. By opposing a relatively elitist Senate to a relatively democratic House, for example, "the framers adopted a middle way that reconciled two systems that were theoretically irreconcilable." The federal government was empowered to enforce its laws even if the states tried to oppose them, unlike earlier weak confederations in Switzerland or Holland, which meant that "the Constitution rests in fact on an entirely new theory, which has to be recognized as a great discovery in the political science of our times." And the provision that decisions of the Supreme Court would be final, short of amending the Constitution itself, showed once again that "theory has been put into practice." (The unwritten British constitution, very differently, was whatever Parliament said it was.) Since thirteen amendments to the Constitution were already in place, moreover, the system clearly had room in it for evolution over time. Yet potent though the Supreme Court was, it could not afford to ignore popular consensus. "Its power is immense," Tocqueville wrote, "but it is a power of opinion. They are all-powerful insofar as the people consent to obey the law, but they can do nothing if the people scorn it . . . They need to be statesmen, able to discern the spirit of their time."

All of these checks and balances were the product of the eighteenth-century founders' preference for a republic controlled by an elite rather than a popular democracy. Adams was a living representative of the old patrician attitude. When Anti-Federalists "assumed the name of Democrats," Adams complained, they were improperly asserting "that democracy is the government of the *whole* people and nothing but the people . . . not the purest, not the strongest, not the wealthiest, not the wisest." Jacksonians did call themselves "the democracy," and they denounced the Senate and the electoral college as elitist anachronisms; their goal was precisely the "democracy without limit" that Tocqueville's Cincinnati informants had deplored. As the election of the year 2000 reminded Americans, the electoral college is inconsistent with majority rule, as is the provision of two senators from each state. Less well-known is the fact that until the Seventeenth Amendment in 1913, senators were chosen by state legislatures rather than by popular vote. Tocqueville approved of the original arrangement, believing that it produced statesmen who were more distinguished than the "vulgar" small-town lawyers and businessmen who filled the House of Representatives.

At bottom, as Hugh Brogan observes, it was Tocqueville's French experience that led him to underestimate the power of the presidency. Partly this was due to the dogmatic view of French liberals that a representative assembly, not the executive, should be supreme. Partly it was due to the historical specter of Napoleon's dictatorship. And partly it was due to the real contrast between the American presidency and the French monarchy of Tocqueville's time. The French king had lifelong tenure and was head of a highly centralized government, whereas the president was head of one of three branches in a decentralized one. The king had the power to dissolve parliament at will, appoint the members of its upper house, and veto legislation with no possibility of being overridden. Nothing like that was true in America.

By now, at any event, the travelers had had more than enough. Beaumont wrote to his mother, "In spite of my efforts to pay attention to the interesting objects around me, I have one perpetual preoccupation, and that's the thought of my return." Tocqueville told Poinsett, who was about to sail for France himself, "I admit that we're already living more in France than in America. Until now your compatriots' agreeable hospitality has made us almost forget that we were far from our own country. We still encounter the same kindness and we still feel the same gratitude, but it's no longer enough. We're realizing for the first time that we're strangers among you."

On February 3, they set off for Philadelphia, and the day after that they were in New York. There had been some thought of returning by way of Liverpool, so as to have a glimpse of England, but a frightening cholera epidemic was spreading through Europe, and there would be a possibility of long delay in quarantine. They resolved, therefore, to sail for Le Havre on the next packet boat, which was scheduled to leave on the tenth. Unfortunately, its departure was canceled, and they ended up idling another ten days away with desultory dinner parties and farewell visits. On February 20, they were finally at sea in the *Henri IV*, and some time in late March they stepped ashore in France.

In the final words of Beaumont's novel, his hero likewise sails from New York for Le Havre, and "on glimpsing the coast of France, which he expected never to see again, he wept with joy. Restored to his dear fatherland, he never left it more." America was to make Beaumont's reputation and Tocqueville's far greater fame, but neither of them ever saw America again.

11

BUILDING A MASTERPIECE

When Tocqueville came home from America with piles of unsorted notes and a trunkful of documents, he was nowhere near ready to write. He knew that if his book was to combine detailed insights into American culture with large views on the theory of democracy, there was still much to learn. First he would need to undertake what has been called his second voyage to America, an interior one this time, with intensive research and thinking that would eventually take eight years to complete. What he knew for certain was that democracy was the wave of the future—a wave, indeed, that might drown his country. "Democracy!" he wrote in an unpublished note. "Don't you recognize that these are the waters of the deluge? Can't you see them advancing ceaselessly with gradual but irresistible force? Already they cover the fields and the towns, they roll over the ruined battlements of castles, they have begun to wash against the steps of thrones . . . Let us attempt, then, to foresee the future with open eyes and steady gaze. Rather than trying to erect impotent dikes, let us seek rather to construct the sacred guardian ark that must carry the human race upon this shoreless sea." The allusion was obvious: Louis XV was supposed to have said "Après moi, le déluge."

Tocqueville was determined to make a difference in the fierce debate between reactionaries who wanted the ancien régime restored unaltered and radicals who wanted to turn everything upside down. But he had a low opinion of the current liberal compromise, the jerry-built constitutional monarchy of Louis-Philippe that was being defended by theorists known as *doctrinaires*, including the historian François Guizot, whose lectures he had attended in Paris some years before. At that time Guizot had given Tocqueville an inspiring vision of what he later called "the river of humanity down to our own day," presenting history as an immense, dynamic process and stressing the triumph of democracy. But now he was just another politician, strongly opposed to universal suffrage and in Tocqueville's view committed to fatal inconsistency, promoting equality in civil rights but inequality in political rights. The contrast with France as it might have been was painful. After Tocqueville had been home for a few months, he wrote to a friend, "I'm trying to avoid making two worlds of it, a moral one in which I can still feel enthusiasm for everything beautiful and good, and a political one where I lie flat on my belly so as to be more comfortable on the dunghill people are trampling."

Meanwhile, the penitentiary report had to be completed, and it was not an inviting task. Fatigue and depression caught up with the highly strung Tocqueville, and he wrote ruefully to Beaumont that he spent all day lounging feebly in a big armchair while waiting for inspiration to strike. "I'm getting weary of this way of 'working,' because I notice that I'm thinking about everything except prisons." Since it was becoming obvious that Tocqueville would never accomplish anything in the armchair, Beaumont persuaded him to travel to some French prisons to obtain material for comparisons. They were shockingly backward, mingling prisoners indiscriminately and allowing them to bribe their jailers for favors, but Tocqueville was equally displeased with a progressive prison in Switzerland that seemed to coddle inmates. "Discipline whose mildness and painstaking details are suitable only for a candy-box prison like the one in Geneva: full-size bed, baths every month, library, recreation on Sunday, limitations on punishments, wages paid at release. Everything is taken care of like a boudoir for a girlfriend."

Tocqueville had more in common than might be supposed with the stern Elam Lynds of Auburn, New York.

It soon became apparent that if the report was ever to get written, it would be up to Beaumont to draft the entire thing, which he did with his usual good cheer, while Tocqueville scribbled such marginal comments as occurred to him along the way. In the volatile political climate of the time, the official document had to be composed with great care, and Tocqueville's respect for the ostensibly liberal regime kept going down. "You would have smiled inwardly," he told Beaumont, "to see with what admirable ease these leaders of the liberalism of 1828, these makers of the revolution of 1830, readily slash to ribbons the fundamental principles of civil liberty, which we ourselves—former royalists—would never abandon at any price. In truth, the world of politics is a dirty arena." After a Paris riot in June that was put down at the cost of eight hundred dead or wounded, the government announced that the rioters would be tried by military courts, not civil ones. Tocqueville commented, "It's distressing to see how rapidly we're reshaping ourselves for tyranny."

On the opposing conservative side, some of Tocqueville's relatives were getting themselves mixed up in a hopeless plot to overthrow Louis-Philippe and reinstate the ancien régime. To his horror, his cousin and close friend Louis de Kergorlay was arrested and committed to prison in Marseille. Tocqueville hastened there to see if he could help, which he couldn't (Kergorlay was eventually tried and acquitted a year later), so he went on to Toulon to pursue the prison investigations. A few days later he picked up a newspaper and was thunderstruck to find that less than two months after their return from America, Beaumont was out of a job. As a test of loyalty, his superiors had ordered him to serve as prosecutor in an unsavory trial that had menacing political implications. A couple of years previously a prince had been found hanged, and although it was ruled a suicide, there were widespread rumors that his mistress had murdered him before he could change his will and leave his fortune to another noble family instead of to the family of Louis-Philippe. With the king's undoubted encouragement, the mistress was now bringing a libel suit against the family that

had lost out, and if Beaumont were to accept the assignment, his relatives and friends would see him as a craven tool of the despised bour-
geois king. So he refused, as his superiors must have expected he
would, and he was immediately fired.

As soon as he learned what had happened, Tocqueville submitted
his own resignation:

> Being at present in Toulon, where I have come to investigate the penal
> ships and other prisons of the town, I have only today learned from the
> *Moniteur* of May 16 of the harsh and, I may say, supremely unjust action
> that Monsieur the Minister of Justice has taken against Monsieur G. de
> Beaumont. Long bound in close friendship to the man whom this dis-
> missal has struck down, whose principles I share, and whose conduct I
> approve, I believe it my duty to associate myself voluntarily with his
> fate and to quit with him a career in which performance and conscien-
> tiousness are no protection against unmerited disgrace. I have the
> honor to request, Monsieur the Public Prosecutor, that you will be so
> good as to bring to the attention of Monsieur the Minister of Justice
> my resignation as *juge suppléant* at the court of Versailles.

"To tell the truth," Beaumont commented much later, "the magistracy
lost more by this action than Alexis de Tocqueville did. By giving up
his duties, he became once more the absolute master of his own time,
of which he was to make such noble use."

On a happier note, Tocqueville resumed his relationship with the
Englishwoman Marie Mottley, and by now he was almost as fluent in
her language as she was in his. She was good-looking and intelligent,
and if her high-strung temperament often caused her emotional distress, it encouraged him to confide in her as a kindred spirit. A year
before their marriage in 1835, which continued to be delayed until he
could finally overcome his family's snobbish resistance, he wrote to her,
"I will never be happy, Marie, that's certain. Nothing in me is harmoni-
ous. Along with limited and incomplete powers I have vast desires; I
have delicate health and an inexpressible need for activity and emo-
tion; I have a taste for the good and passions that lead me astray." At

another time, when he was in Paris and she was staying with his family in the country, he wrote with unusual fervor,

> I'm unhappy, but I love you inexpressibly . . . I'm spending one of the most dismal times of my life here; an unceasing storm has been brewing in the depths of my soul. I've been a perpetual victim of irrational discouragement, of melancholy without an object, of feverish but fruitless activity . . . Who will ever depict the incessant tumult of my heart, who will take the trouble to listen to it, if not you? Who will understand the pettiness that fills my soul and yet the immoderate, enormous desire that draws it forever forward toward what is great?

The attraction was definitely physical as well as spiritual. On one occasion Tocqueville wrote to a friend, "I saw her arrive in the evening, charming from head to toe, tender, witty, a veritable siren . . . The fact is that no one could be more seductive than she was yesterday."

After their marriage they moved into the old family château at Tocqueville and began elaborate renovations; it would always be their favored retreat. "How often has he told me," Beaumont wrote after Tocqueville's death, "that his marriage, criticized by certain 'wise' persons, was the most sensible action of his life!" To be sure, they were often apart for extended periods, and Tocqueville was regularly (not to say compulsively) unfaithful in the style he had found so surprisingly unacceptable to Americans. And to his great disappointment, since dynastic succession meant a lot to him, they never had children.

At about the same time, Beaumont, too, made a happy marriage, with a granddaughter of Lafayette's, and got busy with his own American book. In the hope of attracting readers, he made the unlucky decision to cast it as a novel, admitting ingenuously on the first page, "I know nothing of the novelist's art. Therefore one must not look in this book for plots developed with foresight, nor skillfully managed situations, nor complex events—in a word, none of those things that are commonly used to arouse interest, sustain it, and create suspense." He was right about that. *Marie* is full of valuable information (and has often been quoted in this book), but it is an unusually bad novel, melodramatic and boring at the same time. And was it on purpose that he gave his heroine, who suffers cruel prejudice on account of her mixed blood, the same name as the wife whom Tocqueville had been discouraged from marrying for social reasons?

After a year's work the prison report was published with the title *On the Penitentiary System in the United States and Its Application in France*, and was widely praised for its judiciousness and fullness of detail. At Beaumont's insistence, Tocqueville accepted credit as joint author, and they became so closely identified that caricaturists started calling them "Tocqumont." Privately, Tocqueville acknowledged that Beaumont had written the whole thing. "I contributed only my observations and a few notes."

Whenever he felt boredom and inertia dragging him down, Tocqueville's remedy was travel, and he took this opportunity to visit England, as he had hoped to do before the cholera scare deterred him. (Cholera did rage through England and France—by the time they returned from America, it was killing twelve thousand a month in Paris—but no one in the Tocqueville and Beaumont families was affected.) England was deeply disappointing, and Tocqueville found himself unexpectedly nostalgic for America, where he and Beaumont had been welcome everywhere from mansions to log cabins. The English lived up to their reputation as standoffish snobs, and as an aristocrat himself he felt profoundly insulted. He wrote to Beaumont from London, "It would be difficult to tell you anything about the impressions I've had since I set foot in this immense metropolis. I'm in a constant daze, continually aware of my own nonentity . . . In short, in nothing here do I recognize our America. But be that as it may, here I am, wandering over the surface of London, like a gnat on a haystack."

What did appeal to Tocqueville was feudal relics that stirred his romantic imagination, such as the ruined castle at Kenilworth made famous by Walter Scott. "Imagine an Italian night," he wrote to Marie, "with not a breath of wind, a cloudless sky, and the moon at the full. Add to this a fiery steed moving nimbly between your legs, all the centuries of chivalry in your head, and a bit of youthful fire still coursing in your veins—and then you'll understand that, so to speak, I wasn't touching the ground." Once again the idealized Middle Ages offered a refuge from the modern world, just as they had when he got absorbed in Shakespeare's *Henry V* in a snowbound cabin in Tennessee.

Back at the château and resuming work on his own book, Tocqueville finally began to gather momentum. He wrote provocatively to Beaumont, "Since arriving here, I've hurled myself at America in a sort of fury . . . I think about hardly anything else, even when I'm pulling my cock. My ideas keep getting bigger and more general. Is this good or bad?" But there was nothing playful about the project itself, and at one point he jotted a guiding mantra: "The future of democracy: the sole poetic idea of our time. An immense, indefinite idea. An era of renewal, of total change in the social system of humanity."

Always Tocqueville tried to clarify his analysis by posing large concepts—ideal types, as sociologists would later call them—against each other: North and South, America and France, aristocracy and democracy, past and present. This was a lifelong habit, as well as a principle of analysis in the Aristotelian tradition, and in his opinion it was the only way to gain some distance from unexamined assumptions. "It is one of the singular weaknesses of our mind," he once wrote, "that we can't judge objects and see them in the clear light of day unless we place other objects next to them."

With so much that was novel to describe, Tocqueville found terminology to be a constant problem. At one point he asked Beaumont for advice on a sentence he couldn't get right: "I ended with the word 'states' because I first put 'nations' and then 'peoples'; but 'states' makes a rather feeble impression. And anyway it's not certain that I don't mean 'the United States.' What do you say?" He concluded wryly, "If we go on like this, I'll end up asking your advice on how to sign my own name."

From time to time Tocqueville went to Paris to do research, and he took on a pair of young Americans there as assistants. One of them, Theodore Sedgwick, whom he had met in western Massachusetts, was a valuable resource for ideas and became a lifelong friend. The other, Francis Lippitt, was consigned to more menial tasks, summarizing state and federal statutes. He later embarked on a career in the U.S. Army, rose to the rank of brigadier general, and was one of the signers of the constitution of California. In old age Lippitt offered an astoundingly unrevealing portrait of Tocqueville as he had known him sixty years before: "His physique was not at all striking. He was slightly built, and his height did not exceed five feet six inches [actually it was five feet four] . . . There was certainly nothing about the contour of his head or the expression of his face that indicated him to be a man of more than ordinary intelligence. His manner was quiet and dignified, but somewhat cold . . . He was the most reticent man I ever met. Only twice, so far as I can remember, did he ever volunteer a remark." Lippitt never heard Tocqueville speak English, was unaware that he was writing a book, and was amazed to discover after it was published that "its author was the great political philosopher of the century."

As Tocqueville's working drafts continued to accumulate, they embodied a staggering amount of labor. Each page was divided by a line ruled down the middle, and the text would fill the right-hand side, with a tangle of additions and revisions on the left, further additions on small pieces of paper pasted on top, and yet more revisions pasted over the first ones. After his death, when Beaumont published selections from his letters, the critic Sainte-Beuve commented wonderingly, "No thinker ever created so many preliminary objections for himself before starting work. All the 'but's,' 'if's,' and 'for's' that can enter into a thoughtful mind were debated beforehand and weighed carefully in the balance."

Once he had a coherent draft, Tocqueville sought advice from people he trusted. Nearly the whole of *Democracy in America* was critiqued by his father, his brother Édouard, and his cousin Kergorlay, all of whom made helpful suggestions but predictably urged him to be less critical of aristocracy. Édouard took an especially superior tone: "It would be unfortunate to give the impression that you've come back from America as an American, in the way that people, especially French people, admire what they've gone a long way to see while disparaging what they find at home. I think it might be better, therefore, to show democratic government as less attractive, express more doubts, and maybe be more severe on its vicious aspects." Beaumont was shown this stream of reactionary objections and was disgusted by them, commenting at one point, "All of those pages seem excellent to me, and I strongly urge the author not to make the changes his foolish friends are advising."

On the whole, though, Hervé de Tocqueville was deeply proud of his youngest son, and Édouard, too, was generous when the manuscript was finished: "The overall tone of your work is grave, impartial, and philosophical. You see things from too great a height for your expressions to seem emotional. Your opinions and sympathies can be guessed, but you leave it to the reader to do so; you simply accumulate so many facts and reasons leading to the desired conclusion that the reader is forcibly led there. This is what a strongly thought-out book ought to do."

After all of his second and third and fourth thoughts, Tocqueville did bring coherence to his immense project. It was really a question of focus, as he said in recalling his journey through the northern forest: "All the laws in America derive, in a sense, from the same thoughts. The entire society is, so to speak, founded on a single fact [that is, equality as the basis of democracy], and everything follows from a single principle. America might be compared to a great forest pierced by a multitude of straight paths, all of which end up at the same place. You have only to locate the point where they meet, and everything is revealed at a single glance." He added that in England, with its much longer history and its lack of a written constitution, "the paths crisscross, and you can get a clear idea of the whole only by following out every one of them."

That was in a letter; in *Democracy in America* itself Tocqueville proposed another geographical metaphor. The ideal of social equality was like "a great river toward which every surrounding stream seems to flow." And in still another analogy with the American continent,

I will be like a traveler who emerges from a great city and climbs a nearby hill. The farther away he gets, the more the people behind him disappear from view. Their dwellings merge together, he can no longer recognize the public squares, he can barely make out the streets. But now his eye takes in the contours of the town more easily, and for the first time he grasps its shape. It seems to me that in just this way the entire future of the English race in the New World is revealing itself to me. The details of this immense tableau are still shadowy, but my gaze takes in the ensemble, and I conceive a clear idea of the whole.

In a brilliant commentary Sheldon Wolin explores the richness of Tocqueville's metaphors here: the viewer is a transient, not a native; altitude suggests lofty purpose as well as privileged viewpoint; distance suggests detachment and objectivity; and the whole picture is best understood if its individual parts are blurred and shadowy rather than confusingly distinct.

Toward the end of this first installment of *Democracy in America*, Tocqueville uttered a warning that would seem increasingly prophetic over time. When he consulted the entry on *despotisme* in the classic eighteenth-century *Encyclopédie*, he saw that it had become obsolete: "'Despotism': tyrannical, arbitrary, and absolute government by a single man." As Tocqueville understood, the French Revolution had given birth to something radically new, "the despotism of an assembly under the Republic." Equality and despotism, far from being opposites, could easily coincide. Napoleon held power by winning plebiscites and elections; he was the people's choice, and what they chose was an emperor.

In a manuscript draft Tocqueville elaborated the idea. "Despotism creates, in the souls of those who are subjected to it, a blind passion for tranquillity, a debased liking for obedience, and an incredible kind of self-contempt that ends by making them indifferent to their own interests and enemies of their own rights . . . When someone has reached this point, I will call him, if you like, a peaceable inhabitant, an upright colonist, a good *père de famille*. I'm ready for anything, so long as you don't force me to call him a citizen." Not even Tocqueville could foresee the full extent of this insight. A century later, Hitler would be the people's choice.

Robert Nisbet wrote of *Democracy in America* in 1953, when the Nazis were a recent memory and Communism was at its apogee, "It is an analysis of the nature of totalitarianism that has not been improved upon by even the most brilliant of contemporary students of the subject." What was so original was the realization that however much a totalitarian regime might persecute its scapegoat minorities, it needed its majority to feel that it embodied their deepest yearnings. In this way it could present itself as a secular religion—racial for the Nazis, class based for the Communists—that promised refuge from the anomie of modern mass civilization. One thing it absolutely could not permit would be independent associations of the kind Tocqueville favored, mini-communities that offered refuge from the monolithic state.

The first half of *Democracy in America* ends with another celebrated prophecy. Two vast nations that were still growing and changing were the United States and Russia, but with diametrically opposed ideologies:

> The American's conquests are made with the farmer's plowshare, the Russian's with the soldier's sword. To achieve his goal, the former relies on self-interest and permits the strength and intelligence of individuals to act without direction. The latter concentrates, in a sense, the whole strength of society in a single man. For the former the chief means of action is liberty; for the latter, servitude. Their starting points are different and their ways are diverse, yet each seems called by a hidden providential plan to hold one day the destiny of half the world.

From a Tocquevillean point of view, even the 1918 revolution would have altered this deep structure only superficially. When the Communists overthrew the czars, they inherited the czars' autocracy, just as the French revolutionaries had inherited the centralized bureaucracy of the Bourbon monarchy.

That Tocqueville remained attached to aristocratic values was, paradoxically, an advantage for his life's work. He saw democracy with something of an outsider's perspective, and he tried hard to be objective. After *Democracy in America* was published, he jotted a note titled "My Instinct, My Opinions," in which he declared succinctly, "I have an intellectual attraction to democratic institutions, but by instinct I am aristocratic, which is to say I despise and fear the crowd. I passionately love liberty, legality, and respect for rights, but not democracy. *Voilà*, the depth of my soul." Sainte-Beuve said wittily that "he got married to democracy with deep reservations; it was a marriage of reason and necessity, not inclination." It was this ambivalence that inspired the title of the deepest and most searching modern book on Tocqueville, Sheldon Wolin's *Tocqueville Between Two Worlds*, and as Wolin says, "In large measure he was able to see differently and further because of a premodern or 'archaic' stratum which made him supremely sensitive to the inhospitable aspects of the modern world."

But if Tocqueville often foresaw the future with uncanny prescience, it is important to recognize that he was very much a man of his time, and that despite his admiration for some aspects of democracy he remained antidemocratic in some fundamental ways. One phenomenon that he largely neglected was social class, which socialists in his time were already emphasizing, and which Marx would soon bring to the center of political theory. There was always something paradoxical in the belief Tocqueville formed at the very beginning of his stay, that America was simply one big middle class. It is relevant that he himself inherited a comfortable amount of wealth, and that although he worked hard, it was in the spirit of an aristocrat freely giving his talents; he never needed income from a job. In general, he thought of class in terms of caste and profession, not economic standing. A nobleman could be stony broke and still every inch a nobleman. Similarly, servants in France thought of themselves as a caste and were treated accordingly, whereas American servants preferred to be called the help, and "masters ask nothing from their servants but faithful and strict execution of their contracts. They don't require them to be respectful, they don't demand their love or devotion, and it suffices if they are punctual and honest."

Tocqueville accurately predicted that since most Americans owned property or expected to, there would be little sentiment for abolishing private property or even redistributing it. "They like change," he wrote, "but they dread revolutions . . . There is no country on earth where the feeling for property is more lively and anxious than in the United States, or where the majority shows less inclination for doctrines that threaten to alter in any way how goods are acquired." That was precisely why Jefferson had wanted the typical citizen to be a farmer with enough acres to support his family comfortably, and why he pushed through the Louisiana Purchase to vastly enlarge the land supply. In that way America might avoid the kind of dispossessed urban proletariat that was already causing concern in Europe. Tocqueville's contemporary the economist Michel Chevalier observed that if workers in France were starving, their only recourse was to combat their employers, whereas in America they could make a simple threat: "Raise our wages or we'll go west."

In a footnote, however, Tocqueville acknowledged an ominous possibility. In the big cities there was a growing mass of disaffected poor, mostly immigrants and freed slaves, who might indeed be a source of future unrest. He had already heard of labor strikes in New York and Philadelphia. And although he preferred not to use the word "class" in the narrowly economic sense, he was under no illusion that America was a classless society. On the contrary, he saw wide disparities between rich and poor, so wide in fact that "these classes continue to form something like two distinct nations within the same nation." But America, he went on to say, was far more egalitarian than England, where in law as well as in social experience "the welfare of the poor has often been sacrificed to that of the rich, and the rights of the greater number to the privileges of the few."

As soon as he read this passage, the English economist Nassau William Senior fired off an indignant letter to Tocqueville, arguing that English workers were better paid than workers elsewhere, and that there was no more reason for a farmworker to own his land than for a mill worker to own the mill. Tocqueville returned a deeply considered reply: "It seems to me that you give to the words 'le bien du pauvre' a restricted sense that was not at all mine. You translate it by the word 'wealth,' which applies specifically to riches. I myself meant by it everything that contributes to well-being in life: personal consideration, political rights, ease in obtaining justice, enjoyments of the mind, and a thousand other things that contribute indirectly to happiness. I believe, until it is proved to the contrary, that in England the rich have gradually drawn to themselves almost all the advantages that society bestows upon mankind."

Pondering what the American future might bring, Tocqueville wrote a prescient chapter titled "How an Aristocracy Might Emerge from Industry." In his working notes he commented, "That's what happens in countries where industry is invariably directed by a small number of great capitalists who lay down the law, which a multitude of workers receive." But if this new aristocracy resembled the old by opening up a gap between a few who were very rich and a huge number who were dreadfully poor, in the old days—which Tocqueville always idealized—there had been an affective bond between a seigneur and the people on his estate. In the modern version, on the other hand, the sole connection between worker and employer was the payment of wages. "The manufacturer does not commit himself to protect the worker, nor the worker to defend the manufacturer, and there is no permanent bond that joins them, either of habit or of duty."

Like so much else in Tocqueville's thinking, his attitude in this area was complicated and even at times contradictory. Although he generously lamented the plight of the industrial poor, he was just as committed to laissez-faire as the majority of his contemporaries were. England had recently passed a poor law providing for workhouses, with a rationale that was uncompromisingly stated by Senior, who soon became Tocqueville's correspondent and friend: "No relief shall be given to the able-bodied or to their families except in return for work, and that work shall be as hard as it can be made, or in the workhouse, and that workhouse as disagreeable as it can be made." These ideas had already taken hold in America. By the end of the 1820s the official view in New York City was that assisting the poor only encouraged dissolute behavior, and humane societies that had formerly given food and clothing to the poor were disbanded. Like most people in his time, Tocqueville continued to see poverty in a moral light, and he thought it disastrous for "the most productive, active, and industrious part of the nation to give its help for providing the means of living to those who do nothing, or who make bad use of their labor."

When the manuscript of *Democracy in America* was at long last completed, it was time to seek a publisher, and Tocqueville found one in Charles Gosselin, whose impressive stable of authors included the novelists Victor Hugo, Honoré de Balzac, Walter Scott, and James Fenimore Cooper. Gosselin held out no great hopes for the book, refused to print more than five hundred copies, and was astounded when it became an overnight sensation. With self-deprecating irony, Tocqueville described to Beaumont what happened next. When he went to call on Gosselin, "he received me with the most radiant expression in the world and said, 'Well! It seems you've written a masterpiece!'" Suitably emboldened, Tocqueville rather tentatively proposed that his royalties might be increased. "I advanced this idea as best I could, which is to say very awkwardly and with the air of a little boy in front of his tutor." After Gosselin cheerfully agreed, "I didn't find anything more to say, so after putting on the hat I'd been turning in my hands for the last quarter of an hour, I departed convinced of two things: first, that Gosselin had the best intentions in the world and, second, that I was a big fool in business, which doesn't prevent me from being a small man. *Magnus Alexander corpore parvus erat* [Alexander the Great had a small body]." Tocqueville was always sensitive about his modest height.

Tocqueville had been steeling himself for criticism of his book, or, even worse, for being ignored. He need not have worried. "I'm just getting my head above water at present," he wrote after it had been out for three weeks, "quite astonished at what's happening to me, and absolutely stunned by the praise that's drumming in my ears." What pleased him above all was that his carefully judged moderation was having its desired effect. He told an old friend, "I've tried to show those for whom the word 'democracy' is synonymous with upheaval, anarchy, despoilment, and murder that it could succeed in governing a society while respecting fortunes, recognizing rights, preserving liberty, and honoring beliefs." But he had to admit that his judiciousness made him all things to all men. "Many who hold opposed opinions are pleased with me, not because they understand me, but because by considering my work from just one angle, they find arguments in it that favor their pas-

sion of the moment." *Democracy in America* has been treated that way
ever since.

Standing apart from polemics, Tocqueville was aware that his personal history contributed to his objectivity. After an Englishman named
Henry Reeve translated the book, Tocqueville sent him a revealing
self-portrait:

> They're determined to make me a man of party, and I'm no such thing.
> They impute passions to me, and I have only opinions, or rather just
> one passion, the love of liberty and human dignity . . . I came into the
> world at the end of a long revolution which, after it destroyed the for-
> mer state, created nothing lasting of its own. Aristocracy was already
> dead when I began to live, and democracy didn't yet exist. My instincts,
> therefore, didn't draw me blindly toward either one. I was living in a
> country that for forty years had tried a bit of everything without set-
> tling decisively on anything, so I wasn't easily given to political illu-
> sions. Being a member myself of the old aristocracy of my country, I
> had no innate hatred or jealousy toward it, and since that aristocracy
> had been destroyed, I had no innate love for it either, for one gets
> strongly attached only to that which is alive. I was close enough to
> know it well, and far enough away to judge it dispassionately. I can say
> the same about the democratic element. No family memories or per-
> sonal interest gave me any innate or necessary leaning toward democ-
> racy. But for my own part, I had received no injuries from it, and I had
> no personal motive either to hate it or to love it, apart from those that
> my reason could furnish. In short, I was in such perfect equilibrium
> between the past and the future that I didn't feel naturally and instinc-
> tively attracted toward either one, and it took no great effort to view
> them tranquilly from both sides.

In England, John Stuart Mill called *Democracy in America* "original
and profound," and summarized its purpose acutely: "Not to determine
whether democracy shall come, but how to make the best of it when it
does come." And from Americans came equally gratifying praise. "You

know that I've worked on America," Tocqueville told Beaumont, "rather like Cuvier on the animals before the flood, making constant use of philosophical deductions or analogies. I was afraid therefore that I would sometimes make tremendous blunders, above all in the eyes of the people of that country. It's extremely agreeable to me, as you can well believe, to hear them say that no author before me has penetrated more deeply into the spirit of American institutions, or shown them in better detail."

Soon afterward, John C. Spencer contributed a preface and notes to his American edition of the Reeve translation, with a handsome compliment. "He has described, or rather defined, our Federal government," Spencer wrote, "with an accurate precision unsurpassed even by any American pen." To be sure, Tocqueville's analysis had come in part from Spencer himself, to whom he responded (in English) that no tribute to his work had given him more pleasure, "for I have always set the greatest value on the judgment of enlightened Americans, and I could not presume to hope it would have been so favorable." For many years thereafter the book was widely studied and admired in America. When Henry Adams was working in London as an assistant to his father, the American ambassador, he asserted that he was taking Tocqueville as a model, "and I study his life and works as the Gospel of my private religion. The great principle of democracy is still capable of rewarding a conscientious servant. And I doubt me much whether the advance of years will increase my toleration of its faults."

With his book as a credential—it gained him election to the distinguished Académie des Sciences Morales et Politiques—Tocqueville made up his mind in 1837 to run for a seat in the Chamber of Deputies, representing a constituency in his native Normandy. There was something of noblesse oblige about it; he wrote unenthusiastically to Beaumont, "If it were necessary to pursue politics for very long in this anthill of vices, baseness, and betrayals, I would become a hermit tomorrow." Still, he badly wanted to return to public service and to achieve distinction in practical affairs as his father had done. But his chances were doomed when he high-mindedly refused support offered to him by the prime minister, explaining that he preferred not to be indebted to any party. "So, I've been beaten," he told Beaumont, who also lost, "but not for one moment beaten down." The next year another seat came open and he won it, taking the competition more seriously this time; he reported that he was worn out by his "gastronomico-electoral campaign." As for Beaumont, he lost a second time, but got in shortly afterward by replacing someone who died.

For the next ten years Tocqueville would play a significant role in national politics, but never a leading one. Positioning himself in the Chamber of Deputies was a challenge in the most literal sense; ever since 1789 it had been customary for liberals to sit to the Speaker's left and conservatives to his right (the origin of the expressions "left wing" and "right wing"). To please the voters who had elected him, Tocqueville had to be in the *centre gauche*, the left center. "In the eyes of those people," he told a friend sarcastically, "where you place your rear end is of the highest importance." Tocqueville longed to be at the heart of events, and he was beginning to grasp that he never would. As he told his political mentor, Pierre-Paul Royer-Collard, "A liberal but not revolutionary party, which is the only kind that would suit me, does not exist, and it's certainly not given to me to create it. So I'm pretty much alone, and all I can do is express my personal opinion as best I can on events and laws as they come up, with no hope of altering them. That's an honorable role but a sterile one. I often rebel instinctively against it, for my nature is active and—it's well to admit—ambitious. I would like to have power, if it could be honorably acquired and kept."

Meanwhile, Tocqueville became convinced that he wasn't finished with *Democracy in America* after all. Much remained to be said about the larger implications of democracy. It is sometimes asserted that America vanishes from part 2 and that the real subject is France. To be sure, there are fewer details about America than in part 1, and Tocqueville did try to shape his analysis in ways that might influence his countrymen. But his knowledge of America was his strong suit, and it remained the touchstone in his attempt to understand where democracy might be headed, in France or anywhere else. Throughout the new work, moreover, he returned repeatedly to themes from the first part, which he now understood more profoundly than before, and he ventured predictions of America's future that have proved to be stunningly prophetic.

Returning to writing, Tocqueville felt energized. He wrote to his English translator, Reeve, "I've never worked on anything with such fervor. I think about my subject day and night, and I take pride in being absolutely unsociable. Never would I have imagined that a subject which I had already revolved in so many ways could present itself from so many new points of view." But that turned out to be the problem. How to weave together countless disparate strands of evidence and ideas? He wrote to a friend that he was doing nothing but eating, sleeping, and working, and yet with such uncertainty that "I'm seized by a sort of panic terror." To Mill he sent a lucid analysis of his characteristic habits of thinking and writing: he was constantly seeking clarity and order, but was so open to subtleties that the task became endless. "My subject is starting to weigh on my mind like a nightmare on the stomach of a sleeping person . . . I surrender to the natural movement of my ideas, allowing myself to be carried in good faith from one conclusion to another. The result is that so long as the book remains unfinished, I don't know clearly where I'm going or even if I'll ever get there."

Those comments were made in 1836, when the project was still fresh. Two years later Tocqueville had accumulated a mountain of new notes and drafts but was no nearer to his destination, and the thing had become an incubus. He lamented to Beaumont, "This idée fixe that has pursued me for four years has become so tiresome that I sigh for the day when I'll be able to think about something else. I'm feeling the same painful numbness that someone would who had to stand for a whole day on one leg." Later he added, "At all costs I've got to finish this book. It's a duel to the death between me and it, and either I have to kill it or it has to kill me."

Democracy in America did get finished, of course, with the second part published under the same title as the first, and once again Tocqueville was looking into the future with masterly insight. While working on the book, he wrote a note to himself: "New despotism. It is in the portrayal of this that resides all the originality and depth of my idea. What I said in my first work was hackneyed and superficial." He was attempting to describe an altogether new kind of social contract, for which the old connotations of "despotism" and "tyranny" were inadequate; later writers have sometimes called it "soft despotism." It works not by overt force but by inner conditioning, and is all the more seductive because it claims to be benevolent; when individuals accept direction, they tell themselves they are still free.

Tocqueville's account of the consequences could easily have been written by George Orwell:

> Above them rises an immense tutelary power that alone takes charge of ensuring their pleasures and watching over their fate . . . It is absolute, detailed, regular, farsighted, and mild. It would resemble paternal power if its object was to prepare men for adult life, but it seeks on the contrary to keep them in permanent childhood. It likes citizens to enjoy themselves, so long as all they think about is enjoyment. It labors willingly for their happiness, but it wants to be the sole agent and arbiter of their happiness . . . The sovereign power doesn't break their wills, but it softens, bends, and directs them. It rarely compels action, but it constantly opposes action. It doesn't destroy, but it prevents birth; it doesn't tyrannize, but it hinders, represses, enervates, restrains, and numbs, until it reduces each nation to a mere flock of timid and industrious animals, with government as their shepherd.

Tocqueville thought so highly of this analysis that he wrote in the margin of his manuscript, "In this picture resides all the originality and depth of my thought."

The old anxiety about centralization was never far from his thoughts as well. In America, what mainly impressed him was the remarkably dispersed nature of government. Now, after much reflection, he saw a very different future in store. Individuals might pursue an infinite variety of goals, he observed, but each of them would hope that the government could help him to attain his goals. "The scope of the central power expands imperceptibly in all directions, even though everyone wants it restrained. A democratic government, therefore, increases its power by the mere fact that it continues to exist. Time is on its side.

Every chance event works to its advantage. The passions of individuals assist it without their own knowledge, and one may say that the older a democratic society is, the more centralized it becomes." So the people buy into unperceived bondage, and as for their leaders, it is human nature to love power. "It is easy to see that most of the ambitious and able citizens in a democratic country will work relentlessly to expand the social power, because they hope to control it themselves one day. It is a waste of time to try to prove to them that too much centralization can be harmful to the state, because it's for themselves that they are centralizing it."

Equally remarkable was what Tocqueville now had to say about democracies in wartime. During his travels through the vast and still half-wild American continent, he was naturally struck by the difference between France, surrounded by potential enemies and maintaining a huge standing army, and the United States, separated by thousands of miles of ocean from the militarized world and maintaining therefore an army that was almost preposterously small. But as he reflected further, he could see that the spectacular growth of technology was bound to collapse the gulf between North America and the rest of the world. And in this area, too, the fundamental premise of equality suggested striking consequences for a democracy at war: "There are two things that will always be very difficult for a democratic people—to begin a war, and to end it." The consequence of this, as Tocqueville describes it, is strikingly prophetic of Vietnam and Iraq: "There can be no war that, in a democratic country, does not put liberty at great risk . . . War doesn't always deliver a people over to military rule, but it cannot fail to increase enormously the power of civil government." Moreover, the soldiers themselves would have a natural stake in what a major war could do for their careers. Military rank in Europe had been a privilege of nobility, and there was little opportunity for lower officers to gain promotion. In the United States it would be very different: "In a democratic army all the ambitious men eagerly hope for war, because war opens up vacancies and permits the right of seniority, which is the sole privilege natural to democracy, to be violated. We thus arrive at the remarkable conclusion that of all armies, the ones that desire war most ardently are the democratic ones, even though the peoples who love peace best are the democratic ones. What makes this so extraordinary is that equality produces both of these contradictory effects at the same time."

So the mighty project was finished at last, nearly a decade after the exhilarating journey that had been its inspiration, and although another great book did lie in Tocqueville's future, *Democracy in America* would remain his masterpiece. Deeply pondered and deeply felt, it is a work to return to again and again, the rich distillation of his enthusiastic response to the young nation, his subsequent reading and reflection, and his thoughts about its future prospects. On the whole, the tone is positive, and Americans at the time were right to feel both flattered and inspired. But at bottom the book is haunted by a deep melancholy, akin no doubt to Tocqueville's own constitutional melancholy, and it is this that has seemed increasingly profound to later generations. For even in its positive aspect, the American quest for material well-being was unappeasable. Since there could always be more, there was never enough. This is why, in Ohio, Tocqueville had been convinced that a deep sense of unfulfillment, not just economic pressure, was what impelled people to keep moving on. "They encounter good fortune nearly everywhere, but not happiness. With them the desire for well-being has become an uneasy, burning passion that keeps on growing even while it is being satisfied."

Tocqueville's final formulation, in a chapter titled "Why the Americans Seem So Restless in the Midst of Their Well-Being," is so powerful that it deserves to be read at length:

> When inequality is the common law of a society, the greatest inequalities don't strike the eye, but when everything is more or less at the same level, the slightest inequalities are wounding. This is why the desire for equality becomes ever more insatiable in proportion as equality itself increases. Among democratic peoples men easily attain a certain level of equality, but they don't know how to attain the equality they desire. It keeps receding before them day after day without ever disappearing from view, and as it recedes, it provokes their pursuit.

Endlessly they believe they're going to seize it, and endlessly it escapes their grasp. They see it from close enough to know its charms, but they never get close enough to enjoy them, and they die before fully tasting its delights. These are the reasons for the singular melancholy that inhabitants of democratic countries often experience in the bosom of abundance, and for the disgust with life that sometimes seizes them in the midst of their easy and tranquil existence.

Tocqueville had deep sympathy for this existential longing, with which he was intimately familiar in his own way, and he summoned romantic and even erotic language to emphasize the yearning for this unrequited pursuit. *Charmes*, *douceurs*, and *jouir* describe the charms and delights that ever recede and can never be fully enjoyed.

12

AFTER AMERICA

Election to the Chamber of Deputies, together with the success of *Democracy in America*, gave Tocqueville hope that he was ready to make a major contribution to the France he loved, but the remainder of his life was largely a story of disappointment. In 1841 he told his mentor Royer-Collard that he should probably stay out of politics altogether, "yet I fear this tranquillity of mind will fail me in light of the parliamentary struggle. I still get aroused at the sight of a battle, however petty the fruits of victory may be, and although my reason is strong enough to keep me immobile, it has no power to make me calm. Reason, for me, has always been like a cage that prevents me from acting effectively, but not from gnashing my teeth behind the bars." From then on, though he continued to serve in parliament, he lived in what has been aptly called "internal exile." His literary prestige, at least, continued to grow. In 1841, when he was not yet forty, he received the highest honor in French intellectual life, election as one of the forty Immortals of the Académie Française.

During these years Tocqueville campaigned energetically for the abolition of slavery in the French colonies. He greatly admired the British for emancipating their own colonial slaves. "In one instant," he wrote, "nearly a million people passed from extreme servitude to complete independence, or to put it better, from death to life." In 1848 French slaves too were set free, and Tocqueville played an important role in working out the necessary terms by which their owners were compensated.

Opposition to slavery was one thing; colonialism was a different matter. Tocqueville was not only eager to see his country hold on to the colonies it had; he wanted it to acquire new ones as it was then doing in North Africa, and he thought harsh measures against Arabs and Berbers were entirely appropriate. It was not unusual for a liberal to favor colonialism at the time: Mill believed that England had every right to govern India, and admirers of his classic work *On Liberty* tend to forget a statement in it, "Despotism is a legitimate mode of government in dealing with barbarians, provided the end be their improvement." In Tocqueville's thinking, indeed, the British were providing an admirable example. He approved of the policy by which they played off one Indian ruler against another, and on Algeria he concluded sternly, "Once we had committed this great violence of conquest, I believe we must not flinch from the smaller acts of violence that are absolutely necessary to consolidate it." Like others brought up on the story of the Roman Empire, he was not immune from the conviction that the *gloire* of his country was at stake. "If France should shrink from an enterprise where its only opponents are a difficult terrain and the little tribes of barbarians who inhabit it, it would seem in the eyes of the world to be yielding to its own impotence and succumbing from lack of courage. Every nation that easily relinquishes what it has taken, withdrawing peacefully of its own accord into its former borders, is acknowledging that the great age of its history is over. It is visibly entering its period of decline."

Still, if colonies were acceptable, racism was not, and Tocqueville argued forcibly that the native cultures of North Africa should be respected. When his youthful disciple Arthur de Gobineau began extolling Aryan superiority, Tocqueville told him severely that Caesar might just as easily have dismissed the savages of Britain as an inferior race, and added, "Don't you see that your doctrine naturally gives rise to all the evils that are born of permanent inequality—pride, violence, contempt for one's fellow man, tyranny, and abjection in all its forms?" When Gobineau persisted, Tocqueville broke with him completely.

He also kept up to date on developments in America. In 1856— a year in which Harriet Beecher Stowe sent him a signed copy of *Uncle Tom's Cabin*—he contributed an eloquent statement in English to a Boston abolitionist publication called *The Liberty Bell*:

> As the persevering enemy of despotism everywhere and under all its forms, I am pained and astonished by the fact that the freest people in the world is, at the present time, almost the only one among civilized and Christian nations which yet maintains personal servitude ... An old and sincere friend of America, I am uneasy at seeing slavery retard her progress, tarnish her glory, furnish arms to her detractors, compromise the future career of the Union which is the guarantor of her safety and greatness, and point out to all her enemies in advance the spot where they are to strike. As a man, too, I am moved at the spectacle of man's degradation by man, and I hope to see the day when the law will grant equal civil liberty to all.

In 1854 the Kansas-Nebraska Act repealed the Missouri Compromise, which had prohibited slavery in most of the Louisiana Purchase territory but made an exception for Missouri, and citizens of any new state were now free to permit slavery if they wished. The Republican Party was born in direct reaction to this concession to the South. And when the Democrat James Buchanan was elected president two years after that, with a clear intention of allowing the spread of slavery into the western territories, Tocqueville wrote in deep distress to his former assistant Theodore Sedgwick, whom he had once told, "You know I am half an American citizen":

> On this side of the ocean, the election of the new president looks like the triumph of the cause of slavery, more perhaps than it actually is. For myself, I have never been an abolitionist in the ordinary sense of the word, since I have never believed it possible to destroy slavery in the older states, but I acknowledge that I am violently opposed to extend-

ing that horrible evil beyond the limits, already too large, within which it is confined today. To me that would seem one of the greatest crimes that could be committed against the cause of humanity, and I feel vehement political passion on this point—if a fifty-year-old Frenchman who has seen four or five revolutions can be allowed to have passions of any kind, and to take human affairs seriously.

Meanwhile, a fresh crisis had overturned the political order in France, and given Tocqueville his long-awaited chance to assume a significant role in government. Early in 1848, Louis-Philippe categorically rejected popular demands to enlarge the electoral franchise, and yet another revolution erupted in France. The king was forced to abdicate, the Second Republic was formed, and Tocqueville was elected to a new legislature, declaring to his constituents, "From the moment the Republic was proclaimed, I accepted it without hesitation or reservation. I wanted not only to allow it to survive but to support it with all my strength, and that is what I still desire." Unrest exploded violently in the June Days of 1848, when Paris workers rioted in favor of socialism and filled the streets with barricades. It was 1830 all over again, but much worse. Four thousand rioters were killed, along with sixteen hundred soldiers. Tocqueville was appalled by the specter of class warfare, "with the goal," as he said later in his *Recollections*, "of changing not just the government but the structure of society." He regretted that the workers believed they were being oppressed and were encouraged to take up arms "to open a path toward an imaginary well-being . . . These poor people have been assured that the wealth of the rich was somehow stolen from themselves." Earlier in 1848, Marx and Engels had published *The Communist Manifesto*, and Marx himself was in Paris observing the June Days firsthand.

As always, Tocqueville found himself caught between two worlds, stunningly progressive in his outrage against racial discrimination, but limited in his ability to understand the social and economic upheavals, including the early stirrings of socialism, that were sweeping through the Western world. Again and again, his yearning for an idealized past clouded his capacity to accept modernization. And as an orator, too, he continued to be strangely ineffective. Heinrich Heine said, "His speeches have a certain frigid luster, like sculpted ice." But still, he was finally at the center of power, appointed to help draft a brand-new constitution for France, and he hoped to draw on his deep knowledge of the American model. Socialist theories, he declared in a parliamentary speech, implied "a profound contempt for the individual taken in himself, in his condition as man. What characterizes them all is a continuous, changing, and ceaseless attempt to mutilate, cut down, and hinder human freedom in every way. It is the idea that the state not only should direct society but must also be, so to speak, the master of each man . . . It is a new form of servitude." The delegates responded with hearty applause. In the same speech he declared undiminished admiration for the young nation he had visited sixteen years before. "I shall seek democracy where I have seen it, living, active, and triumphant in the only country on earth where it exists, and where it has succeeded in establishing, up to the present moment, something great and lasting—in America."

The attempt to emulate the American model got nowhere. Tocqueville's colleagues ignored his arguments against centralization, and they dismissed his proposal for a bicameral legislature. His gloomy conclusion was once again that "parties never understand each other; they draw close, they push against each other, they seize hold of each other, but they never see each other at all."

At the end of that eventful year Louis-Napoleon Bonaparte, a nephew of the great emperor, was elected president of the Second Republic, and in 1849 Tocqueville became minister of foreign affairs. In that capacity he conducted various complicated negotiations, none of which turned out to have much historical significance, and he was able to appoint Beaumont ambassador to Vienna, but soon the ministry in which they served fell from power. And in 1851 Louis-Napoleon abruptly dissolved the National Assembly altogether and became Emperor Napoleon III. The Second Republic was at an end, and so was Tocqueville's political career.

In his final years Tocqueville felt more isolated than ever. He visited Germany in the hope of gathering material for a comparative study of political institutions, but complained that subtle cultural differences were hard to understand and that the trip was "completely useless." In a letter he applied to himself a Latin expression, "civis civitatem quaerens," "a citizen in search of a city," and on another occasion he lamented, "I have relatives and neighbors, but my spirit no longer has any family or fatherland. I assure you that this intellectual and moral isolation often gives me a keener sense of solitude than I ever experienced in the forests of America." Even the triumph of *Democracy in America* seemed far away and irrelevant. He told Beaumont, "I've never been able to force myself to reread my *Democracy* since it came out, except when was absolutely necessary in order to insert corrections in successive editions."

Increasingly depressed, Tocqueville wrote bleakly to Gobineau, with whom he was still on good terms at the time, "You won't easily comprehend the degree of apathy I've fallen into. I'm hardly even in the condition of a spectator, since a spectator at least pays attention and I don't take the trouble to. This is due above all to the ever-deepening darkness that overspreads the picture, always so dark, known as the future. Imagine a man traveling on a moonless and foggy December night, and tell me what little pleasure he could get from looking out the window at the landscape. That man is France . . . What a gloomy night! I would prefer daylight, even if it showed us the unavoidable precipice."

Once again the best remedy was a new effort at writing. First Tocqueville completed the lively but deeply disillusioned *Recollections*, recounting his experiences during the 1848 revolution and its aftermath, and he then began the brilliant *Ancien Régime and the Revolution*, intended as prologue to a major reevaluation of the Revolution itself. Recent events had convinced him that revolution was an ongoing affliction in France, and perhaps an incurable one, "which our fathers saw beginning and which we ourselves, in all likelihood, will never see end."

Destructive though the endless revolution had been, Tocqueville was more than ever moved by the idealism that had first inspired it. He had a memorable conversation with an aged monk who remembered those long-ago days and was still passionate about the lost age of ideals.

"'Ah, monsieur!' he exclaimed, 'I think I must be dreaming when I recall the state of minds in my youth—the vivacity, the sincerity of opinions, the respect for oneself and for public opinion, the disinterested political passion. Ah, monsieur!' he added, seizing my hands with the effusiveness and magniloquence of the eighteenth century, 'in those days we had a cause; now there are only interests. There used to be bonds between men; now there are none. It is sad indeed, monsieur, to outlive one's country!'"

Tocqueville's health had been precarious ever since an episode in 1850 in which he vomited large quantities of blood and had to take a leave of absence from parliament. It is now known that tuberculosis, the then-incurable affliction from which he suffered, can lie dormant for long periods and attack intermittently thereafter, and that the slow process of dying can take years. During periods of apparent recovery he struggled to make progress on his writing, hoping to revive something of the excitement with which *Democracy in America* had been composed: "I had youth, ardor, belief in a cause, and hope." The American journey itself remained close to his heart. One winter he wrote to Beaumont from the Compiègne Forest north of Paris, "These tall trees seen through the snow recall to me the woods of Tennessee through which we traveled twenty-five years ago, in even harsher weather. What was most different in that scene was myself, for twenty-five years in a man's life make quite an alteration. I was having these melancholy reflections as I made my way through the snow . . . To cheer myself up, I reflected that until this day I've kept the friend with whom I hunted parakeets at Memphis, and that time has only strengthened the bonds of trust and friendship we had back then." The future held far more shocking surprises than anyone in Tocqueville's day could have imagined: the Compiègne Forest would be the scene of the armistice that ended World War I in 1918, and afterward of the 1940 armistice by which Hitler avenged that defeat.

The book on the French Revolution, which was to have been the culmination of Tocqueville's career, never got written. At the beginning of 1859 his health took an alarming turn for the worse, and he and Marie took up residence in Cannes, hoping that the mild Mediterranean winter might do some good. He wrote to Beaumont in capital letters, "COME. COME. Only you can lead us back into the field!" But he characteristically downplayed his own need, claiming that it was really Marie who required support since she was frantic with worry. Two weeks later he was telling Kergorlay that although his doctors still predicted a full recovery, it was happening "with intolerable slowness." A month after that he was dead, at the age of fifty-three, and was laid to rest in the churchyard at Tocqueville. Marie survived him by five years and Beaumont by seven.

Just two years after Tocqueville's death, the Civil War exploded in America. Before its end a Harvard professor published a new edition of *Democracy in America*, in which he paid tribute to the author's unwavering faith in democracy. "If his life had been spared to witness the terrible ordeal to which the providence of God is now subjecting us, it may confidently be believed that this trust on his part would not have been shaken, even if he should have been compelled to admit that the Federal tie which once bound our large family of democratic States together would probably never be reunited . . . He foresaw, if not the imminence, at least the probability, of the great convulsion which the country is now undergoing; and there can be no clearer indication of the causes which have at last induced it, than that which was made by this wise and impartial foreigner nearly thirty years ago."

After surviving the war, the United States did remain stable, as Tocqueville had hoped it would, and France remained unstable, in the way he feared. In 1870, Prussia dealt France a humiliating military defeat, and Louis-Napoleon went into exile. His empire was replaced by the Third Republic, which lasted until the end of World War II. That in turn gave way to the Fourth Republic, with its volatile legislature and endless changes of administrations, and finally, in 1958, to the Fifth Republic. France now had a president—the masterful Charles de Gaulle—and at long last, as Hugh Brogan remarks, had adopted a Tocquevillean republic, "after trying almost everything else."

Much has changed in America since Tocqueville's time, but much has not. To this day, idealization of the "heartland" treats big cities and big industry as somehow less than fully American. Some years ago

Christopher Lasch deplored "the domination of American political thought by popular mythologies: the frontier, the sturdy yeoman, self-help, God and motherhood." Tocqueville saw and critiqued every one of these, but he also respected them. With sympathy and imagination, he understood why the new nation needed to think of itself in these ways, and also how the mythos had a real connection with American reality. Tocqueville's issues are still with us, and still unresolved.

NOTES

Maddeningly for a reader, many writers on Tocqueville cite by page number only from any one of the numerous translations of *Democracy in America*. Here I give volume, part, and chapter numbers as well as page numbers in the most accessible French edition, volume 2 in the Pléiade *Oeuvres*; and also, although I have made my own translations, page references in Arthur Goldhammer's excellent Library of America edition. Likewise, quotations from Tocqueville's American notebooks are cited from volume 1 of the Pléiade *Oeuvres* and also from the English translation by George Lawrence.

ABBREVIATIONS

Brogan	Hugh Brogan, *Alexis de Tocqueville: A Life* (New Haven, CT: Yale University Press, 2007)
Goldhammer	Alexis de Tocqueville, *Democracy in America*, trans. Arthur Goldhammer (New York: Library of America, 2004)
Jardin	André Jardin, *Alexis de Tocqueville* (Paris: Hachette, 1984); there is an English translation by Lydia Davis and Robert Hemenway, *Tocqueville: A Biography* (Baltimore, MD: Johns Hopkins University Press, 1998)
Journey	Alexis de Tocqueville, *Journey to America*, trans. George Lawrence, ed. J. P. Mayer, rev. A. P. Kerr (New York: Doubleday, 1971)
Lettres choisies	Alexis de Tocqueville, *Lettres choisies, souvenirs*, ed. Françoise Mélonio and Laurence Guellec (Paris: Gallimard, 2003)

Lettres d'Amérique   Gustave de Beaumont, *Lettres d'Amérique, 1831–1832*, ed. André Jardin and George W. Pierson (Paris: Presses Universitaires de France, 1973)

Marie   Gustave de Beaumont, *Marie; ou, L'esclavage aux États-Unis, tableau de moeurs américaines* (Paris: Gosselin, 1835)

Nolla   Alexis de Tocqueville, *De la démocratie en Amérique*, first historicocritical edition, revised and enlarged by Eduardo Nolla (Paris: Vrin, 1990)

"Notice"   Gustave de Beaumont, "Notice sur Alexis de Tocqueville," in *Oeuvres* (Beaumont), 5:5–125

O.C.   Alexis de Tocqueville, *Oeuvres complètes*, 14 vols., ed. J. P. Mayer et al. (Paris: Gallimard, 1954–)

Oeuvres (Beaumont)   *Oeuvres complètes d'Alexis de Tocqueville*, 9 vols., ed. Gustave de Beaumont (Paris: Michel Lévy, 1866)

Oeuvres (Pléiade)   Alexis de Tocqueville, *Oeuvres*, 3 vols., ed. André Jardin et al. (Paris: Gallimard, 1991–2004)

Pierson   George Wilson Pierson, *Tocqueville in America* (Baltimore, MD: Johns Hopkins University Press, 1996); reprint of the 1938 Oxford University Press edition, which was titled *Tocqueville and Beaumont in America*

Schleifer   James T. Schleifer, *The Making of Tocqueville's "Democracy in America"* (Indianapolis: Liberty Fund, 2000)

Voyage   Alexis de Tocqueville, *Voyage en Amérique*, in *Oeuvres* (Pléiade), vol. 1

PREFACE

xv   "certainly the greatest book": Edward C. Banfield, "The Illiberal Tocqueville," in *Interpreting Tocqueville's "Democracy in America,"* ed. Ken Masugi (Savage, MD: Rowman & Littlefield, 1991), 239.

xv   modern writers: David Riesman, *The Lonely Crowd: A Study of the Changing American Character* (New Haven, CT: Yale University Press, 1950); Robert Nisbet, *The Quest for Community: A Study in the Ethics of Order and Freedom* (San Francisco: Institute for Contemporary Studies, 1990; orig. published by Oxford University Press, 1953); Robert N. Bellah et al., *Habits of the Heart: Individualism and Commitment in American Life* (Berkeley: University of California Press, 1996).

xv   "Ideas come in": Tocqueville to his brother Édouard, 28 May 1831, *O.C.*, 14:92.

xvi   "a pitiless questioner": *Quinze jours dans le désert*, in *Voyage*, 1: 375; *Journey*, 366.

xvi   "He had the very rare talent": "Notice," 125.

xvi   "A foreigner often learns": Introduction to *Democracy in America*, in *Oeuvres* (Pléiade), 2:17; Goldhammer, 16.

xvi   "Repose was contrary": "Notice," 23–25.

xvi   "You are always on fire": Tocqueville to Beaumont, 22 April 1838, *Lettres choisies*, 414.

xvi   "a registry": Sheldon S. Wolin, *Tocqueville Between Two Worlds: The Making of a Political and Theoretical Life* (Princeton, NJ: Princeton University Press, 2001), 114.

xvii   "not so much a book of answers": Abraham S. Eisenstadt, introduction to *Reconsidering Tocqueville's "Democracy in America,"* ed. Eisenstadt (New Brunswick, NJ: Rutgers University Press, 1988), 7.

xvii   "Everything he wrote": Larry Siedentop, *Tocqueville* (New York: Oxford University Press, 1994), 138.

xviii   "I know I am treading": *Democracy in America*, 1.2.5, in *Oeuvres* (Pléiade), 2:221; Goldhammer, 224.

xviii   "In America I saw": Ibid., Introduction, in *Oeuvres* (Pléiade), 2:15–18; Goldhammer, 15–17.

xviii   "almost frighteningly prescient": Edward Pessen, "The Egalitarian Myth and the American Social Reality: Wealth, Mobility, and Equality in the 'Era of the Common Man,'" *American Historical Review* 76 (1971), 989.

xviii   "In the picture": *Democracy in America*, 1.2.10, in *Oeuvres* (Pléiade), 2:415; Goldhammer, 413.

xix   "with all the determination": Beaumont to his mother, 7 June 1831, *Lettres d'Amérique*, 59.

xix   "There is not a country": *Voyage*, 1:201; *Journey*, 186.

xix   "This new society": *Democracy in America*, 2.4.8, in *Oeuvres* (Pleiade), 2:850; Goldhammer, 831.

xix   "A momentous rupture": Sean Wilentz, *The Rise of American Democracy: Jefferson to Lincoln* (New York: Norton, 2005), xvii.

xx   unprecedented economic changes: Charles Sellers, *The Market Revolution: Jacksonian America, 1815–1846* (New York: Oxford University Press, 1991); Daniel Walker Howe, *What Hath God Wrought: The Transformation of America, 1815–1848* (New York: Oxford University Press, 2007).

xx   "by the 1820s": Gordon S. Wood, "The Significance of the Early Republic," *Journal of the Early Republic* 8 (1988), 18.

xxi   "two democracies": Jean-Claude Lamberti, *Tocqueville and the Two Democracies*, trans. Arthur Goldhammer (Cambridge, MA: Harvard University Press, 1989).

xxi   "The two parts": Preface to pt. 2 of *Democracy in America*, in *Oeuvres* (Pléiade), 2:509; Goldhammer, 479.

1. WHERE TOCQUEVILLE WAS COMING FROM

3   "in what would be called": Malesherbes to the baron de Breteuil, 24 July 1776, quoted by Benoît Mély, *Jean-Jacques Rousseau: Un intellectuel en rupture* (Paris: Minerve, 1985), 128.

4   historians believe: William Doyle, *The Oxford History of the French Revolution* (New York: Oxford University Press, 1989), 258; Hugh Gough, *The Terror in the French Revolution* (New York: St. Martin's, 1998), 77.

4   repressed romantic: Françoise Mélonio, introduction to *Lettres choisies*, 27.

4   "It's that restlessness": Tocqueville to his brother Édouard, 2 Sept. 1840, *Lettres choisies*, 464.

4   "Why didn't you come with us?": Tocqueville to Lesueur, 4 April 1814, ibid., 109.

5   "Then doubt entered . . . toward sensory objects": Tocqueville to Sophie Swetchine, 26 Feb. 1857, ibid., 1244.

6   "I see that you catch fire": Kergorlay to Tocqueville, 16 May 1823, *O.C.*, 15 (1):62–63.

6   "Nothing is so intolerable": Pascal, *Pensées*, no. 131, in the Léon Brunschvicg numeration.

6   "Mental activity": "Notice," 28.

6   "was born a thinker": *Atlantic Monthly*, Nov. 1861, 552.

7   "I recognize daily . . . made me feel alive": Tocqueville to Kergorlay, 23 July 1827, *Lettres choisies*, 110–11.

8   "a friendship between us": Tocqueville to Beaumont, n.d. (possibly 1829), *O.C.*, 8 (1):75.

8   "like the decanter": Heinrich Heine, *Allemands et Français* (Paris: Calmann Lévy, 1899), 314.

8   "You've taught me": Tocqueville to Beaumont, 25 Oct. 1829, *Lettres choisies*, 139.

8   "You have more chance": Tocqueville to Beaumont, 8 May 1830, ibid., 149.

9   "Fortunately, the mother": Tocqueville to Beaumont, May 1830, ibid., 151.

10   "My conscience doesn't reproach me": Tocqueville to Mottley, 17 Aug. 1830, ibid., 154–55.

10   "His name": "Notice," 9.

11   "The passions of politics": Tocqueville to Beaumont, 25 Oct. 1829, *Lettres choisies*, 140.

11   "Those who never": "Notice," 11.

11   "Behind them": Alfred de Musset, *La confession d'un enfant du siècle*, ed. Claude Duchet and Maurice Allem (Paris: Garnier, 1968), 7–8.

12   "The prison has always": Michel Foucault, *Discipline and Punish: The Birth of the Prison*, trans. Alan Sheridan (New York: Vintage Books, 1995), 200.

12 "books of theory": Tocqueville and Beaumont, *Note sur le système pénitentiaire* (1831), in *O.C.*, 4 (1):51.

12 "which has nothing . . . all other travelers": Tocqueville to Charles Stöffels, 4 Nov. 1830, *Lettres choisies*, 160.

12 "We're going with the intention": Tocqueville to Eugène Stöffels, 21 Feb. 1831, in Beaumont's edition of Tocqueville's *Correspondance et oeuvres posthumes* (Paris: Garnier, 1866), 5:412.

12 "the penitentiary system": Tocqueville to Kergorlay, Jan. 1835, *O.C.*, 13 (1):374.

13 sixty-six days: Tocqueville to his father, 14 May 1831, ibid., 14:88.

13 "it was I . . . on terra firma": Tocqueville to his mother, 26 April 1831, *Lettres choisies*, 163–64.

13 "I was the orchestra": Beaumont to his father, 25 April 1831, *Lettres d'Amérique*, 28.

13 "Although I already knew": Ibid., 26.

14 "Tocqueville is a truly distinguished": Ibid., 27–28.

2. FIRST IMPRESSIONS: NEW YORK CITY

15 "It's a collection": Tocqueville to his mother, 14 May 1831, *Lettres choisies*, 167.

15 "They inspected our baggage": Beaumont to his father, 25 April 1831, *Lettres d'Amérique*, 36.

15 "It's impossible to give an idea": Tocqueville to his mother, 14 May 1831, *Lettres choisies*, 167.

15 "We've arrived": Beaumont to his mother, 14 May 1831, *Lettres d'Amérique*, 37.

16 "In New York": Beaumont to his brother Jules, 4 July 1831, ibid., 80.

16 "The appearance of the town": Tocqueville to his mother, 14 May 1831, *Lettres choisies*, 80.

16 "It's on flat terrain": Beaumont to his brother Jules, 16 Sept. 1831, *Lettres d'Amérique*, 145–46.

17 East Sixty-fourth Street: Pierson, 141.

17 "miserable wooden cottages": James Boardman, *America and the Americans . . . by a Citizen of the World* (London: Longman, Green, 1833), 15, 24.

17 riots defeated: Edwin G. Burrows and Mike Wallace, *Gotham: A History of New York City to 1898* (New York: Oxford University Press, 1999), 477.

17 "The streets of New York . . . have to do with *silence?*": John M. Duncan, *Travels Through Part of the United States and Canada* (Glasgow, 1823); Walt Whitman, in his paper the *New York Aurora* (1842); both quoted by Bayard Still, *Mirror for Gotham: New York as Seen by Contemporaries from Dutch Days to the Present* (New York: New York University Press, 1956), 79–80, 82.

17   "Water should not be drunk": James Flint, *Letters from America* (Edinburgh: Tait, 1822), 8–9. The fatal effects of cold water were also noted by Duke Bernhard von Saxe-Weimar-Eisenach, *Travels by His Highness Duke Bernhard of Saxe-Weimar-Eisenach Through North America in the Years 1825 and 1826*, trans. William Jeronimus (Lanham, MD: University Press of America, 2001), 63.

17   "We're showered with courtesies . . . whistling of the wind": Beaumont to his brother Jules, 26 May 1831, and to his father, 25 April 1831, *Lettres d'Amérique*, 46, 27.

18   "We're accomplishing": Tocqueville to Ernest de Chabrol, 20 June 1831, *Lettres choisies*, 189.

18   "We continue to acquire": Beaumont to his brother Achille, 18 June 1831, *Lettres d'Amérique*, 66.

18   "One can scarcely imagine": "Notice," 23–25.

18   "I've become such an intrepid": Beaumont to his sister Eugénie, 1 Dec. 1831, *Lettres d'Amérique*, 185.

19   "Since our arrival here": Tocqueville to Félix Le Peletier d'Aunay, 7 June 1831, *Lettres choisies*, 183.

19   "They are agreeable people": Beaumont to his father, n.d., *Lettres d'Amérique*, 39.

19   "I'd like to know what use": Beaumont to his brother Achille, 18 June 1831, ibid., 65.

19   *gants glacés*: Tocqueville to his brother Édouard, 28 May 1831, *O.C.*, 14:92. *Gants glacés* are defined in the great eighteenth-century *Encyclopédie* as "ceux qui après avoir été passés du côté de la chair, dans un mélange d'huile d'olive & de jaunes d'oeufs, arrosés d'esprit-de-vin & d'eau, ont été foulés pendant environ un quart d'heure, avec le même mélange sans eau."

19   "Tell Papa": Tocqueville to Lesueur, 28 May 1831, *O.C.*, 14:97.

20   "He is a polished scholar": Quoted by Arthur M. Schlesinger Jr., *The Age of Jackson* (Boston: Little, Brown, 1950), 64.

20   "Madame John Livingston": Beaumont to his brother Jules, 26 May 1831, *Lettres d'Amérique*, 50.

20   "Whenever someone fails": *Souvenirs*, 2.3, in *Oeuvres* (Pléiade), 3:795.

20   "I the undersigned": Beaumont to Tocqueville, 6 June 1831, *O.C.*, 8 (1):107–8.

21   "Remembering that one was supposed to laugh": Tocqueville to his cousin Alexandrine, 20 June 1831, ibid., 14:108–9.

21   "An American told me": *Marie*, 1: 72.

21   "in a word . . . gaiety in the world": Tocqueville to Lesueur, 28 May 1831, *O.C.*, 14:95.

22   "wearing all unconsciously": Francis Underwood, quoted by Jack Larkin, *The Reshaping of Everyday Life, 1790–1840* (New York: Harper & Row, 1988), 149.

22   "there is little": Francis Lieber, *Letters to a Gentleman in Germany* (Philadelphia: Carey, Lea & Blanchard, 1834), 30.

22   "such deadly leaden people": Charles Dickens, *American Notes*, ed. Patricia Ingham (London: Penguin, 2000), 190.

22   "They don't chat": *Marie*, 1:70.

22   "The sole object": Tocqueville to Nassau William Senior, 24 Aug. 1850, *O.C.*, 6 (2):301.

23   "To keep the mind": Tocqueville to Charles Stöffels, 21 April 1830, *Lettres choisies*, 145.

23   "An American doesn't know": *Democracy in America*, 1.2.6, in *Oeuvres* (Pléiade), 2:279; Goldhammer, 279.

23   "The people here": Tocqueville to his mother, 14 May 1831, *Lettres choisies*, 170.

23   "The slightest praise ... lives off itself": *Democracy in America*, 2.3.16, in *Oeuvres* (Pléiade), 2:739–40; Goldhammer, 719–20.

23   "the frank sociability": John Stuart Mill, *Autobiography*, ed. John M. Robson (London: Penguin, 1989), 63.

23   "we've had to give up": Tocqueville to his mother, 14 May 1831, *Lettres choisies*, 169.

23   "Mr. de Tocqueville thanks": Tocqueville to J. W. Francis, 28 June 1831, *O.C.*, 7:27–28.

24   "We're making progress": Beaumont to his mother, 7 June 1831, *Lettres d'Amérique*, 59.

24   "You'll conclude from this": Ibid., 60.

24   "I've often noticed": *Democracy in America*, 2.1.18, in *Oeuvres* (Pléiade), 2:590; Goldhammer, 561.

24   called shops "stores," etc.: Frederick Marryat, *A Diary in America, with Remarks on Its Institutions*, ed. Sydney Jackman (New York: Knopf, 1962), 36, 215, 260, 262, 264, 266, 6.

25   "Business is the very soul": Francis Grund, *The Americans in Their Moral, Social, and Political Relations* (Boston: Marsh, Capen and Lyon, 1837), 202, 204.

25   "materialism, competitiveness": Quoted by Joyce Appleby, *Inheriting the Revolution: The First Generation of Americans* (Cambridge, MA: Harvard University Press, 2000), 251–52.

25   "the almighty dollar": Washington Irving, *New Yorker*, 12 Nov. 1836.

25   "The Americans are a nation": Beaumont to his father, 16 May 1831, *Lettres d'Amérique*, 41.

25   "There are no rich people": Beaumont to his brother Jules, 4 July 1831, ibid., 79–80.

25   "The more deeply": Tocqueville to Chabrol, 9 June 1831, *Lettres choisies*, 186.

25   "So-and-so is worth": *Marie*, 1:386.

26   "A people that seems": Tocqueville to Chabrol, *Lettres choisies*, 187.

26   "The entire society": *Voyage*, 1:292; *Journey*, 290.

26   Modern research: Notably in a classic article by Edward Pessen, "The Egalitarian Myth and the American Social Reality: Wealth, Mobility, and Equality in the 'Era of the Common Man,'" *American Historical Review* 76 (1971), 989–1034. Pessen subsequently augmented his findings at book length in *Riches, Class, and Power: America Before the Civil War* (Lexington, MA: Heath, 1973).

27   Sean Wilentz: *Chants Democratic: New York City and the Rise of the American Working Class, 1788–1850* (New York: Oxford University Press, 1984).

27   "the total want": Basil Hall, *Travels in North America in the Years 1827 and 1828* (Edinburgh: R. Cadell, 1830), 2:80, 156–57.

27   "Servants, whether white": John Fowler, *Journal of a Tour in the State of New York* (London: Whittaker, Treacher, and Arnot, 1831), 218.

27   "'Master' is not a word": Flint, *Letters from America*, 9.

27   "say that they're giving": *Voyage*, 1:237; *Journey*, 225.

27   "Just like everywhere else": *Voyage*, 1:33; *Journey*, 2.

27   "the French have ... of their conditions": *Democracy in America*, 2.3.5, in *Oeuvres* (Pléiade), 2:692, 695; Goldhammer, 670, 673–74.

28   "Among the new objects": Introduction to *Democracy in America*, in *Oeuvres* (Pléiade), 2:3; Goldhammer, 3.

28   New York law of 1821: David S. Reynolds, *Waking Giant: America in the Age of Jackson* (New York: HarperCollins, 2008), 27.

28   "An American": Michel Chevalier, *Lettres sur l'Amérique du Nord* (Paris: Gosselin, 1836), 2:278.

28   "They are subjected": Thomas Hamilton, *Men and Manners in America* (Philadelphia: Carey, Lea & Blanchard, 1833), 57.

28   Lafayette: Mentioned by Harriet Martineau, *Society in America* (London: Saunders & Otley, 1837), 1:196.

28   "In proportion": Quoted by Nolla, 1:263n.

29   one estimate: Burrows and Wallace, *Gotham*, 483–84.

29   "Would you believe": Tocqueville to his brother Édouard, 20 June 1831, unpublished letter, Yale Tocqueville collection, B.I.a.2.

29   "It was the first time": Beaumont to his brother Achille, 18 June 1831, *Lettres d'Amérique*, 65–66.

29   "struck as much": Quoted by Nolla, 2:189n.

30   "The ladies ... when in movement": Frances Trollope, *Domestic Manners of the Americans* (London: Whittacker, Teacher & Co., 1832), 2:102–103.

31   "It's the life": Tocqueville to Émilie, 9 June 1831, *O.C.*, 14:103.

31   "because they're attracted": *Voyage*, 1:242, 278; *Journey*, 231, 275.

31   "the most important": Tocqueville to Hubert de Tocqueville, 23 Feb. 1857, *Lettres choisies*, 1241.

31   "I have often been": *Democracy in America*, 2.3.9–10, in *Oeuvres* (Pléiade), 2:713–15; Goldhammer, 693–95.

32   "The Americans": *Democracy in America*, 2.3.10, in *Oeuvres* (Pléiade), 2:715; Goldhammer, 695.

32   "I admit that": Tocqueville to Émilie, 28 Nov. 1831, *O.C.*, 14:148–49.

33   "I thank you for the care": Tocqueville to Chabrol, 17 Aug. 1831, *Lettres choisies*, 218.

33   "which, as too much experience": Tocqueville to Kergorlay, 27 Sept. 1843, ibid., 522.

34   "infidelity of bad habits": Kergorlay to Marie, 30 Aug. 1843, *O.C.*, 13 (2):114.

35   "Intrigue is his vocation": *Voyage*, 1:177; *Journey*, 161; *Democracy in America*, 1.2.3, in *Oeuvres* (Pléiade), 2:204; Goldhammer, 207 (Tocqueville was quoting the *Vincennes Gazette*).

35   "such slander": Lawrence Frederick Kohl, *The Politics of Individualism: Parties and the American Character in the Jacksonian Era* (New York: Oxford University Press, 1989), 40.

35   "the price of cotton": Tocqueville to his father, 3 June 1831, *Lettres choisies*, 177.

35   "He could not have chosen": Brogan, 153–54.

35   "one of the most fortunate . . . American confederation": Tocqueville to his father, *Lettres choisies*, 176–77.

35   "While the king of France": Beaumont to his brother Jules, 26 May 1831, *Lettres d'Amérique*, 53–54.

36   They found the name peculiar: *Voyage*, 1: 227; *Journey*, 214–15.

36   "their beastly salacity": Quoted by Burrows and Wallace, *Gotham*, 367.

36   "In the United States": Tocqueville to Eugénie de Grancey, 10 Oct. 1831, *Lettres choisies*, 231.

37   "crowding of prisoners": Tocqueville and Beaumont, *Système pénitentiaire aux États-Unis*, in *O.C.*, 4 (1):165–66.

37   "Absolute solitude": Ibid., 159.

37   "They are not to exchange": Quoted by John Luckey, *Life in Sing Sing State Prison, as Seen in a Twelve Years' Chaplaincy* (New York: Tibbals, 1860), 16.

38   the favored implement: Scott Christianson, *With Liberty for Some: 500 Years of Imprisonment in America* (Boston: Northeastern University Press, 1998), 113.

38   a convict was mistakenly accused: Luckey, *Life in Sing Sing State Prison*, 55.

38   "assistant keepers": James Stuart, *Three Years in North America* (New York: J. & J. Harper, 1833), 1:70.

38   "concealed from the observation": Jeremy Bentham, "Panopticon Papers," in *A Bentham Reader*, ed. Mary P. Mack (New York: Pegasus, 1969), 194.

39   "Apart from sleeping": Tocqueville to Le Peletier d'Aunay, 7 June 1831, *Lettres choisies*, 178–79.

39   "We have often walked": Tocqueville and Beaumont, *Système pénitentiaire*, 183.

39   "The rights": Ibid., 194.

39   "All the inmates": Ibid., 183.

39   "unceasing vigilance": Quoted by Daniel Feller, *The Jacksonian Promise: America, 1815–1840* (Baltimore, MD: John Hopkins University Press, 1995), 142.

40   "Is it surprising": Michel Foucault, *Discipline and Punish: The Birth of the Prison*, trans. Alan Sheridan (New York: Vintage Books, 1977), 228.

40   "I'm as unsure": Tocqueville to his father, 7 Oct. 1831, *Lettres choisies*, 227.

40   "I don't think ": *Voyage*, 1:34; *Journey*, 5.

41   "You would never guess": Tocqueville to his father, 3 June 1831, *Lettres choisies*, 174–75.

41   "In the evenings": Beaumont to his mother, 7 June 1831, *Lettres d'Amérique*, 59.

41   "Tocqueville has been waging": Beaumont to his brother Jules, 4 July 1831 (but referring to the earlier incident), *Lettres d'Amérique*, 76.

41   "M. de Beaumont": Newspaper clipping sent by Beaumont to his brother Achille, 18 June 1831, ibid., 67.

42   "I'm weary of men": Beaumont to his father, 29 June 1831, ibid., 72.

42   "We will plunge headfirst": Tocqueville to Chabrol, 20 June 1831, *Lettres choisies*, 189.

3. "EVERYTHING ATTESTS TO A NEW WORLD"

43   the *North America*, etc.: David Lear Buckman, *Old Steamboat Days on the Hudson River* (New York: Grafton Press, 1907), 55, 66, 68, 71.

44   "We were in the position": Tocqueville to his mother, 17 July 1831, *Lettres choisies*, 207.

45   "these same Americans": *Democracy in America*, 2.1.10, in *Oeuvres* (Pléiade), 2:556; Goldhammer, 527.

45   planned obsolescence: *Democracy in America*, 2.1.8, in *Oeuvres* (Pléiade), 544; Goldhammer, 515.

45   "to exclude entirely": Quoted by Daniel Feller, *The Jacksonian Promise: America, 1815–1840* (Baltimore, MD: Johns Hopkins University Press, 1995), 86.

45   "One mustn't expect": Beaumont to his sister Eugénie, 14 July 1831, *Lettres d'Amérique*, 90–92.

46   "artisan independence": Sean Wilentz, *Chants Democratic: New York City and the Rise of the American Working Class, 1788–1850* (New York: Oxford University Press, 1984), 102.

46   "Mixture of amusing": *Voyage*, 1:147; *Journey*, 125.

46   a modern commentator: Roger Boesche, *The Strange Liberalism of Alexis de Tocqueville* (Ithaca, NY: Cornell University Press, 1987), 185.

46   "When it invoked": Tocqueville to Ernest de Chabrol, 16 July 1831, *Lettres choisies*, 205.

47   "Love of country": *Democracy in America*, 1.1.5, in *Oeuvres* (Pléiade), 2:74;
      Goldhammer, 76.

47   "My country, 'tis of thee": Mentioned by Louis P. Masur, *1831: Year of Eclipse*
      (New York: Hill and Wang, 2001), 160.

47   "We expected to stay": Tocqueville to Chabrol, 16 July 1831, *Lettres
      choisies*, 205.

48   "The greatest merit": *Voyage*, 1:182; *Journey*, 167.

48   "New York politics": Richard P. McCormick, *The Second American Party Sys-
      tem: Party Formation in the Jacksonian Era* (Chapel Hill: University of North
      Carolina Press, 1966), 104.

48   "In truth": *Voyage*, 1:89; *Journey*, 64.

49   "You argue like": *Voyage*, 1:99; *Journey*, 75.

49   "What I call": *Voyage*, 1:257–58; *Journey*, 250–51.

49   "Is this theory": Beaumont's query on the manuscript, quoted by Nolla,
      1:138n.

49   "American parties": McCormick, *Second American Party System*, 4.

49   Inspired by a visionary: From Stephen J. Stein, *The Shaker Experience in
      America: A History of the United Society of Believers* (New Haven, CT: Yale
      University Press, 1992).

50   "shakery quakers": quoted from Tocqueville's notes by Nolla, 2:103n.

50   "Their soulless stare": Harriet Martineau, *Society in America* (London: Saun-
      ders & Otley, 1837), 2:60.

50   "Worldly interest": *Marie*, 2:208–9.

50   "Can you imagine": Tocqueville to his mother, 17 July 1831, *Lettres choisies*,
      208–9.

50   "an inordinate desire": Quoted by Charles Sellers, *The Market Revolution: Jack-
      sonian America, 1815–1846* (New York: Oxford University Press, 1991), 158.

50   "throw themselves": *Democracy in America*, 2.2.12, in *Oeuvres* (Pléiade), 2:647;
      Goldhammer, 647.

51   "who go from place to place": *Democracy in America*, 2.2.12, in *Oeuvres*, 2:646;
      Goldhammer, 647.

51   "the greatest revival": Quoted by Masur, *1831*, 64.

51   classic study: Nathan Hatch, *The Democratization of American Christianity*
      (New Haven, CT: Yale University Press, 1989).

52   "I saw": Manuscript note in *Oeuvres* (Pléiade), 2:1123–24n.

52   *The Last of the Mohicans*: Mentioned by Beaumont to his brother Jules, 6 July
      1831, *Lettres d'Amérique*, 84.

52   "In general the whole countryside": *Voyage*, 1:147; *Journey*, 125–26.

53   "the newly-cleared lands": Basil Hall, *Forty Etchings: From Sketches Made
      with the Camera Lucida, in North America, in 1827 and 1828* (Edinburgh:
      Cadell, 1829), unnumbered page facing the illustration.

54 “Send twenty dollars”: Frederick Marryat, *A Diary in America with Remarks on Its Institutions*, ed. Sydney Jackman (New York: Knopf, 1962), 410.

54 “So long as”: *Democracy in America*, 1.2.3, in *Oeuvres* (Pléiade), 2:203; Goldhammer, 206.

54 “After the people”: Quoted by Nolla, 1:141n.

54 Congress promoted: Material drawn from Daniel Walker Howe, *What Hath God Wrought: The Transformation of America 1815–1848* (New York: Oxford University Press, 2007), 225; Sellers, *Market Revolution*, 379; Joyce Appleby, *Inheriting the Revolution: The First Generation of Americans* (Cambridge, MA: Harvard University Press, 2000), 91, 102; Noble E. Cunningham, “Political Dimensions of Everyday Life in the Early Republic,” in *Everyday Life in the Early Republic*, ed. Catherine E. Hutchins (Winterthur, DE: Winterthur Museum, 1994), 5.

54 “a great constitutional question”: *Voyage*, 1:134; *Journey*, 113.

54 “We are under”: Quoted by Howe, *What Hath God Wrought*, 87.

54 “I never saw”: *Voyage*, 1:238; *Journey*, 226.

55 The vehicles had: On stagecoaches, see John A. Jakle, *Images of the Ohio Valley: A Historical Geography of Travel, 1740 to 1860* (New York: Oxford University Press, 1977), 25–27.

55 Dickens complained: Charles Dickens, *American Notes*, ed. Patricia Ingham (London: Penguin, 2000), 209.

55 “The company is generally”: *Common Sights in Town and Country, Delineated and Described for Young Children* (Philadelphia: American Sunday School Union, 1850), unnumbered page facing the illustration.

55 “In this country”: Tocqueville to his mother, 15 May 1831, *Lettres choisies*, 172.

56 “the ante-railroad times”: Harriet Beecher Stowe, *Oldtown Folks* (1869), ed. Henry F. May (Cambridge, MA: Harvard University Press, 1966), 49.

56 “I believe that”: Tocqueville to his mother, 17 July 1831, *Lettres choisies*, 209.

56 “We discover”: *Voyage*, 1:149; *Journey*, 127–28.

57 “How often have I envied . . . channels ever open”: *Voyage au Lac Oneida*, in *Oeuvres* (Pléiade), 1:354–55; *Journey*, 344–46.

57 the true story: See Pierson, 201–4; and *Lettres choisies*, 211n.

57 “In my opinion . . . healthy life”: *Voyage*, 1:36–38; *Journey*, 7–8.

58 “doubtful pecuniary . . . mild and free”: Quoted by O. F. Lewis, *The Development of American Prisons and Prison Customs, 1776–1845* (Albany: Prison Association of New York, 1922), 113–14.

58 “Mr. Morse”: *Voyage*, 1:291; *Journey*, 289.

58 “in some business”: *Voyage*, 1:214; *Journey*, 200.

58 “In aristocratic countries”: *Democracy in America*, 2.2.18, in *Oeuvres* (Pléiade), 2:666; Goldhammer, 642.

58 amazed that a governor: *Marie*, 1:385.

59   "While admiring": Beaumont to his sister Eugénie, 14 July 1831, *Lettres d'Amérique*, 95.

59   "His mind is characterized": *Voyage*, 1:41; *Journey*, 11.

59   "he has described": John C. Spencer, preface to *Democracy in America* (New York: George Dearborn & Co., 1838), viii.

60   "The need for logic . . . occult knowledge": *Voyage*, 1:314, 320; *Journey*, 314, 321.

60   "It adapts itself": *Democracy in America*, 1.2.8, in *Oeuvres* (Pléiade), 2:310; Goldhammer, 311.

60   "To the democratic instincts": *Democracy in America*, 1.2.8, in *Oeuvres* (Pléiade), 2:308–9; Goldhammer, 309.

60   "the most distinguished man . . . never to return": Beaumont to his mother, 22 July 1831, *Lettres d'Amérique*, 98–99.

61   "In addition": Tocqueville to his sister-in-law Émilie, 25 July 1831, *Lettres choisies*, 214.

61   "Our virtue": Tocqueville to Chabrol, 16 July 1831, ibid., 206.

62   "a little town": *Marie*, 2:342.

62   "Unfortunately": Beaumont to his sister Eugénie, 14 July 1831, *Lettres d'Amérique*, 102.

62   "She struck his head": *Quinze jours dans le désert*, in *Oeuvres* (Pléiade), 1:363; *Journey*, 353.

62   "Arrival in Buffalo": *Voyage*, 1:150; *Journey*, 129–30.

62   "Their features told": *Quinze jours dans le désert*, in *Voyage*, 1:362; *Journey*, 352.

63   "The orator": Benjamin Franklin, *The Autobiography and Other Writings*, ed. Kenneth Silverman (London: Penguin, 1986), 122.

63   "All the Indian tribes": *Democracy in America*, 1.2.10, in *Oeuvres* (Pléiade), 2:373; Goldhammer, 373.

63   "We hear the rustling": Quoted by J. O. Lewis, *The North American Aboriginal Port-Folio* (New York: George Adlard, 1839), 56.

64   "The Indian races": *Voyage*, 1:141; *Journey*, 119.

64   "Where today": Quoted by Philip Jenkins, *A History of the United States* (New York: St. Martin's, 1977), 77.

64   "God be thanked": Tocqueville to Chabrol, 17 Aug. 1831, *Lettres choisies*, 217.

64   "Look at the French peasant": *Marie*, 2:261–62.

64   "In all the other nations": *Abolition de l'esclavage*, in *O.C.*, 3 (1):105.

65   "the Americans never use": *Democracy in America*, 1.2.9, in *Oeuvres* (Pléiade), 2:351–52; Goldhammer, 350.

65   "The American farmer": Francis Lieber, *Letters to a Gentleman in Germany* (Philadelphia: Carey, Lea & Blanchard, 1834), 269.

65   "still recovering": Graham Robb, *The Discovery of France: A Historical Geography from the Revolution to the First World War* (New York: Norton, 2007), 216.

65   "When you've traversed": Tocqueville to his mother, 17 July 1831, *Lettres choisies*, 209.

65   "bringing with it": Tocqueville to his mother, 21 Aug. 1831, ibid., 219.

65   "So long as Louis-Philippe is there": Tocqueville to Kergorlay, 29 June 1831, ibid., 202.

4. THE ROMANCE OF THE FOREST

66   "made so famous . . . Europe in arms": *Quinze jours dans le désert*, in *Voyage*, 1:367; *Journey*, 358.

67   "and you'll think": Tocqueville to his father, 15 Aug. 1831, *O.C.*, 14:125.

67   "abominable": Tocqueville to Eugénie de Grancey, 10 Oct. 1831, *Lettres choisies*, 234.

67   "a fine American village": *Voyage*, 1:152; *Journey*, 132.

67   a population of twenty-five hundred: The 1830 census, as reported in M. R. Bartlett, *A Statistical and Chronological View of the United States* (New York: Sleight & Van Norden, 1833), 43.

67   "The man you left behind": *Quinze jours dans le désert*, in *Voyage*, 1:365–66; *Journey*, 356.

67   "From New York": *Marie*, 2:58.

67   "the universal Yankee nation": Quoted by Daniel Feller, *The Jacksonian Promise: America, 1815–1840* (Baltimore, MD: John Hopkins University Press, 1995), 68.

67   "What do you think": Beaumont to Ernest de Chabrol, 2 Aug. 1831, *Lettres d'Amérique*, 108.

68   Henry Adams later observed: Henry Adams, *History of the United States of America* (New York: Scribner, 1891–96), 1:17.

68   "backsettlers . . . trailblazers": J. A. Leo Lemay, "The Frontiersman from Lout to Hero," *Proceedings of the American Antiquarian Society* 88 (1978), 187–223.

68   "It did not happen": Speech at Saratoga in 1840, *The Writings and Speeches of Daniel Webster* (Boston: Little, Brown, 1903), 3:30.

68   "Two years ago": *Voyage*, 1:272; *Journey*, 267–68.

68   profits of speculators: Harriet Martineau, *Society in America* (London: Saunders & Otley, 1837), 1:333, 352.

69   "the West was a migrating region": Frederick Jackson Turner, "The Significance of the Section," in *The Frontier in American History* (New York: Holt, 1953), 203.

69   "American democracy was born": Frederick Jackson Turner, "The West and American Ideals," an address delivered at the University of Washington in

1914, quoted by Henry Nash Smith, *Virgin Land: The American West as Symbol and Myth* (Cambridge, MA: Harvard University Press, 1970), 253. As Smith notes (293), Turner deleted "stark and strong and full of life" when he reprinted the essay in *The Frontier in American History*.

69   "You, who sympathize": Beaumont's notes, quoted by Nolla, 2:256–57n.

70   "You want to see the woods?": *Quinze jours dans le désert*, in *Voyage*, 1:368; *Journey*, 359.

70   "We have no word": Beaumont to his sister Eugénie, 14 July 1831, *Lettres d'Amérique*, 92.

70   " 'new settlers' ": Tocqueville to Chabrol, 17 Aug. 1831, *Lettres choisies*, 216.

70   "We were overcome": *Quinze jours dans le désert*, in *Voyage*, 1:369; *Journey*, 360.

70   Beaumont measured an oak: Beaumont to Chabrol, 2 Aug. 1831, *Lettres d'Amérique*, 113.

70   "He ran with the agility": *Quinze jours dans le désert*, in *Voyage*, 1:383; *Journey*, 374.

71   "Lying on his cloak": *Quinze jours dans le désert*, in *Voyage*, 1: 403–4; *Journey*, 394.

71   "There was no poet": *Marie*, 2:265.

71   "Primitive liberty": François-René de Chateaubriand, *Voyage en Amérique*, ed. Richard Switzer (Paris: Marcel Didier, 1964), 1:133–34.

71   "The wind dies down": *Voyage*, 1:155; *Journey*, 135.

72   "At midday . . . nature's forces were paralyzed": *Quinze jours dans le désert*, in *Voyage*, 1:392–93; *Journey*, 383.

72   Jansenism: Jardin, 127–28.

72   "Men are in darkness": Pascal, *Pensées*, no. 194, in the Léon Brunschvicg numeration.

73   "Suddenly we were startled": *Quinze jours dans le désert*, in *Voyage*, 1:408; *Journey*, 398.

73   "You can't imagine": Tocqueville to Lesueur, 3 Aug. 1831, *O.C.*, 14:123.

73   "Don't go to Michigan": Quoted by Frank B. Woodford and Arthur M. Woodford, *All Our Yesterdays: A Brief History of Detroit* (Detroit: Wayne State University Press, 1969), 165.

73   "but I didn't manage": Beaumont to his father, 1 Aug. 1831, *Lettres d'Amérique*, 106.

73   "the moon revealed": *Quinze jours dans le désert*, in *Voyage*, 1:388; *Journey*, 378–79.

74   "a resinous fire": *Quinze jours dans le désert*, in *Voyage*, 1:399–400; *Journey*, 362.

74   "Focused on": *Quinze jours dans le désert*, in *Voyage*, 1:372; *Journey*, 363.

74   "I often met": *Democracy in America*, 2.3.10, in *Oeuvres* (Pléiade), 2:717; Goldhammer, 697.

75   "On the other side": *Democracy in America*, 3, endnote, in *Oeuvres* (Pléiade), 2:858; Goldhammer, 865.

76   "Civilization has no hold": *Quinze jours dans le désert*, in *Voyage*, 1:396, *Journey*, 386–87.

77   "If he can rake": Mary Graham in 1844, in *Major Problems in the Early Republic, 1787–1848*, ed. Sean Wilentz (Lexington, MA: D. C. Heath, 1992), 191.

77   "Plunged into deep obscurity": *Quinze jours dans le désert*, in *Voyage*, 1:390–91; *Journey*, 381.

77   "Kept awake by the pain": *Quinze jours dans le désert*, in *Voyage*, 1:371–72; *Journey*, 390.

77   "One night": Quoted by Nolla, 2:124.

78   "Don't go too fast": *Quinze jours dans le désert*, in *Voyage*, 1:388–89; *Journey*, 388–89.

78   "Saginaw is the boundary": Beaumont to his father, 1 Aug. 1831, *Lettres d'Amérique*, 105.

79   "is a tireless . . . conveniences of life": *Quinze jours dans le désert*, in *Voyage*, 1:402–3; *Journey*, 392–93.

79   "Dull but capable": Henry David Thoreau, *A Week on the Concord and Merrimack Rivers* (Boston: Houghton Mifflin, 1961), 52–53.

79   "His features": *Quinze jours dans le désert*, in *Voyage*, 1:372; *Journey*, 363.

79   "We asked": *Quinze jours dans le désert*, in *Voyage*, 1:405; *Journey*, 395.

80   "'Why are you being'": *Quinze jours dans le désert*, in *Voyage*, 1:410; *Journey*, 400.

80   "we did . . . our happy return": *Quinze jours dans le désert*, in *Voyage*, 1:412; *Journey*, 402–3.

80   "It was in the midst": *Quinze jours dans le désert*, in *Voyage*, 1:413; *Journey*, 403.

81   "the enchantment . . . raging desire": *Marie*, 2:73–74.

81   "the moon shone": François-René de Chateaubriand, *Atala*, ed. Gérard Gengembre (Paris: Pocket, 1996), 38.

81   "Americans consider": *Marie*, 2:328.

82   "understands the use": James Stuart, *Three Years in North America* (New York: J. & J. Harper, 1833), 1:168, 135.

82   boilers of a saltworks: As reported by Frederick Marryat, *A Diary in America, with Remarks on Its Institutions*, ed. Sydney Jackman (New York: Knopf, 1962), 85.

82   "Tocqueville journeyed": William Serrin, *New York Times*, 2 Jan. 1976, 25.

83   "August 4": *Voyage*, 1:161–65; *Journey*, 142–47.

83   "Village on the bank": *Voyage*, 1:165; *Journey*, 146.

83   Martineau visited Milwaukee: Martineau, *Society in America*, 2:5.

83   "you'll find a little town": Michel Chevalier, *Lettres sur l'Amérique du Nord* (Paris: Gosselin, 1836), 2:163–64.

83 "washed by Lake Michigan": James H. Lanman, *History of Michigan, Civil and Topographical* (New York: E. French, 1839), 316.

84 "They are pretty much": Beaumont to his brother Achille, 11 Aug. 1831, *Lettres d'Amérique*, 120, 118.

84 "Where, thought I": Godfrey Vigne, *Six Months in America* (Philadelphia: Thomas Ash, 1833), 40–41.

84 "We have seldom met": *Detroit Courier*, 1 Sept. 1831, quoted by Pierson, 308.

84 "There was nothing remarkable": Tocqueville to his father, 14 Aug. 1831, *O.C.*, 14:124.

85 "When the ball was over": Beaumont to his brother Achille, 11 Aug. 1831, *Lettres d'Amérique*, 121.

85 "The warning bell": Tocqueville to Eugène Stöffels, 18 Oct. 1831, *Lettres choisies*, 237.

85 "I played the variations": Beaumont to his brother Achille, 11 Aug. 1831, *Lettres d'Amérique*, 122.

86 "The fathers of the Canadians": Tocqueville to Eugénie de Grancey, 10 Oct. 1831, *Lettres choisies*, 233.

86 J. O. Lewis: *The North American Aboriginal Port-Folio* (New York: George Adlard, 1839).

86 "In the forest": *Voyage*, 1:161; *Journey*, 142.

87 "I sometimes wonder . . . do without justice": Beaumont to Chabrol, 2 Aug. 1831, *Lettres d'Amérique*, 110–11.

87 "As with all societies": Tocqueville and Beaumont, *Note sur le système pénitentiaire*, in *O.C.*, 4 (1):49.

87 "I amused myself": Beaumont to his brother Achille, 11 Aug. 1831, *Lettres d'Amérique*, 126.

88 "I found a small piece": Ibid., 125.

88 "The Lutheran": *Quinze jours dans le désert*, in *Voyage*, 1:406; *Journey*, 396.

88 "There is no Indian": *Democracy in America*, 1.2.10, in *Oeuvres* (Pléiade), 2:380–81; Goldhammer, 378–79.

88 "Mild and hospitable": *Democracy in America*, 1.1.1, in *Oeuvres* (Pléiade), 2:26; Goldhammer, 27–28.

88 "They inspire more pity": Tocqueville to Chabrol, 16 July 1831, *Lettres choisies*, 206.

89 "A lady asked me": Martineau, *Society in America*, 3:81.

89 "The gloom of the abyss": Thomas Hamilton, *Men and Manners in America* (Philadelphia: Carey, Lea & Blanchard, 1833), 368.

89 "When I felt how near": Charles Dickens, *American Notes*, ed. Patricia Ingham (London: Penguin, 2000), 220.

89 "The august throne": J. W. Orr, *Pictorial Guide to the Falls of Niagara* (Buffalo: Salisbury and Clapp, 1842), 17–18.

89   "There is a certain satisfaction": Charles A. Dana, *The United States Illustrated, in Views of City and Country, with Descriptive and Historical Articles* (New York: Meyer, 1853), 13.

91   "A description": Tocqueville to Beaumont, 30 Aug. 1829, *O.C.*, 8 (1):78.

91   "In that place": Tocqueville to his mother, 21 Aug. 1831, *Lettres choisies*, 219.

91   "a new political science": Introduction to *Democracy in America*, in *Oeuvres* (Pléiade), 2:8; Goldhammer, 7.

92   "a considerable parish": "Fragment du Journal," in *Lettres d'Amérique*, 137.

92   "Why do you love": *Voyage*, 1:208–9; *Journey*, 195.

92   "The villages we saw": *Voyage*, 1:203; *Journey*, 189.

92   "I don't know why": Beaumont to his brother Jules, 16 Sept. 1831, *Lettres d'Amérique*, 145.

93   "The people are": *Voyage*, 1:211; *Journey*, 198.

93   "This race of men": *Voyage*, 1:206; *Journey*, 192.

93   "They are as French . . . more than money": Tocqueville to Lesueur, 7 Sept. 1831, *Lettres choisies*, 221–22.

5. BOSTON: DEMOCRACY AS A STATE OF MIND

95   "The prisons have bored us": Beaumont to his mother, 7 Oct. 1831, *Lettres d'Amérique*, 160.

95   "The present state": Beaumont to his brother Jules, 16 Sept. 1831, *Lettres d'Amérique*, 147.

96   "a second father": "Notice," 6.

96   "Opening the packet": Tocqueville to his brother Édouard, 10 Sept. 1831, *Lettres choisies*, 223–24.

96   "unlike the thoroughfares": James Boardman, *America and the Americans . . . by a Citizen of the World* (London: Longman, Green, 1833), 273.

96   "We have found here . . . on the same day": Beaumont to his brother Achille, 25 Sept. 1831, *Lettres d'Amérique*, 155.

97   "I chatted": Beaumont to his brother Jules, 16 Sept. 1831, ibid., 147.

98   "men of intelligence": Ellen Coolidge, quoted by Pierson, 392.

98   "Kings we never had": John Adams, *Diary and Autobiography*, ed. L. H. Butterfield (Cambridge, MA: Harvard University Press, 1961), 3:356.

98   "no title of nobility": U.S. Constitution, art. 1, sec. 9.

98   "It seems to us": Beaumont to his brother Jules, 16 Sept. 1831, *Lettres d'Amérique*, 147.

98   "Society": *Voyage*, 1:221; *Journey*, 209.

99   "a man of reserved": Quoted by Charles Sellers, *The Market Revolution: Jacksonian America, 1815–1846* (New York: Oxford University Press, 1991), 95.

99   "Slavery has altered": *Voyage*, 1:74–77; *Journey*, 49–50.

100   "It was hardly a tactful": Brogan, 187.

100   "The political dogma": *Voyage*, 1:73; *Journey*, 47.

100   "1. The majority may be mistaken": *Voyage*, 1:166; *Journey*, 148.

101   "that majority . . . all civilized countries": Jared Sparks to Major Poussin, 1 Feb. 1841, and to William Smyth, 13 Oct. 1841, quoted by Herbert B. Adams, "Jared Sparks and Alexis de Tocqueville," *Johns Hopkins University Studies in Historical and Political Science* 16 (1898), 605–6.

101   "Once an idea": *Democracy in America*, 1.2.3, in *Oeuvres* (Pléiade), 2:210; Goldhammer, 212–13.

102   "In America": *Democracy in America*, 1.2.7, in *Oeuvres* (Pléiade), 2:293–94; Goldhammer, 292–93.

102   "On the contrary": *Voyage*, 1:73; *Journey*, 48.

102   "Interests, passions": *Democracy in America*, 1.1.2, in *Oeuvres* (Pléiade), 2:44; Goldhammer, 45–46.

103   "Massachusetts was": *Voyage*, 1:65; *Journey*, 38.

103   "Not only is each state": "Mr. Clay" (not Henry Clay), *Voyage*, 1:80; *Journey*, 55.

103   "If someone": *Voyage*, 1:66; *Journey*, 39.

103   "the college of Boston": Ronald Story, *The Forging of an Aristocracy: Harvard and the Boston Upper Class, 1800–1870* (Middletown, CT: Wesleyan University Press, 1980), 91.

104   "The conduct of Tocqueville": Pierson, 448n.

104   "a great and fine": Tocqueville to Sparks, 11 Dec. 1852, *O.C.*, 7:148.

104   "flea-bite . . . our demands": Quoted by Van Wyck Brooks, *The Flowering of New England, 1815–1865* (New York: Dutton, 1936), 125.

104   "The whole thing": *Voyage*, 1:246; *Journey*, 236.

104   *crottes de lapin*: Quoted by James T. Schleifer, "Images of America After the Revolution: Alexis de Tocqueville and Gustave de Beaumont Visit the Early Republic," *Yale University Library Gazette* 51 (1977), 136.

104   "No, I cannot believe": *Voyage*, 1:79; *Journey*, 54.

105   two-thirds of the wealthiest: Story, *Forging of an Aristocracy*, 7.

105   "Unitarianism is in general": *Marie*, 2:196.

105   "I have always thought": Tocqueville to Ernest de Chabrol, 26 Oct. 1831, *Lettres choisies*, 244.

105   "When democracy arrives": Quoted by Nolla, 1:57n.

105   "as much a political theory": *Democracy in America*, 1.1.2, in *Oeuvres* (Pléiade), 2:36–38; Goldhammer, 38–39.

106   "The republic": *Voyage*, 1:69; *Journey*, 43.

106   "dead creations": *Journey*, 43; and Pierson, 378.

107 "in which each person": Jean-Jacques Rousseau, *Du contrat social*, 1.6, in *Oeuvres complètes*, ed. Bernard Gagnebin et al. (Paris: Gallimard, 1964), 360–61.

107 three writers whom Tocqueville honored: Tocqueville to Kergorlay, 10 Nov. 1836, *O.C.*, 13 (1):418.

107 "The most important law": Rousseau, *Du contrat social*, 2.2, in *Oeuvres complètes*, 394.

107 "what one might call": *Democracy in America*, 1.2.9, in *Oeuvres* (Pléiade), 2:331; Goldhammer, 331.

107 As Bellah notes: Robert N. Bellah et al., *Habits of the Heart: Individualism and Commitment in American Life* (Berkeley: University of California Press, 1996), 37.

107 "I intend the expression": *Democracy in America*, 1.2.9, in *Oeuvres* (Pléiade), 2:331; Goldhammer, 331.

107 "there is no action": Ibid., 2.1.2, in *Oeuvres* (Pléiade), 2:519; Goldhammer, 489.

108 plenty of publications: Abel Bowen, *Bowen's Picture of Boston* (Boston: Otis, Broaders, 1838), 42–44.

108 "They all consider": *Democracy in America*, 1.2.10, in *Oeuvres* (Pléiade), 2:435; Goldhammer, 432.

108 "I doubt that More": Quoted by Nolla, 2:26n.

108 "living American writers": *Voyage*, 1:212 (not included in *Journey*).

108 an anthology: Mary Russell Mitford, ed., *Stories of American Life* (London: Colburn and Bentley, 1830), noted by Nolla, 2:59n.

108 Christmas tree: Edwin G. Burrows and Mike Wallace, *Gotham: A History of New York City to 1898* (New York: Oxford University Press, 1999), 463.

109 "Sedgwick! Sedgwick!": Brooks, *Flowering of New England*, 382.

109 "Democracy doesn't just . . . do have books": Quoted by Nolla, 2:64n, 65n.

109 "White persons": Bowen, *Bowen's Picture of Boston*, 251, 201, 288.

109 "We are incontestably": Beaumont to his brother Jules, 16 Sept. 1831, *Lettres d'Amérique*, 150.

109 " '*Ma foi*' . . . professions and classes": Francis Lieber, *Letters to a Gentleman in Germany* (Philadelphia: Carey, Lea & Blanchard, 1834), 34–35.

110 "the sheriff executing": *Voyage*, 1:70; *Journey*, 44.

110 "Every innovation": *Democracy in America*, 2.1.10, in *Oeuvres* (Pléiade), 2:555–57; Goldhammer, 526–27.

110 "All around this place": *Voyage en Angleterre et en Irlande de 1835*, in *Oeuvres* (Pléiade), 1:503.

111 "Each day the worker": *Democracy in America*, 2.2.20, in *Oeuvres* (Pléiade), 2:672; Goldhammer, 649.

111 "eighteen distinct operations": Adam Smith, *The Wealth of Nations*, ed. Andrew Skinner (London: Penguin, 1997), 1:110.

111 "In the midst": *Voyage en Angleterre*, 1:504.

111   "It sometimes happens": *Democracy in America*, 1.2.10, in *Oeuvres* (Pléiade), 2:470; Goldhammer, 465–66.

111   "habitually inexact": Schleifer, 308.

112   "I know that in general": Tocqueville to his father, 7 Oct. 1831, *O.C.*, 14:138–39.

112   "Our stay in Boston": Tocqueville to Chabrol, 7 Oct. 1831, unpublished, Yale Tocqueville collection, B.I.a.2.

112   "invincible apathy": *Democracy in America*, 1.1.5, in *Oeuvres* (Pléiade), 2:102n; Goldhammer, 104n.

113   "Will I ever write": Tocqueville to his mother, 27 Sept. 1831, *O.C.*, 14:137.

6. PHILADELPHIA: TOLERATION, ASSOCIATION, AND INCARCERATION

114   "The city is built": Frances Trollope, *Domestic Manners of the Americans*, ed. Pamela Neville-Sington (New York: Penguin, 1997), 201.

114   "I would have given": Charles Dickens, *American Notes*, ed. Patricia Ingham (London: Penguin, 2000), 110.

114   "Philadelphia is mediocrity": Thomas Hamilton, *Men and Manners in America* (Philadelphia: Carey, Lea & Blanchard, 1833), 180.

114   "I believe Philadelphia": Tocqueville to his cousin Alexandrine, 18 Oct. 1831, *O.C.*, 14:141.

115   "I have nothing new": Tocqueville to his mother, 24 Oct. 1831, *O.C.*, 14:143.

115   thirty-two churches: James Flint, *Letters from America* (Edinburgh: Tait, 1822), 30.

115   "I stayed": Fragment titled "Les sectes en Amérique," in Nolla, 2:319–20.

116   "What can public opinion": *Democracy in America*, 1.2.9, in *Oeuvres* (Pléiade), 2:364–65; Goldhammer, 362–63 (the law Tocqueville cites was passed in 1834, after his American trip but before the publication of *Democracy in America*).

116   "when men can speak freely": *Voyage*, 1:234; *Journey*, 222.

116   "The object": *Democracy in America*, 1.2.4, in *Oeuvres* (Pléiade), 2:218; Goldhammer, 200.

116   "like separate nations": *Democracy in America*, 1.2.4, in *Oeuvres* (Pléiade), 2:214; Goldhammer, 216.

117   "No sooner do you set foot": *Democracy in America*, 1.2.6, in *Oeuvres* (Pléiade), 2:278; Goldhammer, 278.

117   "Democracy doesn't give": *Democracy in America*, 1.2.6, in *Oeuvres* (Pléiade), 2:281; Goldhammer, 280–81.

117   "The heart expands": *Democracy in America*, 2.2.5, in *Oeuvres* (Pléiade), 2:623; Goldhammer, 598.

117   "It is easy to foresee": *Democracy in America*, 2.2.5, in *Oeuvres* (Pléiade), 2:623; Goldhammer, 597.

118   "what may enlighten": Michel Foucault, *Discipline and Punish: The Birth of the Prison*, trans. Alan Sheridan (New York: Vintage Books, 1995), 238.

118   "Cut them off . . . scarcely be equaled": O. F. Lewis, *The Development of American Prisons and Prison Customs, 1776–1845* (Albany: Prison Association of New York, 1922), 81, 78.

118   "however good": Ibid., 99.

119   On arrival: For details of punishment, see Scott Christianson, *With Liberty for Some: 500 Years of Imprisonment in America* (Boston: Northeastern University Press, 1998), 132–38.

120   "After the Rev. Mr. Demme . . . with that heart": *First Annual Report of the Inspectors of the Eastern State Penitentiary* (Philadelphia: Thomas Kite, 1831), 8, 19.

121   eighty-seven prisoners: Ibid., 23–24; *Second Annual Report of the Inspectors of the Eastern State Penitentiary* (Philadelphia: Thomas Kite, 1832), 6–9.

121   "In thus addressing ourselves": Letter of 19 Nov. 1831, *O.C.*, 4 (1):505n.

121   "not only the circumstances": Charles Lucas, *De la réforme des prisons* (1836), quoted by Foucault, *Discipline and Punish*, 252.

121   The notebook he compiled: In the Yale Tocqueville collection, Bif.2/16.

121   extended interviews: Tocqueville and Beaumont, *Enquête sur le pénitencier de Philadelphie*, in *O.C.*, 4 (1):328–41.

122   "The interior": Tocqueville's notes, in *O.C.*, 4 (1):40.

123   "He devoted two weeks": "Notice," 20–21.

123   "'God bless you, Sir!'": Harriet Martineau, *Retrospect of Western Travel* (London: Saunders and Otley, 1838), 1:207.

123   "The prisoner": Dickens, *American Notes*, 111, 113.

123   "A considerable number": Quoted by Laura Sullivan, "Solitary Confinement in U.S. Prisons," NPR *Timeline*, www.npr.org/templates/story/story .php?storyId=5579901.

124   "On the haggard face": Charles Dickens, *American Notes*, in *Works of Charles Dickens* (Boston: Houghton, Osgood & Co., 1879), 15:291.

124   "These conversations": "Notice," 21.

125   "When I'm active": Tocqueville to Eugène Stöffels, 18 Oct. 1831, *Lettres choisies*, 258.

7. DEMOCRACY IN "THE WEST"

126   "The trip . . . factories going": Beaumont to his sister Eugénie, 1 Dec. 1831, *Lettres d'Amérique*, 187.

127   "the great turnpikes": Timothy Flint, *A Condensed Geography and History of the Western States* (Cincinnati: E. H. Flint, 1828), 1:212.

127   "rolling its volumed": Edmund Flagg, *The Far West; or, A Tour Beyond the Mountains* (New York: Harper, 1838), 47.

127   "and in a week . . . and the cold": Tocqueville to his brother Édouard, 26 Nov. 1831, *O.C.*, 14: 145–47.

127   "After voyaging": Beaumont to his sister Eugénie, 1 Dec. 1831, *Lettres d'Amérique*, 188.

127   "Your ears freeze": Tocqueville to Chabrol, 6 Dec. 1831, Yale Tocqueville collection, B.I.a.2.

128   "The view": Henry Howe, *Historical Collections of Virginia* (Charleston, SC: Babcock, 1845), 409.

128   "Toward midnight": *Oeuvres* (Beaumont), 5:30–31.

129   "We ran a hundred times": Tocqueville to his brother Édouard, 20 Jan. 1832, *O.C.*, 14:165.

129   a steamboat bearing Lafayette: Lewis Perry, *Boats Against the Current: Revolution and Modernity, 1820–1860* (New York: Oxford University Press, 1993), 18–19.

129   It was very common: Louis C. Hunter, *Steamboats on the Western Rivers: An Economic and Technological History* (Cambridge, MA: Harvard University Press, 1949), 163–67, 282ff.

129   "grand floating hotels": Frances Trollope, *Domestic Manners of the Americans*, ed. Pamela Neville-Sington (New York: Penguin, 1977), 286.

129   "The river Ohio": James Flint, *Letters from America* (Edinburgh: Tait, 1822), 141.

130   *William Parsons*: Mentioned in "Notice," 31.

130   "Without them": Trollope, *Domestic Manners of the Americans*, 35.

130   "A large": Thomas Hamilton, *Men and Manners in America* (Philadelphia: Carey, Lea & Blanchard, 1833), 293.

130   "I suspect": Trollope, *Domestic Manners of the Americans*, 313–14, 95, 78–79.

131   "the man to whose service": Anthony Trollope, *North America* (New York: Knopf, 1951), 77.

131   "a nation of spitters": *American Monthly Review*, quoted by Richard Mullen, *Birds of Passage: Five Englishwomen in Search of America* (London: Duckworth, 1994), 122.

131   "the great experiment": Trollope, *Domestic Manners of the Americans*, 7–8, 161, 80–81.

131   "a sentence elegantly turned:" Ibid., 40, 323–27, 186–87, 133.

132   "the term 'dry goods'": Hamilton, *Men and Manners in America*, 17.

132   other writers complained: Basil Hall, *Travels in North America in the Years 1827 and 1828* (Edinburgh: Robert Cadell, 1830), 1:81, 163; James Stuart, *Three Years in North America* (New York: J. & J. Harper, 1833), 1:201.

132   "a smart fellow": Harriet Martineau, *Society in America* (London: Saunders & Otley, 1837), 1:337.

132   "They are notably lacking": *Voyage*, 1:205; *Journey*, 191.

132 "the perpetual change": *Democracy in America*, 2.1.16, in *Oeuvres* (Pléiade), 2:577; Goldhammer, 548.

132 "It is quite impossible": Quoted by Hall, *Travels in North America*, 2:203.

132 "Everything good and bad": Tocqueville to his mother, 6 Dec. 1831, *O.C.*, 14:152.

133 "a microcosm": Daniel Feller, "Oh Why, Oh Why Ohio?" *Reviews in American History* 17 (1989), 205.

133 "The state of Ohio": M. R. Bartlett, *A Statistical and Chronological View of the United States* (New York: Sleight & Van Norden, 1833), 37.

133 "hundreds of men": John Mason Peck, *A New Guide for Emigrants to the West* (Boston: Gould, Kendall & Lincoln, 1837), 121. Frederick Jackson Turner quotes a long passage from this book in *The Frontier in American History* (New York: Holt, 1953), 19–21.

133 One Illinois woman: Reported by John Woods, *Two Years' Residence in the Settlement on the English Prairie in the Illinois Country* (London: Longman, 1822), 160.

134 "By flattering everyone": *Voyage*, 1:107–8; *Journey*, 85.

134 "What seems most favorable": *Voyage*, 1:109; *Journey*, 86.

135 "The only reason": *Voyage*, 1:113; *Journey*, 91.

135 "The traveler": *Democracy in America*, 1.2.10, in *Oeuvres* (Pléiade), 2:400–401; Goldhammer, 398.

135 "You have passed": *Voyage*, 1:113–14; *Journey*, 91.

135 "It seems to me": *Voyage*, 1:111; *Journey*, 88.

136 "We have pushed": *Voyage*, 1:107–8; *Journey*, 84–85.

136 "absolutely without precedents": Tocqueville to his mother, 6 Dec. 1831, *O.C.*, 14:153.

136 "No one yet knows": *Voyage*, 1:279–80; *Journey*, 276.

136 "It is in the West": *Democracy in America*, 1.1.3, in *Oeuvres* (Pléiade), 2:57; Goldhammer, 58.

137 "Dependence": A reminiscence from Indiana, quoted by Charles Sellers, *The Market Revolution: Jacksonian America, 1815–1846* (New York: Oxford University Press, 1991), 14.

137 "The Puritan": Flint, *Condensed Geography*, 1:207.

137 "They do not love": Francis Grund, *The Americans in Their Moral, Social, and Political Relations* (Boston: Marsh, Capen and Lyon, 1837), 150–51.

137 "the family represents": *Democracy in America*, 1.1.3, in *Oeuvres* (Pléiade), 2:53; Goldhammer, 53.

137 "To flee the paternal": *Democracy in America*, 1.2.9, in *Oeuvres* (Pléiade), 2:328; Goldhammer, 328–29.

138 "languishing for lack": Adolphe Blanqui in 1826, quoted by Graham Robb, *The Discovery of France: A Historical Geography from the Revolution to the First World War* (New York: Norton, 2007), 138.

138 "An American taken at random": *Democracy in America*, 1.2.10, in *Oeuvres* (Pléiade), 2:471; Goldhammer, 467.

138 "Nothing prevents him": Quoted in *Oeuvres* (Pléiade), 2:1041n.

138 "you meet": *Democracy in America*, 1.2.10, in *Oeuvres* (Pléiade), 2:470; Goldhammer, 466.

138 "You may have known": Achille Murat, *The United States of North America* (London: Effingham Wilson, 1833), 335.

138 "If the other thirty-one": *Democracy in America*, 1.2.9, in *Oeuvres* (Pléiade), 2:325; Goldhammer, 325.

138 "In this gradual": *Democracy in America*, 1.2.10, in *Oeuvres* (Pléiade), 2:440; Goldhammer, 437.

139 "In the most recent": Beaumont to his brother Jules, 4 Dec. 1831, *Lettres d'Amérique*, 194.

139 "in an old hat": *Marie*, 2:227.

139 "America demonstrates . . . on earth": *Voyage*, 1:275–76; *Journey*, 271–72.

140 "The hardest task": Quoted by Nolla, 2:114n.

140 "In France": *Voyage*, 1:277–78; *Journey*, 273–75.

140 "a sort of imaginary": *Democracy in America*, 2.3.5, in *Oeuvres* (Pléiade), 2:695; Goldhammer, 674.

140 "Let us trace": *L'ancien régime et la révolution*, in *Oeuvres* (Pléiade), 3:123.

141 "degenerating into": John Stuart Mill, *Autobiography*, ed. John M. Robson (London: Penguin, 1990), 150.

141 "Political virtue": C. L. de Secondat, baron de Montesquieu, *L'esprit des lois*, 4.5, in *Oeuvres complètes*, ed. Roger Callois (Paris: Gallimard, 1951), 2:267.

141 "Imagine if you can": Tocqueville to Chabrol, 9 June 1831, *Lettres choisies*, 185.

142 "The principle": *Voyage*, 1:230; *Journey*, 217–18.

142 As Arthur Goldhammer notes: Arthur Goldhammer, "Translating Tocqueville: Constraints of Classicism," in *The Cambridge Companion to Tocqueville*, ed. Cheryl B. Welch (New York: Cambridge University Press, 2006), 144–49.

142 "The doctrine of interest": *Democracy in America*, 2.2.8, in *Oeuvres* (Pléiade), 2:637; Goldhammer, 612.

142 "If morality": Quoted by Nolla, 1:188n.

142 "Given the total": *Voyage*, 1:278; *Journey*, 274.

143 "Alexis de Tocqueville": "Notice," 45, 25.

143 "The Americans bring": *Democracy in America*, 1.2.10, in *Oeuvres* (Pléiade), 2:469; Goldhammer, 465.

8. DOWNRIVER TO NEW ORLEANS

144   "We're curious to see": Beaumont to his sister-in-law Eugénie, 1 Dec. 1831, *Lettres d'Amérique*, 189.

145   "A big strapping pioneer . . . anything like it": Tocqueville to his father, 20 Dec. 1831, *Lettres choisies*, 251–52.

146   In the East that winter: Pierson, 575, 578.

146   One man who was there: Anita Shafer Goodstein, *Nashville, 1780–1860: From Frontier to City* (Gainesville: University of Florida Press, 1989), 51–52.

146   "Frightful roads": "Notice," 32–33.

146   "Tocqueville and I . . . form the walls": Beaumont to his mother, 15 Dec. 1831, *Lettres d'Amérique*, 196–98.

147   "13 December": "Notice," 33–34.

147   "It's only a cold": Tocqueville to Beaumont, 9 March 1829, *O.C.*, 8 (1):75.

148   "In the evening . . . did get across": Tocqueville to his father, 20 Dec. 1831, *Lettres choisies*, 253–54.

149   "Memphis!!!": "Notice," 35.

149   "A number of steamboats": Tocqueville to his father, 20 Dec. 1831, *Lettres choisies*, 252.

149   "We thus found ourselves . . . ever seen": Tocqueville to his mother, 25 Dec. 1831, *Lettres choisies*, 255.

149   "We killed four": Beaumont to his brother Achille, 25 Dec. 1831, *Lettres d'Amérique*, 203.

150   "At each successive": A Mr. Wilson, quoted by John Howard Hinton, *The History and Topography of the United States* (Boston: Samuel Walker, 1834), 2:114.

150   "as if a brilliantly": John James Audubon, *The Birds of America* (New York: Audubon, 1840–44), 4:307.

151   Audubon: Louis P. Masur, *1831: Year of Eclipse* (New York: Hill and Wang, 2001), 201.

151   "We found Shakespeare": "Notice," 35.

151   Tocqueville later mentioned: *Democracy in America*, 2.1.13, in *Oeuvres* (Pléiade), 2:567; Goldhammer, 538.

151   "While I was reading": Quoted by Nolla, 2:60n.

152   "At last": Tocqueville to his mother, 25 Dec. 1831, *Lettres choisies*, 255.

152   "Their property": Beaumont to his brother Achille, 25 Dec. 1831, *Lettres d'Amérique*, 205.

153   "You must know . . . American nations": Tocqueville to his mother, 25 Dec. 1831, *Lettres choisies*, 257–59.

153   "In this great throng": *Democracy in America*, 1.2.10, in *Oeuvres* (Pléiade), 2:377; Goldhammer, 375.

154   his letter at the time: *Lettres choisies*, 258.

154   "This is a very": C. A. Sainte-Beuve, *Nouveaux lundis* (Paris: Michel Lévy, 1868), 10:288–89.

154   "The valley watered": *Democracy in America*, 1.1.1, in *Oeuvres* (Pléiade), 2:21; Goldhammer, 23.

154   "Traveling": Tocqueville to Ernest de Chabrol, 27 Dec. 1831, *Lettres choisies*, 259.

154   "Distance": Robert Baird, *View of the Valley of the Mississippi; or, The Emigrant's and Traveller's Guide to the West* (Philadelphia: H. S. Tanner, 1832), 265.

155   "looked like": George Rogers Taylor, *The Transportation Revolution, 1815–1860* (New York: Rinehart, 1951), 66.

155   only seventy feet long: For description of steamboats, see John A. Jakle, *Images of the Ohio Valley: A Historical Geography of Travel, 1740 to 1860* (New York: Oxford University Press, 1977), 31–32.

155   Basil Hall: *Travels in North America* (Edinburgh: Robert Cadell, 1830), 3:357–68.

155   "the sameness": Frances Trollope, *Domestic Manners of the Americans*, ed. Pamela Neville-Sington (New York: Penguin, 1997), 30.

155   "an enormous ditch": Charles Dickens, *American Notes*, ed. Patricia Ingham (London: Penguin, 2000), 190.

155   "at the idea": Frederick Marryat, *A Diary in America, with Remarks on Its Institutions*, ed. Sydney Jackman (New York: Knopf, 1962), 220.

155   "The people": Dickens, *American Notes*, 176.

155   "The table was cleared" (and details on meals): Louis C. Hunter, *Steamboats on the Western Rivers: An Economic and Technological History* (Cambridge, MA: Harvard University Press, 1949), 399–403.

156   zoo animals: Thomas Hamilton, *Men and Manners in America* (Philadelphia: Carey, Lea & Blanchard, 1833), 48.

156   "the frightful manner": Trollope, *Domestic Manners of the Americans*, 20.

156   "in private houses": Harriet Martineau, *Society in America* (London: Saunders & Otley, 1837), 3:89.

156   "The cooking": Beaumont to his brother Achille, 25 Dec. 1831, *Lettres d'Amérique*, 204.

156   "boldness": Baird, *View of the Valley of the Mississippi*, 116, 267.

156   "I am an alligator": Quoted by Henry Adams, *History of the United States of America* (New York: Scribner, 1891–96), 1:55.

156   "Behind it stood": John William Ward, *Andrew Jackson: Symbol for an Age* (New York: Oxford University Press, 1955), 13–16.

157   "a regular backwoodsman": Basil Hall, *Forty Etchings: From Sketches Made with the Camera Lucida, in North America, in 1827 and 1828* (Edinburgh: Cadell, 1829), unnumbered page facing the illustration.

157 "a superb stallion": *Voyage*, 1:259; *Journey*, 252.

158 "Know all men": Quoted by Donald Braider, *Solitary Star: A Biography of Sam Houston* (New York: Putnam, 1974), 109.

158 "A succession of injuries": *The Autobiography of Sam Houston*, ed. Donald Day and Harry Herbert Ullom (Norman: University of Oklahoma Press, 1954), 7, 62.

159 "The Indian": *Voyage*, 1:261; *Journey*, 254.

159 "We shot them": Andrew Burstein, *The Passions of Andrew Jackson* (New York: Knopf, 2003), 100, 106.

160 "The entire operation": Robert Remini, *The Legacy of Andrew Jackson* (Baton Rouge: Louisana State University Press, 1988), 67.

160 "the quiet progress": Francis Grund, *The Americans in Their Moral, Social, and Political Relations* (Boston: Marsh, Capen and Lyon, 1837), 225–26.

160 "The social bond . . . laws of humanity": *Democracy in America*, 1.2.10, in *Oeuvres* (Pléiade), 2:376, 393; Goldhammer, 374, 391.

161 "The fatigue": Hamilton, *Men and Manners in America*, 319, 322–23, 331.

161 "sold down the river": Peter Kolchin, *American Slavery, 1619–1877* (New York: Hill and Wang, 2003), 98.

161 second only to New York: Daniel Walker Howe, *What Hath God Wrought: The Transformation of America, 1815–1848* (New York: Oxford University Press, 2007), 10.

162 "When people tell you": Tocqueville to Chabrol, 16 Jan. 1832, Yale Tocqueville collection, B.I.a.2.

162 "If there is no conversation": Archille Murat, *The United States of North America* (London: Effingham Wilson, 1833), 353–54.

162 "The Creole of Louisiana": Tyrone Power, *Impressions of America, During the Years 1833, 1834, and 1835* (Philadelphia: Carey, Lea & Blanchard, 1836), 2:147–48.

162 "Alas!": "24 Hours in New Orleans," in *Journey*, 412 (translated into English from a lost French original, and therefore not in *Voyage*).

163 "In locking people up": Tocqueville and Beaumont, *Système pénitentiaire aux États-Unis*, in *O.C.*, 4 (1):166.

163 Tocqueville was told: *Voyage*, 1:119; *Journey*, 96.

163 "the offspring": Baird, *View of the Valley of the Mississippi*, 69.

163 "In the American South": *Marie*, 2:103.

163 by-products of the slave trade: Howe, *What Hath God Wrought*, 24, 403.

163 "Strange sight": *Voyage*, 1:180; *Journey*, 165.

164 "many quadroons": Duke Bernhard von Saxe-Weimar-Eisenach, *Travels by His Highness Duke Bernhard of Saxe-Weimar-Eisenach Through North America in the Years 1825 and 1826*, trans. William Jeronimus (Lanham, MD: University Press of America, 2001), 346, 368.

9. ROAD TRIP THROUGH THE SOUTH

165 "le Midi": *Voyage*, 1:126; *Journey*, 104.

165 "bridges out": Beaumont to his father, 16 Jan. 1832, *Lettres d'Amérique*, 206.

165 "our meeting": Harriet Martineau, *Society in America* (London: Saunders & Otley, 1837), 2:173.

166 "It would be absurd": *Voyage*, 1:287; *Journey*, 284.

166 "If ever I write": Tocqueville to his cousin Alexandrine, 16 Jan. 1832, *O.C.*, 14:163.

166 "He who meditates": Diderot to the abbé Le Monnier, 15 Sept. 1755, in *Correspondance*, ed. Laurent Versini (Paris: Robert Laffont, 1997), 51.

166 "Whoever does not want": "Droit naturel," in the *Encyclopédie*, cited by Raymond Trousson, *Jean-Jacques Rousseau: La marche à la gloire* (Paris: Tallandier, 1988), 1:331.

166 "a charming little": *Voyage*, 1:184–85; *Journey*, 170–71.

167 "Why is it": quoted by Nolla, 1:247n.

167 potent incentive: Joyce Appleby, *Inheriting the Revolution: The First Generation of Americans* (Cambridge, MA: Harvard University Press, 2000), 59, 71.

167 "more of the established": James L. Crouthamel, "Tocqueville's South," *Journal of the Early Republic* 2 (1982), 401.

167 "I am speaking": *Democracy in America*, 2.3.18, in *Oeuvres* (Pléiade), 2:750; Goldhammer, 730.

168 "The Southerner": *Democracy in America*, 1.2.10, in *Oeuvres* (Pléiade), 2:437; Goldhammer, 434.

168 "What distinguishes": *Voyage*, 1:90; *Journey*, 66.

168 "Coldly burning": *Voyage*, 1:192; *Journey*, 179.

168 "devote themselves": *Voyage*, 1:75; *Journey*, 50.

168 "one could learn nothing": Henry Adams, *The Education of Henry Adams*, ed. Ira B. Nadel (New York: Oxford University Press, 1999), 88.

168 "the highest toned . . . the felons": Quoted by Drew Gilpin Faust, *James Henry Hammond and the Old South* (Baton Rouge: Louisiana State University Press, 1982), 176–77, 199.

169 "Q. Is it true": *Voyage*, 1:124–25; *Journey*, 102–3.

169 "no day had passed": Martineau, *Society in America*, 1:308.

169 It has been suggested: Kenneth S. Greenberg, "The Duel as Social Drama," in *Masters and Statesmen: The Political Culture of American Slavery* (Baltimore, MD: Johns Hopkins University Press, 1985), 23–41.

170 "In Europe": *Voyage*, 1:236; *Journey*, 224.

170 "a little old man": From the draft of a letter to an unidentified recipient, 8 Nov. 1831, Yale Tocqueville collection, B.I.a.2.

170 "the strongest aristocracy": Gordon S. Wood, *The Radicalism of the American Revolution* (New York: Random House, 1991), 71.

170 "very well preserved": Beaumont to his brother Achille, 8 Nov. 1831, *Lettres d'Amérique*, 173–74.

170 "gay, cheerful": *The Diary of Philip Hone, 1828–1851*, ed. Bayard Tuckerman (New York: Dodd, Mead, 1910), 13.

171 "This race of men": *Voyage*, 1:102; *Journey*, 79.

171 "All, all dead!": Jefferson to Francis Vanderkemp, 11 Jan. 1825, quoted by Joseph J. Ellis, *American Sphinx: The Character of Thomas Jefferson* (New York: Vintage Books, 1998), 278.

171 "I consider this": Quoted by Louis P. Masur, *1831: Year of Eclipse* (New York: Hill and Wang, 2001), 173.

171 "A mere democracy": *Voyage*, 1:102; *Journey*, 78.

171 one-tenth of 1 percent: Peter Kolchin, *American Slavery, 1619–1877* (New York: Hill and Wang, 2003), 101.

171 four-fifths of the black people: Daniel Walker Howe, *What Hath God Wrought: The Transformation of America, 1815–1848* (New York: Oxford University Press, 2007), 54.

171 "when a Negro took": *Voyage*, 1:173–74; *Journey*, 157.

171 "It would degrade": *Marie*, 2:169.

172 "Today we saw": *Voyage*, 1:175–176; *Journey*, 159.

172 "There was something": Beaumont to his brother Achille, 8 Nov. 1831, *Lettres d'Amérique*, 175–76.

173 "Many a time": Martineau, *Society in America*, 1:185.

174 "the cast-iron": Harriet Martineau, *Retrospect of Western Travel* (London: Saunders & Otley, 1837), 1:243–44.

174 "No, the nullifiers": *Voyage*, 1:131–32; *Journey*, 110.

174 "The answer is easy": *Democracy in America*, 1.2.10, in *Oeuvres* (Pléiade), 2:444; Goldhammer, 440.

174 "openly violating . . . remaining loyal": *Democracy in America*, 1.1.8 and 2.3.26, in *Oeuvres* (Pléiade), 2:176, 805; Goldhammer, 177, 784.

175 sexual mores: *Voyage*, 1:130, 136; *Journey*, 109, 115.

175 "I cannot enter . . . consent of the governed": Martineau, *Society in America*, 1:199, 205; 2:338, 328; 1:207.

176 "In the South": *Democracy in America*, 1.2.10, in *Oeuvres* (Pléiade), 2:420; Goldhammer, 418.

176 "a great evil . . . at his death": *Voyage*, 1:133; *Journey*, 111–12.

177 "the climate . . . the two races": Basil Hall, *Travels in North America* (Edinburgh: Robert Cadell, 1830), 3:117, 191.

177 "the most contented . . . people": Martineau, *Society in America* 2:131, 152.

177 "All men are equal": Albert G. Brown, quoted by Charles Sellers, *The Market Revolution: Jacksonian America, 1815–1846* (New York: Oxford University Press, 1991), 281.

178 "Break down slavery": Henry A. Wise, quoted by Harry L. Watson, *Liberty and Power: The Politics of Jacksonian America* (New York: Hill and Wang, 1990), 53.

178 "that most hideous": Charles Dickens, *American Notes*, ed. Patricia Ingham (London: Penguin, 2000), 34.

178 "the ghost of slavery": Dickens to Samuel Cartwright, 29 Jan. 1868, *The Letters of Charles Dickens*, ed. Madeleine House et al. (Oxford: Clarendon Press, 2002), 12:26.

178 "and to make him . . . soda water": Frederick Marryat, *A Diary in America with Remarks on Its Institutions*, ed. Sydney Jackman (New York: Knopf, 1962), 218, 248.

178 "The ordinary Negro": *Voyage*, 1:261; *Journey*, 254.

179 "The Negro, as a result": Quoted by Nolla, 1:248n.

179 "The Negro is placed . . . a fatherland": *Democracy in America*, 1.2.10, in *Oeuvres* (Pléiade), 2:370, 368; Goldhammer, 368, 366.

179 "It is impossible": *Democracy in America*, 1.2.10, in *Oeuvres* (Pléiade), 2:465; Goldhammer, 461.

179 Beaumont noted: *Marie*, 1: 191.

180 "Christianity had abolished": *Democracy in America*, 1.2.10, in *Oeuvres* (Pléiade), 2:395; Goldhammer, 393.

180 "he would make": Martineau, *Society in America*, 2:153.

180 American Colonization Society: Daniel Feller, *The Jacksonian Promise: America, 1815–1840* (Baltimore, MD: John Hopkins University Press, 1995), 65, 111.

180 "I am in earnest": "To the Public," inaugural number of *The Liberator*, 1 Jan. 1831.

180 "the laws": Martineau, *Society in America*, 2:344–45, 136.

180 "The threat . . . the two races": *Democracy in America*, 1.2.10, in *Oeuvres* (Pléiade), 2:416–18; Goldhammer, 413–16.

181 "I avow": Quoted by Nolla, 1:276n.

181 "His remarks": John C. Spencer, preface to *Democracy in America* (New York: George Dearborn & Co., 1838), v.

181 "I have only": Tocqueville to his brother Édouard, 29 Jan. 1832, *O.C.*, 14:165.

10. THE NATION'S DISAPPOINTING CAPITAL

182 "Take away from America": *Marie*, 2:259.

182 "In the center": *Democracy in America*, 2.1.12, in *Oeuvres* (Pléiade), 2:565; Goldhammer, 536.

183   "the population never": Tocqueville to his father, 24 Jan. 1832, *O.C.*, 14:167.

183   "he found himself": Henry Adams, *The Education of Henry Adams*, ed. Ira B. Nadel (New York: Oxford University Press, 1999), 42.

183   Back in Philadelphia: Beaumont to his father, 17 Nov. 1831, *Lettres d'Amérique*, 180.

183   "During our stay": Beaumont to his father, 16 Jan. 1832, ibid., 207.

183   "This letter . . . the present moment": Tocqueville to his father, 24 Jan. 1832, *O.C.*, 14:166.

184   "I've talked": Tocqueville to his brother Édouard, 20 Jan. 1832, ibid., 165.

184   "you'd think . . . twenty-two times": Beaumont to his mother, 20 Jan. 1832, *Lettres d'Amérique*, 212, 211.

185   "It's not a matter": Tocqueville to his father, 24 Jan. 1832, *O.C.*, 14:166.

185   "The debates": Beaumont to his mother, 20 Jan. 1832, *Lettres d'Amérique*, 211.

185   "You may see": Francis Lieber, *Letters to a Gentleman in Germany* (Philadelphia: Carey, Lea & Blanchard, 1834), 29.

185   "in the most unseemly": Frances Trollope, *Domestic Manners of the Americans*, ed. Pamela Neville-Sington (New York: Penguin, 1997), 171.

185   "incessant": Charles Dickens, *American Notes*, ed. Patricia Ingham (London: Penguin, 2000), 25.

186   "He is not a man": Beaumont to his mother, 20 Jan. 1832, *Lettres d'Amérique*, 210.

186   "took the opportunity": Paul C. Nagel, *John Quincy Adams: A Public Life, a Private Life* (Cambridge, MA: Harvard University Press, 1997), 307.

187   "a man of violent": *Democracy in America*, 1.2.9, in *Oeuvres* (Pléiade), 2:318; Goldhammer, 320.

187   "How could one doubt": *Voyage*, 1:174; *Journey*, 158.

187   "I do not wish": *Democracy in America*, 2.3.22, in *Oeuvres* (Pléiade), 2:787; Goldhammer, 765.

187   "*La gloire*": *Voyage en Angleterre* (1833), in *Oeuvres* (Pléiade), 1:420.

188   book on America: Achille Murat, *The United States of North America* (London: Effingham Wilson, 1833), 261–64, 74.

188   "That's due almost entirely": *Voyage*, 1:137; *Journey*, 116.

188   "who always carried": Jackson to George W. Martin, 2 Jan. 1824, *The Correspondence of Andrew Jackson*, ed. John S. Bassett (Washington, DC: Carnegie Institution, 1935), 2:222.

188   bought a buffalo: Dell Upton, "Another City: The Urban Cultural Landscape in the Early Republic," in *Everyday Life in the Early Republic*, ed. Catherine E. Hutchins (Winterthur, DE: Winterthur Museum, 1994), 101.

188   "He was the most candid": James Parton, *Life of Andrew Jackson* (1861), quoted by Andrew Burstein, *The Passions of Andrew Jackson* (New York: Knopf, 2003), xvii.

188   "trample his personal enemies": *Democracy in America*, 1.2.10, in *Oeuvres* (Pléiade), 2:457; Goldhammer, 454.

189   "the desire to be": *Democracy in America*, 1.1.8, in *Oeuvres* (Pléiade), 2:152–54; Goldhammer, 154-55.

189   "After having thus": *Democracy in America*, 1.2.10, in *Oeuvres* (Pléiade), 2:457; Goldhammer, 454.

189   Second Bank of the United States: This account of banking is drawn from Daniel Walker Howe, *What Hath God Wrought: The Transformation of America, 1815–1848* (New York: Oxford University Press, 2007); Charles Sellers, *The Market Revolution: Jacksonian America, 1815–1846* (New York: Oxford University Press, 1991); Daniel Feller, *The Jacksonian Promise: America, 1815–1840* (Baltimore, MD: Johns Hopkins University Press, 1995); and Harry L. Watson, *Liberty and Power: The Politics of Jacksonian America* (New York: Hill and Wang, 1990).

190   "not in the light of day": William Allen (1838), quoted by Lawrence Frederick Kohl, *The Politics of Individualism: Parties and the American Character in the Jacksonian Era* (New York: Oxford University Press, 1989), 25.

190   "One of the important functions": Kohl, *Politics of Individualism*, 50.

190   "All the flourishing cities": Quoted by Watson, *Liberty and Power*, 39.

191   the ethical principle: C. B. Macpherson, *The Life and Times of Liberal Democracy* (New York: Oxford University Press, 1977), 25.

191   the model of economic individualism: Steven Lukes, *Individualism* (Oxford: Basil Blackwell, 1973), 154.

191   "history's most revolutionary": Sellers, *Market Revolution*, 4.

191   "the framers adopted": *Democracy in America*, 1.1.8, in *Oeuvres* (Pléiade), 2:131; Goldhammer, 133.

191   "the Constitution rests": *Democracy in America*, 1.1.8, in *Oeuvres* (Pléiade), 2:175; Goldhammer, 176.

191   "theory has been put": *Democracy in America*, 1.1.8, in *Oeuvres* (Pléiade), 2:168; Goldhammer, 169.

192   "Its power is immense": Ibid.

192   "assumed the name": John Quincy Adams, *The Social Compact, Exemplified in the Constitution of the Commonwealth of Massachusetts* (Providence, RI: Knowles and Vose, 1842), 31.

192   "vulgar": *Democracy in America*, 1.2.5, in *Oeuvres* (Pléiade), 2:226; Goldhammer, 229.

192   French experience: Hugh Brogan, "Tocqueville and the American Presidency," *Journal of American Studies* 15 (1981), 357–75.

193   "In spite of my efforts": Beaumont to his mother, 20 Jan. 1832, *Lettres d'Amérique*, 213.

193   "I admit": Tocqueville to Poinsett, 1 Feb. 1832, *O.C.*, 7:45.

193   next packet boat: There is some confusion among Tocqueville's biographers about the ships to France, but accurate details are given in *O.C.*, 14:164n.

193   "on glimpsing": *Marie*, 2:180.

11. BUILDING A MASTERPIECE

194   what has been called: Schleifer, pt. 1.

194   "Democracy!": *Democracy in America*, drafts, Yale Tocqueville collection, C.V.h, packet 3, notebook 3, p. 28.

195   "the river of humanity": *Mémoire sur le paupérisme*, in *Oeuvres* (Pléiade), 1:1156.

195   "I'm trying to avoid": Tocqueville to Eugène Stöffels, 12 Jan. 1833, *Lettres choisies*, 284.

195   "I'm getting weary": Tocqueville to Beaumont, 4 April 1832, *O.C.*, 8 (1):112.

195   "Discipline whose mildness": Notes made in 1832, ibid., 4 (1):21.

196   "You would have smiled": Tocqueville to Beaumont, 4 April 1832, *Lettres choisies*, 279.

196   "It's distressing": Tocqueville to Blanche de Kergorlay, 16 June 1832, ibid., 283.

196   unsavory trial: Explained by Brogan, 218–19.

197   "Being at present": Tocqueville to the *procureur-général*, 21 May 1832, *Oeuvres* (Beaumont), 5:37–38.

197   "To tell the truth": "Notice," 38.

197   "I will never be happy": Tocqueville to Marie Mottley, 23 Aug. 1834, *Lettres choisies*, 305.

198   "I'm unhappy": Tocqueville to Marie, 26 Dec. 1837, ibid., 399–401.

198   "I saw her arrive": Tocqueville to the comtesse de Circourt, 14 Feb. 1854, *Oeuvres* (Beaumont), 6:173.

198   "How often": "Notice," 46.

198   "I know nothing": *Marie*, 1:ii.

199   "Tocqumont": Introduction to *Lettres choisies*, 45.

199   "I contributed only": Tocqueville to F.-A. Mignet, *Lettres choisies*, 49–50.

199   Cholera did rage: Mentioned in *Lettres choisies*, 265.

199   "It would be difficult": Tocqueville to Beaumont, 13 Aug. 1833, ibid., 288.

199   "Imagine an Italian night": Tocqueville to Marie, 30 Aug. 1833, ibid., 292–93.

200   "Since arriving here": Tocqueville to Beaumont, 1 Nov. 1833, *O.C.*, 8 (1):136.

200   "The future of democracy": Quoted by Nolla, 2:72n.

200   "It is one of the singular": Tocqueville to Pierre Freslon, 30 July 1854, *Lettres choisies*, 1107.

201   "I ended with the word": Tocqueville to Beaumont, 24 Oct. 1834, *O.C.*, 8 (1):144.

201   "His physique": Quoted by Daniel C. Gilman, "Alexis de Tocqueville and His Book on America—Sixty Years After," *Century Illustrated Monthly Magazine* 56 (1898), 707.

201   "No thinker": C. A. Sainte-Beuve, *Nouveaux lundis* (Paris: Michel Lévy, 1868), 10:320–21.

201   "It would be unfortunate": Quoted by Nolla, 1:180n.

202   "All of those pages": Ibid., 1:104n.

202   "The overall tone": Édouard to Tocqueville, 15 June 1834, Yale Tocqueville collection, C.III.b.2, 63–65.

202   "All the laws": Tocqueville to the comte Molé, Aug. 1835, *Oeuvres* (Beaumont), 7:135.

202   "a great river": *Democracy in America*, 2.2.1, in *Oeuvres* (Pléiade), 2:608; Goldhammer, 582.

202   "I will be like": *Democracy in America*, 1.2.10, in *Oeuvres* (Pléiade), 2:474–75; Goldhammer, 470.

203   brilliant commentary: Sheldon S. Wolin, *Tocqueville Between Two Worlds: The Making of a Political and Theoretical Life* (Princeton, NJ: Princeton University Press, 2001), 138.

203   "the despotism": From the notes collected under the heading "Rubish," quoted by Nolla, 2:263n.

203   "Despotism creates": Quoted by Nolla, 1:185.

203   "It is an analysis": Robert Nisbet, *The Quest for Community: A Study in the Ethics of Order and Freedom* (San Francisco: Institute for Contemporary Studies, 1990; orig. published by Oxford University Press, 1953), 170.

204   "The American's conquests": *Democracy in America*, 1.2.10, in *Oeuvres* (Pléiade), 2:480; Goldhammer, 475–76.

204   "I have an intellectual attraction": Quoted by Antoine Rédier, *Comme disait Monsieur de Tocqueville* (Paris: Perrin, 1925), 48.

205   "he got married": Sainte-Beuve, *Nouveaux lundis*, 10:318.

205   "In large measure": Wolin, *Tocqueville Between Two Worlds*, 565.

205   "masters ask nothing": *Democracy in America*, 2.3.5, in *Oeuvres* (Pléiade), 2:697; Goldhammer, 676.

205   "They like change": *Democracy in America*, 2.3.21, in *Oeuvres* (Pléiade), 2:773; Goldhammer, 752.

206   "Raise our wages": Michel Chevalier, *Lettres sur l'Amérique du Nord* (Paris: Gosselin, 1836), 1:237.

206   In a footnote: *Democracy in America*, 1.2.9, in *Oeuvres* (Pléiade), 2:320n; Goldhammer, 320–21n.

206   "these classes continue": *Democracy in America*, 1.2.6, in *Oeuvres* (Pléiade), 2:267–68; Goldhammer, 264–66.

206   "It seems to me": Tocqueville to Senior, 21 Feb. 1835, *O.C.*, 6 (2):70.

207   "How an Aristocracy": *Democracy in America*, 2.2.20, in *Oeuvres* (Pléiade), 2:671; Goldhammer, 649.

207   "That's what happens": Quoted by Nolla, 2:139.

207   "The manufacturer": *Democracy in America*, 2.2.20, in *Oeuvres* (Pléiade), 2:674–75; Goldhammer, 652.

207   "No relief": Quoted by John Brewer, "England: The Big Change," *New York Review of Books*, 26 June 2008, 55.

207   official view in New York City: Edwin G. Burrows and Mike Wallace, *Gotham: A History of New York City to 1898* (New York: Oxford University Press, 1999), 493–94.

207   "the most productive": *Mémoire sur le paupérisme*, in *Oeuvres* (Pléiade), 1:1168.

208   "he received me": Tocqueville to Beaumont, 1 April 1835, *Lettres choisies*, 315–16.

208   "I'm just getting my head": Tocqueville to Eugène Stöffels, 16 Feb. 1835, ibid., 313.

208   "I've tried to show": Tocqueville to Eugène Stöffels, 21 Feb. 1835, ibid., 314–15.

209   "They're determined": Tocqueville to Reeve, 22 March 1837, ibid., 377.

209   "original and profound": John Stuart Mill, "De Tocqueville on Democracy in America (I)," in Mill, *Essays on Politics and Society*, ed. J. M. Robson (Toronto: University of Toronto Press, 1977), 49–50.

209   "You know": Tocqueville to Beaumont, 22 Nov. 1836, *O.C.*, 8 (1):175.

210   "He has described": John C. Spencer, preface to *Democracy in America* (New York: George Dearborn & Co., 1838), viii.

210   "for I have always": Tocqueville to Spencer, 20 Sept. 1838, *O.C.*, 7:71.

210   "and I study": Henry Adams to Charles Francis Adams Jr., 1 May 1863, *A Cycle of Adams Letters, 1861–1865*, ed. Worthington Chauncey Ford (Boston: Houghton Mifflin, 1920), 1:282.

210   "If it were necessary": Tocqueville to Beaumont, 9 July 1837, *O.C.*, 8 (1):207.

211   "So, I've been beaten": Tocqueville to Beaumont, 12 Nov. 1837, *Lettres choisies*, 394.

211   "gastronomico-electoral": Tocqueville to Beaumont, 30 Sept. 1838, ibid., 316.

211   "In the eyes": Tocqueville to F. de Corcelle, 10 March 1839, *O.C.*, 15 (1):125.

211   "A liberal": Tocqueville to Royer-Collard, 27 Sept. 1841, *Lettres choisies*, 485.

212   "I've never worked": Tocqueville to Reeve, 21 Nov. 1836, *O.C.*, 6 (1): 35.

212   "I'm seized": Tocqueville to Louis Bouchitté, 26 May 1836, *Oeuvres* (Beaumont), 7:149.

212   "My subject": Tocqueville to Mill, 19 Nov. 1836, *O.C.*, 6 (1):314.

212   "This idée fixe": Tocqueville to Beaumont, 8 July 1838, *Lettres choisies*, 418.

212   "At all costs": Tocqueville to Beaumont, 8 Oct. 1839, ibid., 450.

212   "New despotism": Unpublished note quoted by Jean-Claude Lamberti, "The Ways of Conceiving the Republic," in *Interpreting Tocqueville's Democracy in America*, ed. Ken Masugi (Savage, MD: Rowman & Littlefield, 1991), 18.

213   "Above them rises": *Democracy in America*, 2.4.6, in *Oeuvres* (Pléiade), 2:837; Goldhammer, 818–19.

213   "In this picture": Quoted in *Oeuvres* (Pléiade), 2:1177n.

213   "The scope": *Democracy in America*, 2.4.3, in *Oeuvres* (Pléiade), 2:813n; Goldhammer, 813n.

214   "It is easy to see": Tocqueville's notes at the end of *Democracy in America*, in *Oeuvres* (Pléiade), 2:861; Goldhammer, 868.

214   "There are two things": *Democracy in America*, 2.3.22, in *Oeuvres* (Pléiade), 2:787; Goldhammer, 765–66.

214   "In a democratic army": *Democracy in America*, 2.3.22, in *Oeuvres* (Pléiade), 2:784–85; Goldhammer, 763.

215   "They encounter": *Democracy in America*, 1.2.9, in *Oeuvres* (Pléiade), 2:326; Goldhammer, 326.

215   "When inequality": *Democracy in America*, 2.2.13, in *Oeuvres* (Pléiade), 2:651; Goldhammer, 627–28.

12. AFTER AMERICA

217   "yet I fear": Tocqueville to Royer-Collard, 27 Sept. 1841, *Lettres choisies*, 486.

217   "internal exile": François Furet, "Tocqueville," in *A Critical Dictionary of the French Revolution*, ed. Furet and Mona Ozouf, trans. Arthur Goldhammer (Cambridge, MA: Harvard University Press, 1989), 1022.

217   "In one instant": *L'émancipation des esclaves*, in *O.C.*, 3 (1):79–80.

218   "Despotism is a legitimate": John Stuart Mill, *On Liberty*, in *On Liberty and Other Writings*, ed. Stefan Collini (Cambridge: Cambridge University Press, 1989), 13.

218   "Once we had committed": Tocqueville to Louis de Lamoricière, 5 April 1846, *Lettres choisies*, 565.

218   "If France should shrink": *Travail sur l'Algérie* (1841), in *O.C.*, 1:691.

218   "Don't you see": Tocqueville to Gobineau, 17 Nov. 1853, *Lettres choisies*, 1092–93.

219 "As the persevering enemy": Tocqueville's letter to *The Liberty Bell*, in *O.C.*, 7:164.

219 "You know": Tocqueville to Sedgwick, 4 Dec. 1852, ibid., 7:146.

219 "On this side": Tocqueville to Sedgwick, 10 Jan. 1857, ibid., 189–90.

220 "From the moment": Quoted in *Lettres choisies*, 68.

220 "with the goal": *Souvenirs*, chap. 9, in *Oeuvres* (Pléiade), 3:842.

221 "His speeches": Heinrich Heine, *Allemands et Français* (Paris: Calmann Lévy, 1899), 314.

221 "a profound contempt": Discourse of 12 Sept. 1848, in *Oeuvres* (Pléiade), 1:1142–43, 1146.

221 "parties never": Tocqueville, *Souvenirs* 2.8, in *Oeuvres* (Pléiade), 3:841.

222 "completely useless": Tocqueville to F. de Corcelle, 2 Oct. 1854, *Lettres choisies*, 1115.

222 "civis civitatem": Tocqueville to Pierre Freslon, 30 July 1854, ibid., 1108.

222 "I have relatives": Tocqueville to Sophie Swetchine, 20 Oct. 1856, *Oeuvres* (Beaumont), 6:350–51.

222 "I've never been able": Tocqueville to Beaumont, 22 Feb. 1656, *O.C.*, 8 (3):374.

222 "You won't easily": Tocqueville to Gobineau, 7 Jan. 1850, *Lettres choisies*, 678.

222 "which our fathers": *Souvenirs*, 1.1, in *Oeuvres* (Pléiade), 3:728.

223 "'Ah, monsieur!'": Tocqueville to Freslon, 16 March 1858, *Lettres choisies*, 1300.

223 "I had youth": Tocqueville to Marie, 18 April 1858, ibid., 1302.

223 "These tall trees": Tocqueville to Beaumont, 21 Feb. 1855, ibid., 1126.

224 "COME. COME": Tocqueville to Beaumont, 4 March 1859, ibid., 1334.

224 "with intolerable slowness": Tocqueville to Kergorlay, 18 March 1859, ibid., 1336.

224 "If his life": Francis Bowen, introduction to his revision of the Reeve translation, *Democracy in America* (Cambridge, MA: Sever and Francis, 1863), iv–v.

224 "after trying": Brogan, 269.

225 "the domination": Christopher Lasch, introduction to *The American Political Tradition and the Men Who Made It*, by Richard Hofstadter (New York: Knopf, 1973), xii.

INDEX

Page numbers in *italics* refer to illustrations.